More praise for

# *The Fabulist*

"A lively account of Santos and his fall from grace. . . . Among the high points of its reporting, *The Fabulist* paints a picture of someone who really doesn't know what survival means. . . . When the cameras go cold, Santos may find himself alone with the person he had always wished to avoid."

—*The New York Review of Books*

"An engrossing look at Santos's rise and crashing fall. With detail and wry humor, Chiusano fillets his subject. *The Fabulist* is an amalgam of dish and supporting receipts, an ideal stocking stuffer for political junkies and voyeurs. This is a book Santos never wanted published. Truly."

—*The Guardian*

"Chiusano's book offers not just a contextualization of [Santos's] deceptions but also a fuller, even compassionate story, a piecing together of a complex character. . . . A comprehensive portrait of a grand fabricator and the society that created him."

—*Newsday*

"Aside from delivering an avalanche of bizarre new scooplets and anecdotes about the life and times of George Santos, the book does something that few have been able to do: It humanizes him . . . [painting] a complex portrait of a real human being who seems to lie as a way of life."

—*Business Insider*

"The deceits, frauds, and unlikely triumphs of the Republican congressman from New York are untangled in this labyrinthine exposé. . . . Combining punchy reportage with thoughtful analysis, Chiusano's richly textured profile makes Santos into a fitting embodiment of today's declining public faith in politics."

—*Publishers Weekly*

"Chiusano's book called out, siren-like, from the new-books section of my local public library, and I succumbed. What I learned is that my idea of Santos had been much too charitable. . . . [I]n Chiusano's account, almost all of Santos's life is vaporware. . . . Santos's saga really does mark something new in the annals of America's Congress."

—The Bulwark

"Dogged reporting . . . As if channeling Herman Melville's novel *The Confidence-Man*, Chiusano suggests that America is a nation of wolves and sheep, where the wolves always win. . . . In a well-researched book, Chiusano offers fair warning to anyone who might consider voting for his con man subject."

—*Kirkus Reviews*

"A fabulous, sizzling, and sometimes sassy book, excelling both as real-time reportage and an incisive review of the time and places that made the rise and fall of George Santos possible."

—Our Town

"Followers of politics and readers who've been watching the saga of George Santos will devour *The Fabulist*. If you love a good, romping head-shaker, pull this one off the shelves."

—Terri Schlichenmeyer, OutSFL

# *The Fabulist*

## THE LYING, HUSTLING, GRIFTING, STEALING, AND VERY AMERICAN LEGEND OF GEORGE SANTOS

---

# MARK CHIUSANO

**ONE SIGNAL**
**PUBLISHERS**

---

**ATRIA**

New York | London | Toronto | Sydney | New Delhi

ONE SIGNAL
PUBLISHERS

ATRIA

An Imprint of Simon & Schuster, LLC
1230 Avenue of the Americas
New York, NY 10020

First One Signal Publishers/Atria Paperback edition September 2024

ONE SIGNAL PUBLISHERS / ATRIA PAPERBACK and colophon
are trademarks of Simon & Schuster, LLC.

Simon & Schuster: Celebrating 100 Years of Publishing in 2024

For information about special discounts for bulk purchases,
please contact Simon & Schuster Special Sales at 1-866-506-1949
or business@simonandschuster.com.

The Simon & Schuster Speakers Bureau can bring authors to your
live event. For more information or to book an event, contact the
Simon & Schuster Speakers Bureau at 1-866-248-3049 or visit
our website at www.simonspeakers.com.

Interior design by Joy O'Meara

Manufactured in the United States of America

1   3   5   7   9   10   8   6   4   2

Library of Congress Control Number: 2023944338

ISBN 978-1-6680-4367-7
ISBN 978-1-6680-4368-4 (pbk)
ISBN 978-1-6680-4369-1 (ebook)

*For Charlotte*

*You two green-horns! Money, you think, is the sole motive
to pains and hazard, deception and deviltry, in this world.
How much money did the devil make by gulling Eve?*

—Herman Melville, *The Confidence-Man*


*He said out loud and by himself:
—I'm very intelligent, I'll end up a congressman.*

—Clarice Lispector, *The Hour of the Star*

# Contents

Preface to the Paperback Edition     xi

*Author's Note*: Talking to George Santos     xv

Introduction     xxi

## *Part One*
## The Scammer

**1.** Escape from the Tower of Babel     1

**2.** Up from the Basement     15

**3.** Kitara at the Bingo Table     33

**4.** Grift City     57

**5.** And Then Came the Dogs     75

## *Part Two*
## The Candidate

**6.** Choosing Politics     91

**7.** The Excellent Messy Awesomeness of 2020
Or, How Santos Got COVID and Learned to Stop the Steal     113

# CONTENTS

**8.** The Coattail Candidate     139

**9.** *The Producers*, Part 2     165

**10.** The Perfect-Storm Election     187

**11.** Keep Posting     213

Epilogue     229

A Note on Sources     241

Acknowledgments     243

Notes     247

Index     273

# Preface to the Paperback Edition

*I*n a feat of incredible (and lucky) timing, this book was originally published the very week George Santos was thrown out of Congress.

It is a capsule, then, of Santos's rise and fall on the national stage, a narrative of his captivating road to infamy.

It's also the story of a figure out of Twain, Melville, or even *Goodfellas*, the tale of a grifter from Queens who was always looking for a quick buck and a fun time. Santos was a gambler in more ways than one. He loved the world of entertainment, before he endeavored to entertain the world. He tried out different fields and biographies, sampled call center cubicles and small-time hustles. But he didn't make it big until he put on the costume of a politician and entered history. In doing so, he exposed the rot at the heart of American politics. He was the perfect symbol of almost everything that is wrong with that staid, officious world, and also a warning of what might be to come.

He served eleven ignominious months before he finally got pushed out, at the end of 2023, vowing to wear his expulsion like a "badge of honor," à la Donald Trump. Unsurprisingly, the hustle continued. Santos's first quick fix was selling video clips to civilians on Cameo, agreeing to say anything, even "Happy Hanukkah," for the right price. As usual with Santos, it worked—for a while. The disgraced former congressman broke the record for biggest first day, week, and month on Cameo, the company cofounder and CEO told me earlier this year.

Those videos were fun, as were so many aspects of the Santos saga, but they were only confectionary sprinkles decorating a much more perplexing story. What makes someone lie the way Santos did? And what does it say about the United States that the hustle worked so long—and so well?

That's what drew me to this project in the first place. I set out to investigate Santos's background and life in New York City and Brazil, to measure the chip on his shoulder and the depth of his dissembling, which began long before he made the fateful choice to perform his way into office. He has had a wild ride, not one that many people could stomach. But certainly there is something interesting—even relatable—about his shameless self-transformation, his desperate bid for celebrity and riches, his attempt to bluster into the stratosphere where titans of power seem to be effortlessly earning just by being beautiful or amusing or loud. Couldn't he be all those things, and more?

He was a product of America, after all, shaped by a culture that encourages mythmakers to rise and thrive. Through his crazy hijinks and dumb luck, he became an American legend, another hustler who got away with the con for a minute, using every trick in the book. He did not break our political system—he just showed how broken it already was.

Though Santos's brief moment in Congress is (mostly) receding into the past, these issues are even more urgent. His story shows how easy it is to suck up attention and invent a persona, to stave off consequence and leave a trail of victims while still crying victimization. He understood that liars and losers can win in this country simply by blustering and being outrageous and shameless—and persistent. He's not alone.

Mark Chiusano, March 2024

# Author's Note

## Talking to George Santos

*T*he first time I spoke to George Santos was by phone in November 2019, three years before his brush with infamy.

It was for a routine political write-up about this little-known Republican newcomer making a longshot bid for Congress in New York. There was very little to suggest that he could win—and Santos ended up losing solidly to the Democratic incumbent in that first run—but a few impressions stuck out even in that inaugural conversation.

He was practiced at papering over mistakes or inconsistencies with excuses. In rapid succession he let slip both that he was in Florida for a work conference as we talked, and also that today— that exact day, the day of our phone call—should be considered the official launch of his campaign. Why was he launching his campaign for a New York district from Florida, I asked? He explained that there had been a slight bit of miscommunication with his lovely team about his travels, he was in the Sunshine State only for the night, and he'd be back home the next day.

He was already getting dexterous with the political lingo of immigration and guns and taxes; he was happy to stretch himself ideologically to have things both ways. But beneath the talking points he also exuded an intense and deeply personal fixation on status, arguing that nothing was handed to him, this first-generation American (his phrase), born and raised in New York to Brazilian immigrant parents. He told me defiantly that he had been able to grow and advance on his own merits. About his business life, he claimed (falsely) that he had worked in private equity for his entire professional career, but that he was "not a one percenter." Rather, "I work for the one percent." Later, he would launch scheme after scheme in an attempt to bring in serious one-percent money. He'd brag about buying an Hermès bag and he'd drive a Mercedes. But as he launched his political career, he was still stuck in the outsider-looking-in mode that informs the origin story of so many strivers and hustlers.

This mode had an uneasiness to it. He seemed even then to be on edge—though at the time, I thought it was simply the typical nervousness of an inexperienced candidate, as opposed to the anxiety of a serial grifter and fabulist.

Santos remained pretty available for comment to me in the coming years. He had to. I was writing for *Newsday*, his district's local paper, and few other people were doing much keyboard tapping about his political attempts. He was thirsty for press clips, though he wasn't always happy with what he got. Our conversations were often marked by the same uneasy edge that had been present in that first phone call, particularly when I was calling with questions about yet another of his bizarre moves—such as not being clear about whether he lived in the district, or holding a pretty-mask-free indoor fundraiser during the COVID-19 pandemic, or opening a "recount" campaign committee to raise money for a race he'd definitely lost.

He was guarded with me, a little combative, but he always tried to cover all that with an ooze of explanations and wan humor. During campaign number two, when I asked something about his decision to run for Congress after his first loss, he told me (accurately, it turns out), "Second time's the charm."

By the time that ultimately successful campaign came around, Santos was in a very different situation. Multiple political currents and lucky breaks meant this neophyte actually had a real chance of making it to the House, and in his interactions with me, the nasty started outweighing the courting. Sometime down the line he blocked me on Twitter, a dubious distinction he'd soon grant to other reporters and political observers. But it struck me as another oddity. Thin-skinned behavior. I could easily see what he was tweeting via an incognito browser.

Strange too was the encounter we had in *Newsday*'s cavernous restroom before a Third Congressional District debate. On that occasion, I first ran into Santos's opponent at the sink and then Santos himself as he came through the door. Seeing me, he spun around and left. I'm not sure if he ended up hitting the urinals before that debate, but he went on to say puzzling things that evening on the debate stage, such as, "I have no record."

Soon the whole world would learn just what Santos's record actually was, starting with the *New York Times*' explosive December 2022 look into his fakeries. He would go from a replacement-level congressman-elect to an internationally known—and ridiculed—figure, someone on the tongue of late-night hosts and subway commuters, the character of the moment on Twitter and in comic roasts, famous and deluged and surrounded and certainly no longer in need of phone calls from a local reporter.

No surprise, then, that Santos and his team became not particularly responsive to my queries for a little while. But old habits die hard. When this book was announced, he couldn't help taking to Twitter and giving everyone a couple of preemptive takes about the pages you are about to read.

He did not, however, talk to me for this book, as is his right. Although I reached out multiple times—including with a request to fact-check the voluminous information I'd learned about his fascinating life—he refused to speak to me.

Actually, that's not entirely true. He did pick up once in May when I called, and he asked "How was your trip to Brazil?" a line that he uttered with the old mix of sarcasm, jokey politeness, and almost-threat that I'd become used to from him over time. He then said he hoped I enjoyed the reporting sojourn (I did), and not to call again. He himself called back moments later, and said not to contact him or his family, "they're not interested, we're not interested, have fun with your book; I respect your freedom of speech and your ability to go do it but I will not be lending my voice." I lent him my ears and kept my recorder running. He added repeatedly that he wished me luck, and warned, "Just make sure you don't put any liability on the publisher and on yourself." When I asked if there was a staff member I could perhaps talk to, he said, "Nobody is interested in talking to you. . . . Mark, nobody is interested."

He hung up. Later that afternoon, after I reiterated my request by text, he responded with the following:

"This is my last warning for you to stop contacting me and my family. I will go to the depths of hell to get a restraining order form [*sic*] you.

STOP!

We have video proof of you trespassing inside various buildings where my family members reside and leaving notes under their doors."

He was apparently referring to some standard shoe-leather reporting practiced by all journalists worth their pads: I had tracked down addresses for some of his relatives, politely knocked on their house or apartment doors, and sometimes left a piece of paper with my contact information in case they wanted to get in touch. Guilty. My aim was to learn as much as I could about him, to provide the most complete and three-dimensional picture of the talented Mr. Santos. Yet he saw something more sinister:

"They haven't gone to the police because I asked them not too [*sic*], but I will move forward with legal ramifications if you do not stop."

A few weeks after that, in response to another request to talk, he texted:

"Mark I am going to respectfully advise you if you don't stop contacting me I will file a police report for harassment."

When it came time to fact-check this book, I once again offered him the opportunity to respond to my reporting, to comment, clarify, or criticize, and to have those remarks reflected in this book. He responded by text that he would not be giving me "cover."

"This is your journey. Now own up your short coming [*sic*] and know I will challenge any and all thing [*sic*] inaccurate in your book."

I followed up with the suggestion that responses from him might provide a fuller picture for readers, including those who happened to be residents of the Third Congressional District of New York. He appears to have seen the text, because in the year of our Lord 2023 his cell phone still alerted correspondents that messages had been read. But he did not respond.

It has been radio silence since then.

# Introduction

**W**hen he looked in the mirror, there were things he wanted to change, and maybe this was where the lies came from in the first place.

There was nothing really wrong in the mirror. Round cheeks, friendly eyes, an open face. George Santos had an expressive mouth, a large build, and smooth skin. But what he wanted was something different.

Or so he told people.

There was one campaign aide in 2022 who'd be driving around and then her phone would ring—it was Santos. He had just gotten back from having his lips done, he'd gush. The doctor was amazing. "New lips kicked in lol," he texted once. Or Santos would confide about getting liposuction.

Such procedures did not become public knowledge, but these were not the only conversations he had about sculpting his body.

Later, to one former volunteer, he said he'd recently shed weight and also spent big for his Botox.[1] He told a reporter that he'd lost six pounds from walking in his first days in DC.[2] He mentioned these details in passing, but they were deeply tied to his self-worth, which was clear when he brought the matter up once in an important political meeting. He was pitching himself to some of Long Island's GOP leadership, arguing that he could really win. He'd be serious; he'd present an appealing version of himself to voters. So he said he was getting lap band surgery.

Or in the darker moments of Election Night 2022, when he thought he had lost to his well-coiffed Democratic opponent: "Fuck," he joked, loudly enough that others heard, "I guess he does have better lip filler than me." As if that was how voters made their decision.

The vote tally turned his way, however, and that's what brings us here today—George Santos, the lying congressman, the man who made up almost everything. His college diplomas and his Wall Street jobs.[3] His Holocaust-fleeing grandparents.[4] His education at the fancy private high school, Horace Mann.[5] The four employees lost in the Pulse nightclub shooting.[6] The Broadway-producer gig for *Spider-Man*.[7] On and on. Each claim more like a mirage, at best a wild exaggeration. He is a fabulist. These were all just stories he told.

That was something his mother used to say, years before his political career, when she was confronted with yet another lie: "Oh my god, Anthony and his stories." She said it repeatedly, one ex-roommate remembers. "Don't listen to him," she would say of her son with a tone of exasperation. His fake jobs, his fake life, his fake anecdotes. Just stories.

But they were so easy, these stories, they were so simple to tell. They smoothed life, like the suction tube does to stomachs.

From the beginning Santos had this drive toward a more attractive, higher-class existence, and so he fretted over his looks and he made up fantasies. But the changes were unsatisfying, and never more than temporary. They were a shortcut, like Ozempic and its variants, the miracle drugs celebrities started using to drop pounds right around when Santos got into national politics. So of course Santos would want to follow suit. In fact he said so at a Ronald Reagan Republican Club gathering in Commack, New York, where he raved about the results he had seen from his own Ozempic use—and claimed he had stock in the company, too.

This was at a meet-the-candidate night at Mario's Pizzeria, the April before he won, before he made history. He was still anonymous then, just a guy with a big smile talking next to a silhouette of the trim, forgiving Gipper. You could have a thought about cholesterol at an event like this, looking out at the trays of pepperoni, the pale senior citizens clutching canes or pill-box-conveyor purses. Santos stood in front of a line of silver catering trays in the pizzeria's back room, and he did his stump speech, with Ozempic thrown in.

What you have to understand about Santos is that he was great at this—stories. He knew which ones to share, and when, and with whom. He was a world-class mimic and trickster, one of the twenty-first century's great chameleons. He could don the costume of a private equity maven, a media executive, or a beauty pageant performer. He could engagingly cycle among subjects and tales so fast that one veteran of the Santos experience once wondered with awe if the guy had attention deficit disorder. Once, he was interviewed on a podcast by a former NYPD detective, who said confidently, "My art is sniffing through bullshit." This law enforcement professional, one of New York's finest, reiterated that he could "smell a bullshit artist a mile away." But as for Santos? "You're legit, you know your stuff."[8]

Something like that was happening at Mario's Pizzeria: Santos spinning. He talked about taking Ozempic and how it caused his weight loss, yes, but the point of that story was that other people, too, should be allowed to use the drug like he did and refashion their body anew. The federal government wouldn't approve it widely, he said, and *wasn't that just typical for this whole sector*—bad priorities from the pharma people who wanted you to get these COVID vaccines. It was vintage Santos, weaving a story that both connected him with a crowd—this one a right-leaning set still furious about vaccine mandates—but also made him look a little better, classier, skinnier than them. He was halfway toward the fashion uniform for which he would become famous[9]—blue blazer over sweater, thick glasses, all of it screaming "approachable" and "friendly" and "nothing unusual to see here." This particular sweater was zip-up, but maybe that was even better for the nonpreppy audience. He knew the populist harangues they wanted to hear, one listener recalled. Hence the monologue Santos went on about how "America is not for sale," how "we're definitely not in the business of making politicians rich at the cost of the American taxpayer."[10]

Well, even good liars sometimes let their cards fall a little. He was a politician in the midst of getting rich at that very moment. Politics worked nicely for him. It would be the best of his cons. He had not been rich before, and who knows if he ever really did shell out to use Ozempic or get liposuction or lap band surgery. Those stories. He told so many. Who knows if he really did have stock in Ozempic's parent company either. His disclosure forms don't mention the company, even though, ironically, his opponent's did, in a retirement account.[11] One can't trust much about Santos's paperwork, however. It's studded with lies.

The lies have finally caught up with him. Legally speaking, of course—starting with his twenty-three-count federal indictment for money laundering and wire fraud and more—but also in the public mind. So much does the legend of George Santos precede him that in the course of reporting this book I was told, unprompted, the most bonkers and totally factually unverifiable stories: like one person's belief that Santos performed a hex on her through macumba magic; or another's claim that someone told them Santos once took feminine hormone pills. There is another rumor that Santos made all his money from pimping. I must stress that these have to be considered fictional stories, and I include them here merely to differentiate from the much more documented and wild-enough lies and stories he did in fact tell, and to show what blossoms from those fables.

A family member of his likes to say that with Santos, it's "a pebble of truth and a mountain of lies." The mountains, rising higher and higher, are defenses against a deep sense of self-doubt. He himself on a local morning show once spit out the word *insecurities* when asked about his résumé myths.[12] His happy-go-lucky and even optimistic exterior lies above a churn of enviousness, plus the kind of anxiety that once made him rush back to his campaign staff in the basement of a church in Whitestone, Queens, one freezing New York evening, storming over and lighting into them about the fleece-type vest he was wearing.

"I can't believe that nobody told me what I look like in this vest," he could be overheard saying, remarking on a garment that was perhaps a little too small (a passerby had noted as much). "I'm out there looking like this in front of this crowd of people," he went on. "It's embarrassing." He turned nasty, displaying the threatening side of him that poked out when he felt attacked, like when as a young man he texted a Brazilian immigrant "You are in my country" and "I am the one dealing the cards" after she called him a crook. Here in Whitestone, there was no threat. This was a friendly crowd for Santos, one that was on his side no matter what he looked like or wore—which goes to show how deeply embedded was the insecurity, outweighing logic, outweighing reality. This was the kind of crowd where a guy with a Santos button told a questioner about once being a Democrat but then switching since he didn't believe in killing babies after they're born. The questioner did not know what to say to that. Lies are contagious and, when they spread, make the whole system sick.

This is George Santos on the inside, the man behind the headlines, the turmoil within that launched this young New Yorker on an absolutely wild journey—lying his way up the food chain, leaving victims in a Brazilian favela and Queens apartments, crafting a most American story and then succeeding in a most American way, always a step away from disaster, until his implosion on the nation's highest stage. This book is an effort to understand what drove Santos, his never-ending hustle, what made him lie and steal so compulsively, so much so that he landed himself in the great pantheon of American con artists and thieves.

This book is also an effort to probe what it was about America that allowed him to rise so quickly, what bedrock national principles this son of immigrants successfully channeled, and what changes in the country's consciousness have brought lies and scams so directly into the political realm. This book is a case study for how a scammer and fantasy creator could worm his way into national politics, aided by apathy, gatekeepers' blunders, the pallor of the media ecosystem, the continued international rise of right-wing populism, and a money-swamped political system in which it often seems that everything and everyone is for sale. George Santos matters because he won't be the last fabulist to chart this route—least of all in the dawning age of misinformation, when institutions have lost people's trust and conspiracies spread at the swipe of a finger.

Santos has long modeled himself after former president Donald Trump, from the speech patterns of his fellow Queens native to a fondness for what Trump's senior adviser called "alternative facts." Trump was a pioneer on this particular blustering path to success, but Santos shows that path can be marched too by ordinary tricksters and clowns. He is part of a new generation—a sort of Shameless Caucus—that includes Trump descendants like Marjorie Taylor Greene, Lauren Boebert, and Paul Gosar, who followed their mentor's way in politics by embracing controversy and the limelight and little else.

And for Santos, the shamelessness is a way of life that goes far beyond politics.

"Americans have always been fascinated by the con artist who can get away with things that the rest of [us] can't," writes Baylor psychiatry professor Glen O. Gabbard in his book *The Psychology of the Sopranos*. "Many of us secretly admire the smooth-talking, antisocial person who manages to write his own laws and follow his own moral code."[13]

Hence Tony Soprano, the sympathetic psychopath mobster, but also Herman Melville's confidence man on a steamboat; and F. Scott Fitzgerald's Gatsby, who is generally accepted to be a resident of the district Santos won; and the real-life Silicon Valley founders and Manhattan scammers from Elizabeth Holmes to Anna Delvey who fake it until they make it, since that's what the market rewards.

But Santos is in a counterfeit class of his own.

He has told stories about his parents' jobs, his mugging on Fifth Avenue and Fifty-Fifth Street in Manhattan (they took his shoes!),[14] an attempt on his life,[15] his mom fleeing socialism in Europe,[16] and also her highly questionable escape from Ground Zero.[17] He was married to a woman at the same time as he was dating men.[18] He has claimed he "used to" go to the Met Gala,[19] and also that he was among the first people in the entire United States to get COVID-19.[20] Once, he regaled an audience about accidentally flipping a table on Stephen Schwarzman, the CEO of Blackstone, who upon inquiry stated that he does not think they've ever met.[21] Santos has said that he survived a brain tumor[22] and also purports to be a Mets fan, even though he once posted a video singing the classic "Let's Go Mets" chant in the absolutely incorrect cadence, as if he'd never heard it before in his life.[23]

The stories span genres. They include tales about filling up his gas tank three times a week (implausible, according to an auto expert),[24] a claim that he helped "develop and fundraise for" carbon-capture technology in his career (he also said he had a "very extensive role in gas and oil in this country"),[25] and make-believe about owning real estate all over the New York metropolitan area (though public records show instead that he has actually faced multiple eviction proceedings).[26]

While such lies might have a minor political or personal purpose, such as boosting his story of wealth, they are often simply gratuitous. Like the time Santos claimed that he'd just sold one of his properties in the Hamptons because he was looking to buy on Fire Island, a popular beachy destination a fellow Republican was discussing during a fundraiser.

What was the point? He could have just vamped about the weather.

But lying had become a brazen game for Santos.

He lied even after people knew he had been a liar, as when journalist Marisa Kabas surfaced a picture of Santos dressed in drag as a teenager in Brazil.[27] Santos pooh-poohed the drag queen allegation: he had just been a young man who "had fun at a festival."[28] This is not how people described it to me when I went to Niterói, the city next to Rio de Janeiro where Santos spent time on and off during his adolescence. One family friend called him, simply, a "drag queen." Other people remembered different moments that he dressed in women's clothes. A young girl, who considered Santos to be something of an uncle, told stories about how the future politician—very sweetly—would entertain her. They would dance, Santos wearing a bra and a towel wrapped around his head, singing Lady Gaga's "Bad Romance."

He returned to some favorite fibs, groping them like rosary beads as if for comfort, lies that would morph and shift to suit the need, the conversation, or just Santos's mood. Those lies included his saga of volleyball greatness at Baruch College, a school he did not attend, which hosted a team that he certainly wasn't on; and, of course, his ongoing flirtation with being Jewish, him and his mother and grandparents.

Besides some controversial armchair debates about Trump's psychological makeup, mental health professionals often shy away from diagnosing prominent figures in public, dating back at least to the rounds of speculation about Barry Goldwater's mental fitness during the 1964 presidential campaign. But for Santos, taken together, the scope of lying certainly seems to go beyond dishonesty or dissembling for monetary gain alone. It may approach something more clinical—like pseudologia fantastica, defined by *Kaplan & Sadock's Synopsis of Psychiatry* as "a type of lying in which a person appears to believe in the reality of his or her fantasies and acts on them." Factual material is mixed with belabored, creative fluff. Patients "give false and conflicting accounts" of their lives and assume the identities of prestigious others: "Men, for example, report being war heroes and attribute their surgical scars to wounds received during battle or in other dramatic and dangerous exploits."[29]

Santos has not (to my knowledge) fabricated a military background for himself. But his inventions paint a ghostly picture of the American heights he wanted to climb. His made-up character is a bionic hero that says a lot about what Santos yearned to see when he looked in the mirror, what America rewards these days, and what prizes felt so out of reach. This hero was contoured and svelte, wealthy and suave, a Wall Street whiz and owner of land, a man who wore Brioni suits and a Cartier family heirloom watch. A well-educated cosmopolitan man whose inherited family riches he had expanded, whose parents immigrated legally and proudly before taking up fabulous jobs of their own. A man who rose deservedly through the meritocratic ranks en route to a graduate degree; who understood the economy and helped people manage their money, which was how he made his own money. A man who got into politics to just bring some sanity back to the proceedings in that unmathematical, emotionally charged field.

This was the man Santos wanted to be, and was anything but. He was often poor, always mooching, rarely gainfully employed for long. He squeezed into shared apartments and wished he could look better and lose a few pounds. His parents had struggled before him, trying strenuously to scratch out a life between two countries. They could not afford fancy private school, the kind that serves as a smooth feeder to elite East Coast colleges, and so he did not graduate from any college at all.[30] He was self-taught, always on edge, sometimes bumbling, had difficulty finding a score in a modern economy that seems to produce little but money for other people, and he jumped into politics because of the grand carnival stage it offered, the only platform he could force his way onto, one that occasionally allows those who do not inherit power to earn it instead. It is a democracy, after all.

This book also aims to illuminate the lives of the people who bought Santos's stories, who suffered his lies and scams or partnered with him in his exploits. Those kinds of people, no matter which side of the law they are on, don't often get to Congress or even interact much with that hallowed chamber. Yet their unstable lives can explain more about the state of the country than many a DC hearing or debate.

Santos himself sought to outrun this instability, and he earned a lot with his stories, because he was stealing much of the time he was talking. He nabbed $24,744 in unemployment insurance benefits that shouldn't have been his, according to the federal government. He took from those closest to him. He scammed a sixteen-year-old who didn't speak English. He conned a phone insurance company and New York City landlords.[31] He convinced people to give him, just hand him, tens of thousands of dollars. Ultimately, that included some of America's most actually wealthy men.[32]

Along the way, with all the money, with the accretion of successful lie after successful lie, he did achieve something: He became, or he appeared to become, confident. He did change his circumstances in life. He achieved the dream. For a while.

That was what struck Hector Gavilla at that Ronald Reagan

Republican Club dinner with Santos, the one where he talked about Ozempic and won over the pizzeria crowd. Gavilla, who went on to become president of that club, had once been a promising local GOP candidate himself. Santos had met with him for advice, in fact, sometime around 2019. Gavilla was charmed. At a function not long after, the future congressman handed over a business card, and Gavilla glanced down at the four unwieldy names. George and Anthony and Devolder and Santos.

*You know what you should do*, Gavilla swears he said, *you should change your name to George Santos*: "It has a nice ring to it."

So it does.

But in the pizzeria, Gavilla kept returning to this sense of confidence from the newcomer in front of him. Santos recited a litany of successes: Wall Street. Self-made millions. Wins in business. His triumphant American story. Gavilla looked at the cocky kid in front of the catering trays and thought, *What did I do wrong? Where's my money?* Gavilla was a real estate broker, had operated and then sold his own brokerage. He considered himself somewhat successful. But here was this young guy, doing even better. On his way to greatness, even. Looking and feeling good. "I guess the bigger the lie, the more people believe it," Gavilla said.

Santos was telling a better story. The story of his life.

# Part One

## The Scammer

# 1

## Escape from the Tower of Babel

*T*he Dish Network call center in College Point, Queens, was not regarded as a particularly luxurious outpost. It was situated in a squat little building underneath the flight path from LaGuardia Airport, where smoke breakers struggled to hear their own gossip over the *rip-rip* of planes. The hardly decorated exterior was sandwiched between Home Depot and Con Ed gas and power. An industrial yard with piles of dirt glowered nearby, full of machinery belching dust that would sometimes settle onto the call center's windows and the cars.

Which is not to complain about the setting per se—there were plenty of things that workers in or out of the smoking circle might want to complain about, the jobsite and its distance from public transit merely being one of them. But certainly this location and basically just the regularity of everything around clashed strangely with what Barbara Hurdas heard on her first day on the job, when she sat next to George Santos in the training class, and he started bragging about the money his family came from in Brazil.

Outside, the wind whistled along the glass. Cement mixers and garbage trucks barreled down the roads, a sign of the roads' emptiness, or, you could even say, desolation. You could only just make out the moneymaking skyscrapers of Manhattan. Yet inside the call center, Santos was talking dollar signs, about how the family had property on Nantucket.

"It didn't make sense," Hurdas remembers.

But who has time to dwell much on small perceptions? It was their shared first day; there was lots to learn and a paycheck to await. Even if this new guy's economic background didn't match the general vibes of twelve-dollar-an-hour call center work, one thing was clear: he was good on the phone.[1]

"He certainly had the gift of gab," says John Rijo.

Rijo is a customer service lifer. In the fall of 2011, when the twenty-three-year-old Santos showed up at Dish, Rijo was already there for a tour of duty alongside him. Among the things he's seen in the industry was, decades ago, a gimmick in which the phone operators for an airline were supposed to pick up by saying, "Thank you for calling the airline, my name is John Courtesy." Daisy Ling would say, "Thank you for calling, this is Daisy Courtesy." And so on and so forth. Some study or other said the *Courtesy* got stuck beneficially in callers' heads.

But gimmicks like this go only so far. Call center culture is not for the timid or easily cowed. The good representatives have something innate that no number of prepared scripts can beat.

Back then, Rijo listened in to a few of Santos's calls in his capacity as a supervisor. And the outgoing new kid was good.

He was an upseller, the currency of the land at a place like Dish, which had more than 13.9 million US customers and was the nation's third-largest pay-TV provider at the time. Key to its business model was, as Dish business filings put it, "better educating our customers about our products and services, and resolving customer problems promptly and effectively when they arise."[2] In other words, hustling on the phones.

This kind of customer service work is challenging and often rote, but also good training for a would-be con artist—or even a politician. Certainly that was true for Santos. The Dish representatives had to learn how to size up a mark—a customer—quickly, while they pitched the many movie packages available with just a mutter of one's credit card number. They had to be able to expound on the wisdom of purchasing insurance, sounding authoritative and adjusting their pitches effortlessly. If movies weren't the customer's style, there were also pay-per-view soccer matches. And the fabulist-in-training learns that it takes real skill to hold a story together. It's cognitively hard to spin, and even harder to lie.

Most of all, the agents would learn to savor the thrill of having pulled off a sale, of tacking on a big purchase to a customer who didn't necessarily want one. Bonuses were available for the best customer service agents at the end of the month.

There was money to be made, in other words, and Santos's colleagues felt that he could smell that possibility. Congress was nowhere in the future here at Dish. He was simply eager, at least in the beginning, to get promoted.

Marcia Ritchie, who came from the same Brazilian region as much of Santos's family and thus had an "immediate commonality" with him, remembered that he was ambitious from the jump, suggesting to her that in a year, he'd be on his way to something greater. He'd be a manager, for example. It was only a matter of time, and he was never patient. She remembered him pushing back from his desk and going to the director's office to try to befriend that person; and peering surreptitiously at the screen of a talented team leader, trying to learn tricks to get good metrics.

He had the ability to focus, often shockingly, on what it was that he wanted, at least when it suited him. Some colleagues felt a sense sometimes that he was thinking, *What can I get out of this*?

There was the time when somebody from corporate came calling, and Hurdas remembers how strangely friendly, even kiss-ass-y, Santos became with this higher-up. This was Dish, a company with many thousands of workers at many levels. The corporate ladder is high and vice presidencies loom large. Hurdas is Greek from Queens, and in some ways that's not so dissimilar to being Brazilian in the borough when it comes to the friendliness and the hugging and the kissing. But Santos's behavior was different—he was adamant about making himself known professionally to this corporate man. On the crowded office floor with its thick windows that couldn't be opened, Santos was looking to the suit as if he had the key to something better. He wanted his attention.

---

*The corporate honcho was meeting* George Santos at a very special moment in the latter's life: it seems to be among the first moments when he stuck for so long and so grimly to what might be termed a "regular job." Santos did not graduate from an institution of higher learning, but this was, metaphorically speaking, his first job out of college. It was his main introduction, postadolescence, to the office-based working world.

It was also close to the last time he ever submitted himself to such nonflashy work, as far as many who knew him can tell. It was a hinge moment when he gave the whole desk-job situation a shot, and in this formative period he learned what type of life he wanted.

To his dismay, the life he currently had at Dish was that of a small cog in an enormous wheel. He was paid accordingly (probably around $12, no more than $15 an hour); his responsibilities matched his still-green skills. And he was not slapping shoulders with wealthy C-suite plutocrats. Many of his colleagues, who certainly had their own ambitions, were focused at a more basic level on earning steady salaries and keeping their heads above choppy waters. Many, in fact, had come to New York City specifically for a tough but dependable job like this. They were immigrants and the sons and daughters of immigrants, from all the corners of the world.

The Dish call center, for all its unflashy surroundings, was a fairly unique specimen in the way it served as a haven for the newly arrived. One of the company's calling cards was providing some two hundred seventy-five of what it called "Latino and international channels," satisfying the needs of immigrants far from home.[3] This was a significant niche in the home entertainment business, just one of the ways that immigrants make their presence felt in the enormous girth of the American economy. Those who pick up and leave for a new country, as Santos's parents did, often want some audiovisual reminder of the place they left behind. That wasn't easily available with standard cable, so Dish earned loyal customers by beaming in a package from India or Brazil straight to your new home in the United States.

And in order to serve this sizable immigrant clientele, Dish needed customer service agents who could respond to questions in German and Urdu and Spanish and Russian and the other tongues of earth. In other words, it needed immigrants, and their sons and daughters.

This straightforward situation of supply and demand kept the company's phones humming and provided needed jobs to newcomers in Santos's backyard of Queens, one of the most diverse and immigrant-rich places in the United States. The workers' languages of birth or heritage got them in the door, and now they used the weapons of that and English to feed their families. Santos was no different. Perhaps one edge he had on his peers was that his Portuguese was good but he could really dip and dart in English. He could be nimble, a godsend in a gig that trains representatives in calming customers down. The workers called this *deescalation*, a word that would come into wider vogue in later years in relation to the NYPD, a more heavily armed customer service outfit whose fancy new academy was then under construction, also in College Point, just down the road.

It is not generally Santos's style to settle for what everyone around him has. It must have been uncomfortable for him to get going in this new gig and realize that he was just one in a large pack; good, but not so good that anyone was putting him in charge. It was the familiar deadening sensation that many people feel once the first-day adrenaline runs out, and the long stretch of a career looms ahead. Some people savor happy hours, or grit their teeth and keep working, or find some other way to cope.

Soon, Santos was testing what he could get away with. The workers knew that someone from the company could be listening in on their calls, but at some point in the day, Ritchie says, that person left, and then the shenanigans could begin. One key metric was the amount of time you spent on the line, and so if no one was listening, a shortcut-taking worker might drop a call, or dial up different friends to complete quick connections, lowering your average. It took many workers weeks of experimenting to get their call times down, but Santos figured it out right away.

This practice in being a quick study would become one of his signatures. It's what allowed him to sound reasonably knowledge-able as a politician or businessman, even if he knew almost nothing about the subject at hand.

At times, he embraced the social life of the job. Some colleagues remember him as a happy-go-lucky kid, eager to chop it up or walk outside with the gang for a smoke break. He would hug and kiss those he liked, and there was one woman he called his "work mom." But he also seemed obsessed with showing that he was better than the rest, that he felt marooned in this first role, destined for greater things at Dish and beyond. He acted unconcerned about obeying the rank-and-file attendance rules, playing hooky and going to Macy's to pick up some Calvin Klein and Ralph Lauren. His peers, many of whom came from humble backgrounds, were too scared to test those waters. They were single mothers, hustling newcomers, supporting children. They faced long commutes and many bills. This was Santos's reality too, in fact, but confronted with it, he leaned into the story of a fictional Santos accustomed to comfort and money. There was all that talk of property and multigenerational wealth, a divider between him and his colleagues. He'd walk around comfortably in, for example, an untucked pink button-down shirt, sleeves rolled up. Once he showed pictures from what he said was a fancy vacation—*A vacation?*, some of his new friends might have wondered. *What's that?* Peering closer at the pictures, one shrewd colleague had some questions: Why was he not in any of the pictures? Were those stock photos—of Dubai?

But people made excuses for the kid. He was young. Being an adult is hard. He was figuring it all out. When they tried to square his story, they sometimes contorted: maybe he's studying business, and wants to see the American economy from the ground up.

Ground level was definitely how this job often felt. It was not the easiest work in the world. Like all work that bosses pay underlings to do, the job Santos held was not done just for fun. Sitting on a phone might not be as physically taxing as the work of the contractors who buzzed around Home Depot down the road, or that of the Con Ed hard hats descending into manholes. But that's what someone says when they have not sat without moving and completed fifty to one hundred call center calls a day. Where the calls must be answered in a matter of seconds.

There was a sound to the job. A *doot doot* in the headphones. It meant another call coming in. If you wanted to catch your breath for three or fifteen seconds you might put yourself on a particular "After Call" setting, but the company didn't like that: it went against metrics.

Lunch was an unsatisfying respite, particularly for someone who values his meals, as Santos has said he does. The trek to Sparky's deli for a sandwich meant a diesel-smelling walk or drive past a sanitation facility. Or there were the food trucks that sometimes showed up in front of Home Depot. Someone had once cut a little hole in the garbage-collecting fence between the call center and Home Depot, so the workers could duck through. The hole helped the workers shave a few minutes off their walk, save a little more for eating or gossiping or smoking in their designated outdoor area, anything that wasn't politely assuaging the egos of

America's angry watchers of television, be they foreign or native born. Perhaps an immigrant truly becomes an American when they learn to ask for a manager.

The callers were agitated people, pissed about an extra dollar on their monthly bill, irate at the loss of an expected, family-favorite program. Or maybe their TV remote wasn't working, and the call center worker wasn't helping, and there was a need to elevate the engagement or risk the person canceling it all. Transfers to the loyalty or retention departments sometimes happened too early, or too late. It added up to a job whose stress did not comport with the amount of money cleared each payday. Yet as the months went by, Santos's behavior continued to give off the sense that he didn't need the work—such as suggesting he had so much money that when a colleague announced she was getting married, Santos promised he would pay for the woman's dress. (A fellow employee confirmed he didn't.)

The workers had their own issues going on, but this Santos guy continued attracting fascination. Again and again his actions raised burning questions, for those whose financial circumstances meant they really needed to be at the drab College Point site: Why, if he had money, would he work at a job that could run eleven hours a day, four days a week? Why would he work for less than what would become, a few years later, the state's minimum wage? If he really was rolling in dough, why would he trek to this distant office outpost? Why would he work in a call center at all?

---

*It turned out that Santos* did have other options beyond the Dish drudgery. Or he was searching for them. Something beyond the cubicle was calling to him.

One such call was a woman named Uadla. Santos would mention this woman Uadla sometimes, the colleagues remember, perhaps even post her on social media—but not in the way of a romantic date or flirtatious getaway. It might be more on the order of going to Home Depot. Or a park in Queens.

Other people who knew Santos had similar stories—that when they met this woman Uadla she might be introduced as a friend, and Santos always had many of those. He would not indicate that she was or would be anything more. People who crossed paths with her at the time remarked on her beauty, and beauty was certainly something that Santos valued. She was someone who might come over and hang out on a weekend, or go to the nightclubs with Santos and his friends; in an Instagram post from a few years later the crew was at her apartment drinking Patrón, the shot glasses decorated with pictures of famous twentieth-century gangsters and robbers. A hashtagged good time.

But in the beginning, one of Santos's stories that made the rounds with Dish employees was that there was a trust fund he needed to access, and in order to retrieve it he needed to be married. And so, he was getting married to Uadla.

The inevitable deadpan, when he announced to one colleague that he was tying the knot. Pause, pause: *To a woman?* the colleague asked.

It was not that he wore anything particularly flamboyant, but there was not much doubting of Santos's sexuality in the smoke circle and cubicle row. "I always knew George to be gay," Hurdas says. So what was up with this woman?

His colleagues wondered. Perhaps they had met in Brazil, where she seemed to be from, and she came back with him. Maybe his family was so against his sexuality that he felt, in order to please them, he had to get married. Some other immigrant workers from conservative families could understand this possibility. Santos did talk often about his mother, never his father. People do self-destructive things to please the ones they love. The workers heard this trust fund possibility; perhaps that had something to do with it. And there was another whisper, among people accustomed to hearing stories about fellow strivers making ends meet: Did he marry her for immigration purposes? Did he get paid?

Santos did not provide clear answers, yet as usual, his colleagues in or out of the gossipy smoking circle wrote in their own conjecture around his avoidances. Plenty of the things he said at the call center or to the call center workers, you had to wonder: The money, his not needing the job. His mother being from Belgium. Her having Jewish ancestry. There was the generous assumption that maybe she was Sephardic. Hurdas even remembers Santos saying he was born in Brazil. The marriage was just another detail that didn't quite add up.

It was not a marriage to last forever. In 2013, a year after the Manhattan-based nuptials, court records show a move to end the union. Though such records are restricted in New York, we do know that in the coming years, the partnership helped Uadla become a legal permanent resident and then citizen. And in 2019, she and Santos ended the union for good.[4]

An outside political vulnerability study during candidate Santos's congressional run found the marriage to be "questionable."[5] Reporters who have visited Uadla's house since her ex-husband became famous have staked out her block in Elizabeth, New Jersey. She has sometimes been seen walking quickly into or outside the house with a young child, and sometimes she or a woman who answers her buzzer will ask who it is and, when told it has something to do with George Santos, will say only "No. Goodbye."

Though she'd rather not speak and has declined to address her union with Santos, her block tells its own story. It is a place with signs of other immigrant strivers, who might have fallen into a job at that dusty Queens call center. The house faces La Ideal Supermarket, where men stand outside passing the time with scratch-offs, one of the store's popular items, along with Newports and chances for the New Jersey Lottery. An advertisement in the window alerts people that a $50,000 ticket was sold there in May 2016. That is a long time ago now, but people can daydream. How much would it take to leave your workaday job behind? Maybe today will be the day you get lucky, when a windfall changes your life.

----

*Agents had always cycled in* and out of the Dish call center, leaving for other customer service gigs, or just disappearing without saying much. The veteran phone man Rijo remembers that you'd know workers were gone only "because all of a sudden, they were asking people that spoke a specific language to work overtime or to stay longer, because they were short staffed."

It was something like that with Santos, of whom another colleague said, "I don't think that call center was for him." Years later, Santos himself would say on a podcast that "idea makers make more money than the laborers" in this country, a hard lesson you don't learn, not really, if you haven't spent some time in and then escaped the laboring field.[6]

There was the impression that he may have been passed over for advancement, or that in some form or another he didn't get what he wanted at Dish. It seemed very millennial to Ritchie, this need to move up toward higher places quickly—Santos had been doing the work just a little under a year. But the call center workers were not really sure they ever knew the real George Santos. One thing was clear: the work and the life offered at Dish was not the one for him.

His departure prompted a personal category shift, not just a search for a slightly better occupation: he saw himself as part of a different New York tribe, one far away from office drudgery under a flickering fluorescent tube, and definitely far from College Point. It was not long before Santos was saying goodbye to all that. He left in July, and the next month he got married.

Everyone in New York aligns with some tribe eventually, when they decide how they want to make a living. Another tribe was far away on Wall Street, for example, a world of fleece vests and well-tailored suits, a world Santos would later pretend he had been inhabiting when he was actually answering customer service calls. Yet another tribe is an even more rarefied one, whose members refuse to be held down by jealous roots, who are willing to make their money off a little of this and a little of that and simply waltz their way as best they can into whatever group strikes their fancy. That was the way for Santos. He would not be confined by plastic headsets and quality control. He might have been brethren with the immigrants and second-generation kids and outer-borough workers of the Dish call center, but he did not want to remain one of them. And so he went in search of a field that would bring him real fortune, and maybe even fame.

# 2

## Up from the Basement

*T*he way George Santos tells his story, he was special from the beginning. That's because he was "born at twenty-four weeks gestation."[1]

It's an eyebrow-raising claim to make, even if it came as part of an argument on a political podcast about his anti-abortion beliefs. One study culminating in October 1988, the year Santos came into the world, found a survival rate of just 34 percent at twenty-four weeks.[2] In New York City alone in 1988, there were 250 fetal deaths in the twenty-four-to-twenty-seven-week gestation period.[3] But true or not, it makes a good story. And with this one, Santos's story was set: he was an overcomer from the beginning.

And wasn't the world stacked against him, in all truth? He was born into relative privation, relying on America's creaky public systems in various forms. He would later say he had "survived" the experience of being born at Elmhurst Hospital in Queens.[4] He had a point that it was not a place of privilege at that time: a last resort for victims of gunshots and car crashes, a place to test the blood of DUI suspects, a destination for prisoners, a safety net facility that by federal calculations in 1988 had abnormally high death rates among Medicare patients, and where, the month before Santos was born, early or not, a Black man was rushed after being viciously attacked by a gang of white men for offering to help a woman near the Suite Bar in Jackson Heights.[5]

This was the section of city that Santos and his Brazilian immigrant parents would come to call home, the multicultural neighborhood where Santos's American tale began. Santos has described these early years as "abject poverty,"[6] and has suggested that his family used welfare programs to survive: "I was poor for many years, very poor indeed."[7] Among the issues with their basement apartment were the rats, "bigger than me when I was born."[8] At night he'd surrender the ground because that was their playtime.[9]

Hanging over it all, ghostly impressions on the skin of every Santos story, are his parents, who provided the bottom from which he would try to claw his way up to great heights and riches. They were never exactly who he said they were.

They hailed from different parts of Brazil, but came together in Queens. Both followed family members there, and worked to make their own way. His father, Gercino, was often the primary breadwinner, working as a house and building painter to support the family. Fatima, George's mother, cared for the child when he was young, and also worked cleaning houses along with other relatives. Fatima and Gercino met at a dance performance in New York, one family friend remembers.

It seemed like there was a great love between the two, or at least a love Fatima often reminisced over after the relationship was through. They were poor, but they had established a little beachhead here in the world's city, had left their only homes in search of the old staple, opportunity. Their relatives cycled in and out from this new perch, too. And now, here in this basement, their American boy.

Family members and friends alike say that Santos was spoiled from early on. Fatima and Gercino would give him everything. He liked dolls, and clothes, and cooking. There is a story of him wearing an apron as a little kid and singing in a kitchen. His aunt Elma doted on him, buying him things to eat. Whatever George wanted. He was everyone's sweetheart. It was a little like the line in Mário de Andrade's epic novel *Macunaíma*, the story of a shape-shifter who wanders around the Brazil that Santos's family left behind. After the birth of a tyke, the reader is told: "All anybody ever did now was think about the little squirt." And who wouldn't be obsessed with a firstborn, given the lack of givens in life back home?

The child in the book dies young.

The Jackson Heights apartment could be boisterous. Holidays were a big deal. There was kibe, the fried Brazilian delicacy, a touchstone for the past. A relative remembers the TV was almost always running, tuned to the Globo network from back in South America, or telenovelas, or talk shows like *Laura en América*. The family was addicted to the screen, a very American condition.

Their little world allowed them to be both Brazilian and American. In the nearby neighborhood of Astoria there are Brazilian restaurants and spas that have been there for years, places like Pão de Queijo and Point Brazil, where the dishes smell like Rio and where workers say Santos himself used to show up. It is a place where communities are jammed next to each other, so that on a single street you may fall into shops called Cairo, Cafe de Colombia, or Roxelana Fine Gifts from Istanbul to New York. This is one of those exceptional international aspects of Queens, which a 2019 analysis found to have an astronomical probability that two county dwellers chosen randomly would be of a different race or ethnicity. Queens's figure—76.4 percent—came in higher than that of the other boroughs or any big county around the country.[10] The clashes and tenuous alliances of cultures can sway political races—including the one that Santos would win many years later. But here the borderlines of the world can also collapse toward proximity, so that each country's café outpost is mere feet from another's, all selling and swapping their own particular strain and preparation of coffee.

The borders collapse in public school, too, which Santos intermittently attended. At IS 125 in Woodside, Queens, he experienced what a visiting *New York Times* columnist around that time called "modern New York in miniature." It was a middle school attended by some kids for whom the free lunch was the only meal of the day. The school's own principal told the columnist that "we're not a great school. . . . But we are a good school."[11]

Santos often seemed invested in being allowed to fit in, according to his classmate Tiffany Bogosian. She remembers him participating in English as a Second Language programs, not uncommon among the diverse student body. He would also offer to take girls shopping in the intoxicating air of the Queens Center Mall, sampling the wares at JC Penney and Macy's.

Bogosian didn't accept the largesse. She figured that nothing in life was really free. It seemed a little thirsty and sad of Santos to be making the offer—a sign of an outsider mentality. She did not know him to be out of the closet, but his interests were not very well concealed. This was a time of universally baggy Ecko sweatshirts and drawing those Stüssy *S*'s with two stacks of three lines; when veering off the typical path could mean social trouble. Santos was flamboyant, and opinionated.

Not long after Bogosian and Santos became friends, she says she stuck up for him against a bully, a boy who was threatening to lay hands on Santos. This struck Bogosian, who would later become a lawyer, as unjust: picking on a kid dealing with his own issues. Only many years later would she be told, by another Santos friend, that the story was perhaps more complicated, as it often is with him. Santos had a habit of making fun of this boy's girlfriend. "Oh my god," he'd say to her, "you don't dress well." Little jabs. After the jabbing, he took the girl to shop at the mall, sort of a peace gesture. The little psychodrama drew the attention of the protective boyfriend.

He'd jab and get jabbed back. He'd make friends and then become sharp tongued, going a little too far. He could turn nasty, particularly when he felt threatened or unstable. Despite the surely embarrassing eighth-grade ponytail he claims he once sported,[12] he was obsessed with appearances, his own and that of others. These were patterns he would repeat for the rest of his life, an uneasy means of social relations that he never fully escaped.

School itself was a comparative refuge. Tom Taglienti, a onetime science teacher at 125, remembers serving as a sub in a few of Santos's classes, and he describes the future congressman as having a certain social intelligence, an outgoing nature while also being well behaved. Some teachers remember him being bright—one educator who had him in class told a fellow colleague that Santos would sometimes come up after the period and ask what he could do to get better in his studies.

This respectful inquisitiveness was not allowed to fully flower in a school setting after Santos moved on. He did not graduate from a high school, and instead got his GED. Yet he has repeatedly claimed that after middle school he spent time at Horace Mann, the fabulously expensive and exclusive New York City private school, which has found no record of his attendance under his various names. A Horace Mann spokesman said the school looked fruitlessly as far back as the 1930s. Santos nevertheless clings to the prep school story, even sparring with talk show host Piers Morgan to insist he had attended Horace Mann for six months of ninth grade in 2004.[13]

It is a strange, painfully couched retort. Of all the things from Santos's biography that he has eventually admitted to making up, he has repeatedly doubled down on this easily verifiable point. So it seemed worthwhile to turn 1,600 pages of Horace Mann yearbooks for 2003, 2004, and 2005, covering the period Santos seems to be saying he was there. This exercise in carpal tunnel did not yield up a George Santos, an Anthony Devolder, or even a Zabrovsky—another nom de con—nor any photo that looked remotely like him. In the last hundred pages of the last yearbook there was, however, a Gabriela Santos, who answered diplomatically when asked if a guy named Santos had been her classmate: "Not to my recollection." But then she thought it through some more:

There were not many kids in her class, certainly fewer than two hundred. She knew people the year above and below. Would she have remembered another Brazilian kid also named Santos? This is a school—unlike IS 125—where diversity is a—shall we say—work in progress. Yes, she would have.

The more useful part of this yearbook exercise was a crash course in why Santos might care about Horace Mann at all. There are plenty of brainy NYC schools that Santos, the inquisitive student, could have told stories about attending, but he didn't choose a competitive public one like Bronx Science. Instead he revealed his more status-conscious side, thrusting himself into an intricate, inaccessible world of privilege, one whose yearbooks show scenes of students riding horses, or relaxing in the first-class sections of planes. The inside jokes—like "I'm an HMer but all my clothing still says Spence"—hint at an expensive world approximately three trains and a bus from Jackson Heights.

There are different ways to get the money that can start collapsing those physical and psychological distances, for those who really want to, the crisp bills that can buy your way into a different environment. You can ask your parents, but even the generous ones have a limit. Chores or fast-food restaurant shifts are earning possibilities, as well as ways to inculcate a work ethic that lingers for a lifetime. Gercino was the kind of father who wanted his son to know how to grind. Santos once told an interviewer that his dad insisted he at least consider being a painter for his career. "It's good money," was the argument. But this was not what Santos had in mind. "I've painted a wall or two in my life, and by the end of the day I'm like, 'Oh my god, whatever happened to my lower back,'" he said in the same interview. He laughed. "I killed it!"[14]

There is, of course another way to get money, particularly from people who spoil you and love you, or those whom you make surrender their love. Santos seems to have stolen from his aunt Elma, according to a family member and a friend. One version of it, as per the relative, was that Elma gave her nephew money to pay her bills, and rather than passing it along to cover his aunt's debts, he kept the money. Elma was smart and hardworking, moving from cleaning houses to working at a bank and the post office. But she was not so smart with him. She realized what happened when the proverbial creditors came calling. But she didn't do anything about it. This was her blood. She did not return multiple requests for comment about this allegation or any other.

Fatima too was lenient. "She was always making up excuses for what he did," one relative said. It was just George for so long, and then his sister, Tiffany. Theirs was a small family unit. In a 2016 Facebook post, not long before Fatima died, she explained in Portuguese: "I love my children, they are my everything ♥♥♥♥♥"

---

*There is one subject that* does seem to move Santos with consistency, an emotion that always seems to be true: he is a "card-carrying" mama's boy, he has said.[15] He has repeatedly called Fatima his "mentor" and "best friend."[16]

One person who helped on a Santos political campaign remembers his voice getting shaky whenever he'd bring up his mother, even long after her 2016 death from cancer.

There were moments throughout Santos's life when his mother would leave him for a spell in one place or another. He would stay with a relative while she went to Brazil. One time, when he was grown and she returned to New York, Fatima's roommate remembered Santos frequently checking in on his mother, even though he lived some distance away. It seemed that Santos missed her.

At various points, they cohabitated, even when he was an adult. It could sometimes be tense. Another roommate remembers them fighting about everything you can imagine—cigarettes, money—

and sometimes, Fatima would retreat to her bedroom and just cry. Santos would say horrible things to her, tell her to leave the house—"his" house, he'd say. This too would become a trait of his; he'd flip a switch, and threaten the nearest of friends or kin.

But with his mother, there was something often pushing him back to the woman who had brought him into the world, after however-many weeks in the womb.

Santos's sister, Tiffany, once left a "review" on his political Facebook page calling him a "son who dedicated his life to give our mother the most comfortable life when she was loosing [sic] her fight to cancer." Santos's care for Fatima is even stenciled into Queens public records. On Christmas Eve 2015, Santos appeared in housing court for failing to pay $2,250 in rent, and the complete audio recording of the proceeding reveals him saying matter-of-factly that his mother was staying with him, "for health issues."[17]

He talks not only about his deep feelings for his mother, but also his great pride in her life. Santos has called Fatima "the first female executive at a major financial institution."[18] He cites her prominence in local Republican politics, calling her "active with the party as a donor for over two decades." He fondly remembers her leaving her "nine to five" to canvass for Rudy Giuliani, and bringing young Santos along.[19] And he has clucked about her escape from the South Tower on 9/11, the way she got caught up in the "ash cloud."[20] There is good reason to believe that none of this is true.

City, state, and federal campaign finance databases show no evidence of political donations. She does not appear to have been a registered voter in New York, and her immigration records betray no sign that she was even a US citizen, though she worked for years to legalize her status and at one point had a green card.[21] The 9/11 story is also questionable at best: In her own immigration paperwork, she claimed she was not in the United States that year. One entry from June 2001—just before the attacks—lists her current address as Niterói, Brazil. Santos continues to insist his mother was at Ground Zero, and perhaps she reentered or remained in the country in a way not reflected in the documents. Immigrants and employers sometimes tell tall tales on their applications about dates, details, and locations. But the son's full claim about his mother's 9/11 experience has further holes, including the campaign bio in which he says in successive sentences that Fatima was a financial executive and that she was "in her office in the South Tower" on the tragic day. People who knew her remember nothing about Wall Street jobs or Wall Street wealth.

There is something touching about Santos's ambition to construct a pioneering, world-bestriding life for his mother, constructing a false memory palace in her honor, boosting her to heights she was never quite able to see. Over the years, he has told whoppers about his father, exaggerating Gercino's achievements as well. But on the public stage it was to his mother's memory that he returned over and over again.

Fatima's genuine American story began sometime in the 1980s. Immigration records suggest that she came across the southern border in the San Diego area, and found work in Florida.

Her introduction to American life was more *Grapes of Wrath* than *Gatsby*, far from the life of wealth and privilege Santos pretended she'd led. Fatima's paperwork for legalization says she spent 110 days picking beans and squash on David Jones's farm in Goulds, Florida. Steve Jones, son of the namesake farmer, told me the fields were full of immigrants then, working sunup to sundown, in the 90- to 100-degree Florida heat. They donned long-sleeve shirts and towels on the neck to provide a miserly shade. Men and women and sometimes their kids worked together, shoving food into their mouths from Tupperware for quick sustenance. The beans were tossed into hampers that earned the picker five or seven dollars per.

There were dangers: Crack hit some of the workers hard in the mid-1980s. Cold snaps dried out the available work too. Some pickers stayed years, while others continued on to other fields or places like New York, which is where the immigration records suggest Fatima ventured next.

The housekeeping work that Fatima found there had its own precarities. There were new spaces to navigate, fancy homes to learn. She had to figure out how to communicate in a foreign tongue: she spoke Portuguese, Spanish, and "Little English," she claimed to federal officials. A 1989 form letter from someone who employed her as a housekeeper affirmed that she was a person of "good moral character and sound judgment." Between 1990 and 1996 she also worked for Charles Goodman of the Upper West Side. This kind of household work was certainly not the high-flying financial wizardry to which Santos claimed his mother belonged, but it did bring her into its proximity at least. Her boss's family had founded Marvel Comics decades prior,[22] connecting Fatima in a way to Stan Lee, Spider-Man, the Black Panther, and over $29 billion of film revenue.[23] She was known as an excellent cook and a hard worker, minding the five-day-a-week job until an abrupt end to her employment when items were found missing, according to a source close to the family.

This was typical work, with typical opportunities and challenges, for many people in the Brazilian diaspora that gathered in the apartments and houses of Queens. Other members of Santos's family spent at least some time working in other people's homes.

His aunt Victoria appears to have worked for years as a top-level household staffer for someone legitimately high up in the business world, according to a friend and a family member. It's an intimate act to clean or cook or look after the home of someone who has more money than you. You are touching the same linens, dusting the same books, overhearing the same phone calls in which masters of the universe shout or chortle or complain. You are so close, even if you leave and get on the subway or bus to your own place and cares. Tomorrow you'll be back. It makes sense that someone with an active imagination, like Santos, would place himself and those he loved in more expensive shoes.

It was the stuff of fantasy. There may be heroes and boldfaced names in Santos's family tree, as far as the genealogists can figure: a respected classical pianist, a distant ancestor considered a martyr in a revolt against the Portuguese. But his parents were people who worked onerously in whatever ways they could to support their families. They scratched and earned and took chances. They built a life. It's the story of America. It's what people remember on their deathbeds, and Fatima reached hers too soon. For almost everyone, a life of work and family is as good as things get. But it was never enough for George Santos.

Perhaps he looked around him and was not satisfied with what he saw. There was a Queens church called Saint Rita's he used to go to on Eleventh Street, along with his mother and sister. For twenty years the church has had a regular Sunday Mass in Portuguese that draws Brazilians from all over the five boroughs and also Long Island and New Jersey. There are some doctors and lawyers but many housekeepers and painters, those who work in construction, people who might have an immigration issue after skipping an ICE check-in. People like his own people.

The church gets packed on Christmas and Easter. Other days, people give each other the peace of the Lord and take tabs on who is there. But even on an average spring Sunday there are dozens who come out for the sense of community, young men in colorful T-shirts and blond highlights mixing with kids keeping their backs ramrod straight in the pews, looking at the red banners with English words exhorting the flock toward "Reverence" and "Right Judgement."

Fatima is still remembered there. Whether or not it was really true that she "instituted a grassroots daily operation to distribute sandwiches around the Northeast Queens area to homeless individuals," as Santos claimed she did, she was a mother. She loved her children. And she died and was memorialized by this church in 2016.

It must have been excruciating for Santos. Even their fights showed how much they meant to each other. A December 2016 fundraising post said he had been busy nursing her and also that he needed monetary help to pay for a wake: "Fatima left two children who were not working because she needed 24 hours of care and now they need our help in this delicate moment."[24]

Luckily, the church came to his side, this flock of his peers. They may not have had much, and they may not have come from the worlds Santos dreamed of, but they opened their wallets now. For typical Sunday services, the collection box is a cloth bag given structural support by a wire basket. This basket is placed in front of the altar, within sight of the priest, a deterrent to someone skimming off the top as the dollars pile up. Here, the parishioners come to the front to drop their offerings into the clean white cloth of the bag, the color of First Communion outfits, the color of the ties worn by children who bear their mouths to the Father;

a white that signifies, with all its unsubtle connotations, purity, rectitude, the lamb of whose blood etc., etc. A saintliness not exactly exhibited by what Santos apparently did with a bucket almost identical to that one.

The church's collection was handed right to him. The amount is lost to history but was significant.[25] Yet a source familiar with the funereal situation says the funeral home was never paid its debt, as of the spring of 2023. This was not chump change: similar mortuary work in 2016 used to cost in the $6,000 range and often higher.

It seems to George Santos, even the death of the mother he loved, his mentor, his friend, the woman he dreamed with and dreamed for, could become an opportunity.

———————

*Santos was walking around Queens* one day in 2011 when he had an encounter he had anticipated but hoped to avoid.

"Oh shit," he said later to a friend. "I just met my father."

Not for the first time, of course. But there were periods when they did not see each other much. Here was the end of one. Santos was in his early twenties and recently back from Brazil, and his father knew he was home. Soon after, Gercino would visit Santos's new apartment, to judge how it was that his son lived.

It was a small place, remembers the friend, Adriana Parizzi. She and her young daughter were sharing it with Santos. Gercino was the type of worker who wakes up at five to get to the construction site by seven. He looked over the apartment with his professional eye. When he reached the bedroom, where he saw Parizzi's daughter sleeping, he paused. He seemed to soften. George was a room away, out of earshot from Gercino.

"Let me tell you something," Gercino said to Parizzi. "It's my son, but be careful."

From the beginning, there were rifts between Santos and his father, and between Fatima and Gercino.

Santos has said there was a "dispute"[26] between his parents about what to name him, and this is how he ended up with two first names. Anthony seems to have been his mother's choice, and that is what she and many others called him.

Santos's parents did not stay together long. In the Brazilian state of Minas Girais, where Gercino is from and to where he often returned, Gercino's birth certificate logs a marriage between him and another woman in 1998. Santos would have been around ten. For much of his life he seems to have been more Fatima's son.

Gercino remained a specter in Santos's life, though. When the son got around to running for office, he once told an interviewer that his father was an "independent thinker."

"He likes Clinton, hates Bush, hates Obama. He's okay with Trump. So . . ."

Santos laughs nervously, and then the interviewer asks that obvious question: "Does he like you? Is he going to vote for you?"

There is an excruciating pause and then Santos says stiffly, "Well, he put his money where his mouth is."[27] It seems to be a reference to a donation made in Gercino's name to Santos's campaign. (Though this itself is not evidence of contribution, since Santos's campaign charted multiple bogus donations from relatives.)[28]

On the Father's Day that came during his second run for office, someone in Santos's campaign posted the expected picture of the candidate and his dad with the innocuous caption "Happy Father's Day to all the dads out there!"

In the picture, Gercino is dressed simply in a dark coat and jeans, one hand in one pocket and the other behind his son's back. He is smiling. Santos is wearing a neat white sweater, and they are standing in front of a Christmas tree full of lights and baubles, a red ribbon on top. It is a warm scene, but why use a wintry picture for a June holiday?

Santos's sister, flagging the picture for Santos, provided her own evidence of a strained relationship.

"You must be fucking kidding with me," she messaged Santos on Instagram. "I hope this shit was posted by one of those fucking bitches that works for your campaign. I really do."

Signs of Gercino and Santos's complicated father-son connection were evident in court in 2023, when, after everything, it came time for someone to secure the son's bond. This was a solemn moment. In a sealed bond hearing that May, the judge explained that the people who signed for George Santos did not have to put up the $500,000, but they'd be on the hook for it. "This could go against your credit rating, your ability to get a mortgage. You'd owe that money to the government," the judge said. "So I want to make sure that you both understand that."

It was Gercino and Aunt Elma to whom the judge spoke. These two blood relatives were the ones who stood up for Santos and put their reputations and livelihoods on the line, even after he'd lied to them so many times. Even after he'd stolen from Elma. When the judge asked Elma about her relationship with Santos, she said, "It's a good relationship even though I don't speak with him on a regular basis."

Gercino said much the same. "I see him I'd say every forty-five, fifty days. We don't see enough."

He noted that lately they spoke often, "but in the past, not as much."

At one point in the hearing out in Central Islip, Gercino asked what would happen if his son got caught going to areas forbidden by his bond agreement. It signaled a level of concern for his son's well-being. This day was one of multiple times over the years when Gercino seems to have tried to help his son toward a better if quieter path, to show that you can overcome adversity by slow and steady progress, by earning one dollar at a time and putting one workday behind you and resting up for the next one. But his son was always looking for shortcuts.

Santos's old childhood friend Tiffany Bogosian lost track of him for a while after middle school, but a mutual friend later told her a story about another scheme Santos had supposedly tried. He was eighteen or so, and there was a particular bag in his father's home that had important documents, passports, maybe money. The story was that Santos told this friend to take the bag and walk out the front, and he'd go out the back. But out on the street, Gercino saw the friend with this very important bag and grabbed her.

"Look," he said, "I know that you're trying to help him. But I'm telling you now, you're only going to cause problems."

The friend called out to Santos, and he dutifully came over. Gercino took the bag, and his son, and they went back upstairs.

# 3

## Kitara at the Bingo Table

*T*he first big gay pride parade in Niterói in 2005 was a mess. Which is to say that it was fun, a lot more fun than some people anticipated. The authorities, for one. There was this idea that maybe it would just be a small gathering. Then there were thousands of people frolicking by Icaraí Beach.

*Frolicking* is maybe not a strong-enough word. People were stretching out the old rainbow flags and having sex under them. On the main avenue overlooking the water. You don't get that at the Bank of America–sponsored stuff in Manhattan. There were cross-dressers, shirtless men and women, and people in costume made up to look like genderless machines. There was advocacy for the importance of coming out and being who you are, how seeming different is normal. And there were people yelling and screaming and hooking up. A letter to the editor in *O Globo* later said that the whole city was happily singing and dancing in the streets that day.[1] There is a bad joke that the best thing about Niterói is the view of proud Rio de Janeiro across the water. But even the Cariocas might agree about this night in particular: Niterói was hopping.

One guy who certainly would agree with that was a young New Yorker in a black dress, his long black hair, wig or not, tied into a ponytail that bounces with his every move.

The young man bears an exceptionally striking resemblance to George Santos, and both he and the scene around him can be viewed on tape today because they were captured in a brief video interview. The interviewee—who is indeed Santos, according to friends and ex-friends of the future congressman—has the confidence of youth (he's not yet twenty), the breathlessness of a party, of nighttime, of being one among many and not alone. He is far from Queens. He is unfettered by familial authority figures and restrictions. He revels in this permissive, affirming culture, just a nice change in general from the same-old, same-old atmosphere back home. He nonchalantly grabs a pair of sunglasses off a less-than-fully clad man next to him, dons them (the sunglasses) with the explanation that they're required since he fudged his makeup. He lights up when a microphone enters the frame. True to current form, Santos also gets in some self-promotion, about his "presentations," or performances, at the big Rio drag clubs of the era like Cascadura and even Le Boy. Then the interview ends with Santos's hand skimming smoothly across the semi-bare chest of the formerly sunglassed man he'd used for a TV-ready accessory.[2]

It is a beautiful night in Niterói. It is a beautiful time to be uninhibited, to be alive.

Why would it not be? What could stop Santos, at this moment?

He is confident and assured about himself and his future. Indeed, he says it all the time:

"I'm gonna be rich! I'm gonna be rich!"

That is how the drag artist known as Eula Rochard remembers it: Santos's chorus during their frequent leafy walks from Rochard's house to the Boa Viagem Beach, to meet friends from the city's gay scene. The closer one gets to the beach, the more expensive the houses get, as they do in every city, in every country.

"I'm gonna be rich!"

It grated on Rochard a little, to be honest, Santos's insistence that he was going to marry a rich man. Santos even claimed sometimes that he was already in good financial shape—that his father was wealthy and traveled a lot, and met famous people. Rochard would scoff. Rochard knew Santos's mother cleaned houses, knew that sometimes Santos could not afford the bus. Bluster. It was just another one of his stories. Yet Rochard tolerated the young American.

Eula Rochard has never been to the United States but has notoriety of a sort at home in Brazil. There are newspaper articles about Rochard that follow a certain form: by day, this resident of Niterói does things as a man, like going for a run, exercising at the gym, reporting to work at a nonprofit. But at night, this man takes the ferry to Rio and transforms into a woman: Eula Rochard. Makeup is done en route as the boat coasts over the water; wigs and costumes are pulled from plastic bags. She performs at bars and parties and nightclubs, or acts as a hostess, lip-syncs, makes people laugh and think she is beautiful, dancing the moon into sun.

It was sometime in 2004 or 2005 that Rochard remembers first seeing a lot of Santos, when the two became friends. They were both at that first Niterói parade, certainly, Rochard in a fabulous, busty pink outfit, talking wisely about the importance of Niterói getting an event like this. Santos would spend time at Rochard's home, and should count himself lucky for it—it would be like an aspiring young American drag queen being in Ru Paul's home, that kind of proximity to one of Brazil's drag greats. (That is Rochard's opinion.)

Her apartment is crowded with bags full of costumes, with artifacts from the Amazon, with international gay guides that include her visage, and pictures of her in headdresses and beads and chokers and bracelets and wigs, always wigs, some made with real human hair. And it was in this apartment that Santos sat and learned the drag life: how to get dressed the right way, Rochard says, how to brush wigs, to choose earrings, to move in the world.

"I would teach him," Rochard says now.

Did it matter whether Santos was good or not? Whether he really learned? Rochard told the journalist Marisa Kabas that Santos "did not have what it takes to be a professional. George did not have the glamour for that."[3] He wasn't, Rochard has made clear, at the same level as other drag artists. He could also sometimes be annoying, the way he always tried to nab people's attention. But Rochard had a certain dark fondness for him, a shaking of one's head, in the way that another provincial newcomer to Rio was described in Clarice Lispector's 1977 classic, *The Hour of the Star*: the girl was "so dumb that she sometimes smiles at other people on the street. Nobody smiles back because they don't even look at her." But people sometimes looked at Santos in those years, taken in by his youth and lustrous hair.

Santos was beautiful then, Rochard told me one afternoon in Niterói. "A beautiful boy." She sometimes switches pronouns when talking about Santos these days: sometimes he, sometimes she. It's all fluid.

Rochard wasn't Santos's only friend, and vice versa. She remembers Santos disappearing for a while, and then being back a few years later. This time, Santos actually had money. He wasn't rich, but he was rich for Niterói, in a way, or in one particular way—he came with money and materials for a new dress.

He had patches and huge glittering earrings and a certain kind of costume jewelry that was hard to get in the Brazilian drag community at the time, Rochard says. It was a rock that glinted in daylight or in nightclubs, such was its versatile shine. In bulk, it could almost weigh a dress down. Maybe one could get these pieces in America, or Italy, or France or India, but not in Niterói. Yet here Santos was, with the means to make himself even more beautiful. Where did Santos get this influx of money? Rochard didn't know, but she did feel that Santos had grown since returning. Now the young American was ready to test his beauty and learning above and beyond just fitting in: he tried for a dream of his, to be one of the "Misses" at a Rio gay beauty pageant.

To win is another matter. One does not simply show up and become Miss Rio de Janeiro Gay. One does not laugh about it and come away with the trophy. Consider Isabelita dos Patins, the transformista and friend of Rochard's who once kissed a Brazilian finance minister and future president at carnival, and who is now in her seventies but has judged at this particular Rio pageant in the past. It takes her hours to put on her makeup, her lipstick, her long red nails, her tiara and tight-fitting dress and layers of necklaces and brocades and rings—so many rings. So much outfitting that she basically can't go to the bathroom for the duration, so long would it take her to take everything off in a small stall. It is something similar for the pageant's participants, who belabor their faces, clothes, and hair, making sure everything's perfect. And on the night of the pageant itself, when hundreds of people stand or pay for the privilege of sitting at one of dozens of tables, the participants must be able to do the walk.

Their walking must be beautiful, explains Isabelita. Their movement must be careful and contain a certain charisma. It is a game for the young, and for the hopeful, because the winners get not necessarily fame but a very heavy trophy and the simple acknowledgment of their looks and skill.

The rumor is that there is a VHS tape of this beauty pageant, the one featuring Santos, which no amount of money has yet surfaced. And plenty of money has been waved in front of the faces or computer screens of those who crossed paths with Santos years ago. But what that tape would show is another victor, another beautiful dresser. The winner that year—it was either 2007 or 2008, depending on the recollection of people involved—was not George Santos, who participated but lost, according to the contest's organizer, Orlando Almeida.

Who needs beauty pageants, though? When the need arose, Santos could make himself pretty. As was the case in 2007, once again at the Niterói pride parade, along the avenue beside the beach. And once again there is an image, of Eula Rochard with Santos, featuring the alluring drag name he had adopted—Kitara Ravache. All of it immortalized in one of the defunct gay newspapers once kept afloat by nightclubs. Eula and Kitara. Kitara and Eula. It is a photo, a newspaper clip, that had been waiting like an unused costume in a low drawer of Rochard's home for these many years. It surfaced only one night in 2022 when Rochard, reclining under a seductive painting of herself done by her aunt, saw a TV program about this Brazilian American politician George Santos. But that was *Kitara*, Rochard gasped. Soon she found the photo to prove it.

This time, in this photo, Santos has ditched his plain black outfit, his reliance on a wave of hair for his transformation toward femininity. Now he looks more like his mentor Rochard. He is wearing a bold red dress, full of those fancy and eye-catching foreign stones; he displays long, glittering earrings, with which he stands out among the crowd. If he is not rich or pageant-ready he has certainly won something—the interest of a photographer, the respect of his peers in dresses or out. A new name. And Rochard in her white dress, tight over a firm bosom, stands beside Santos in the fond but distant manner of a teacher, a godmother, one who has seen the rise and fall of many gay friends and lovers, drag artists and marchers, and who knows exactly how winding the road can be.

---

*Even the very taking of* this picture and the place in which it was printed was a sign of the complicated queer history of Brazil.

The snapshot is one of multiple little portraits of people at that 2007 pride parade,[4] an event that was still in its infancy. The short article that goes along with the pictures says the theme that year was resistance against sexism, racism, and homophobia. Along with the great outfits and carousing, the day also featured a case of aggression against a queer couple, the article says. A group of boys yelled at the couple that Niterói wasn't a place for them, and then attacked the pair with stones and bottles and kicks.

There had been so much violence like that, for so long, and

Rochard lived through it. She was born in 1965, during the military dictatorship of Brazil, not exactly a high point of gay rights in the country. Her father did not know she dressed in drag. As a teenager, Rochard discovered the Dionne Warwick song "I'll Never Love This Way Again," learning how to perform to it. Something deep and electrifying flowed through her. She saw her future.

Use of the word *drag* is relatively recent in Brazil, though it's an old concept, common in the everything-goes ethos of carnival, or the nightclubs of Rio. Members of an earlier generation, including Rochard and Isabelita, sometimes call themselves *transformistas*, or transformers. They are people who change through clothing, through makeup, through characterization. They become someone else. Or, as Isabelita says, "I'm a boy during the day, I'm a butterfly at night." There is an artistry to it, apart from sexuality. It is a skill and a calling—a sight to behold. And Rochard learned how to put it on display, in the performances she would give in venues across the city, and the "hostessing" that she helped pioneer—coming, in full drag regalia, to entertain the long lines of people waiting to enter a club, getting them loose and ready to have fun. It started with the "transformer" at the door.

This transformation, this change, is at the heart of what historian and political scientist Thiago Coacci calls a "peculiar history" regarding LGBTQ rights in Brazil. The nation sports a rich gay culture with values of acceptance and openness alongside powerful evangelical and conservative factions—ones that have boosted the career of former president Jair Bolsonaro.

Coacci studies LGBTQ issues and is also an aide to Duda Salabert, one of the first trans women to serve in the Brazilian congress. Salabert is from Belo Horizonte, the relatively conservative and traditional area where Santos's father, Gercino, was born.

There is something of a paradox in the way gay Brazilians have gained acceptance and civil rights over the years, even as they face real violence and discrimination, including from the authorities. Rochard, for example, remembers riding the bus home once from working the big nightclubs in the south zone of Rio—popular destinations, patronized by thousands, straight and gay, places where she was sort of a star. But on the bus, police were frisking people to check if they carried drugs. When they got to her purse, they pulled out her wig, sneered and held it up for everyone to see. *Is this yours? Is this yours?*

Others suffered worse.

Then there were the plagues that none could escape. Brazil's handling of the AIDS crisis in the 1980s and '90s was hailed as one of the most enlightened in the world. Yet Rochard and her community were still hit hard. Before she started performing, a different bus would carry her and dozens of her gay friends to a joyful nearby nightclub. Of that group, only a handful remain.

The life of gay Brazilians improved in many ways with the end of the dictatorship, as states across the country began to encode LGBTQ rights into their constitutions. Big cities like Rio and São Paulo began hosting huge pride parades in the 1990s. And Luiz Inácio Lula da Silva (better known as Lula), the champion of the Brazilian Left and three-time president who came out of the working-class labor movement, took power in 2003 on a platform that included strong support for gay rights. Money flowed to gay causes, and the high courts began awarding more rights. This was the political backdrop during the years Santos spent a lot of time in Brazil: the period was an "explosion" for the movement, Coacci says. Certainly Santos benefited.

He had been a shy and effeminate child, according to one

relative, who says George was sometimes the target of bullying by his cousins: "The whole gay issue wasn't easy for him in the family." The public period of cross-dressing started in his later teenage years when he was in Brazil for long stretches, according to this family member. Luckily, it was a moment of acceptance in public society, with pride parades finally making it out of the biggest metropolises and reaching secondary places like Niterói.

So Santos found a community. He even befriended some activists, and handed out pamphlets at LGBTQ events.[5] Rochard remembers doing with him some of the things Santos would be doing only if he were lonely, or at least searching for his people. That included tagging along to the grocery store, or walking under the canopy of trees to the beach. There at Boa Viajem you could watch the airplanes to Rio fly in and out, walking along the rocky cliffs in search of a private cave, or bush, where the romantically desiring could have sex. Rochard didn't engage in the public sexcapade—there were rats and snakes down there by the bushes—but one could stay busy with that crowd and in that place just by talking, strolling, and preening. At night, along with the hoots of the owls that hunted the rats and snakes, there were the murmurs and yelps of gossip—who had AIDS, who was fucking who, or wanted to. It was a place to find friends and partners, a place to connect. Here Santos might start yapping again about his quest to become rich or his already-rich family— Rochard would cut him off. Lies spread when they're not quashed. But many lies or jokes or tall tales were told, certainly, over time, among those shambling rocks.

Farther along the coast was the route where the pride parades took place, but these informal beach gatherings were less a parade and more what passed for social media in that time, the community that was available to the gays of Niterói. It served the same purpose that those small newspapers did, in whose service people used their Kodaks to snap pictures of outfits and couples and poses. Before the cacophony of cell phones, the beach was a place where Santos could learn how to act and flirt and behave in the world, and feel safe while doing so, a reality that was not the case everywhere.

Because in Brazil, beneath the embrace of fantastic, glittering dresses, of the tolerance of parades and the pursuit of fun, there was a lurking conservatism that was waiting for its moment to reemerge. The way Rochard puts it is that the prejudice was put to sleep, but woke up with Jair Bolsonaro.

Even in the time Santos was living and learning and experimenting in Brazil, the rise of Bolsonaro was underway. The former army captain was open in his homophobia, saying in 2002 that if he saw two men kissing in the street, "I'll beat them up." He made similar warnings about those closer to him, telling *Playboy* in 2011 that he would be "incapable of loving a homosexual son."[6]

Bolsonaro's openly derogatory beliefs and language extended to race and beyond—he once answered a question about what he'd do if his son fell in love with a Black woman by saying, "I don't run that risk because my sons were very well educated."[7] But his comments about gay people could be particularly unsubtle. In a bizarre 2016 sit-down with the actor now known as Elliot Page, Bolsonaro noted that if he was a cadet in the military academy and saw Page, he'd whistle due to Page's attractiveness. He said he believed that for a majority of gay people, "it's a behavioral issue."[8]

Rhetoric like this helped Bolsonaro harness the advocacy and power of the evangelical movement in Brazil on his route to the presidency, which he attained in 2018.

Santos admired Bolsonaro and his movement. He defended the South American leader on Twitter during his own political run,[9] and one day posed for a grinning, thumbs-up picture with Bolsonaro's far-right congressional ally Carla Zambelli.[10] He had experience with conservative viewpoints in the Bolsonaro vein from an early age. Santos's family members have posted repeatedly—and negatively—on social media about Lula, who has been a titanic figure on the left in Brazilian politics for decades. The religion his family embraced could also be a powerful political force. The church he and his sister and mother attended in Queens—Saint Rita's—boasts a tomblike statue outside its doors labeled IN LOVING MEMORY OF THE INNOCENT UNBORN.

Santos himself sometimes talked about politically adjacent issues as a young man—hating Lula, loving the military, admiring power and the sensation of taking charge. Yet he was noncommittal in the politics section of his account for Orkut, the now-defunct social media platform.

He was able to pass. There was a peace dividend that he was living off, one that came after the suffering and struggles of the gay Brazilians and transformers who came before him. Now he could fill his Orkut account instead with phrases about self-knowledge and being happy in love. And years before he and his American political party would characterize drag queens as a greater threat to children than guns, he would dress the way he wanted. He would wear jewelry if he felt the urge. He would make himself beautiful.

Given the amount that Santos exaggerates and story-tells, it is difficult to know how often he really did perform in drag, as he himself described on video. People—including his onetime dressmaker—remember some shows at a club or beachside kiosk. After one, the dressmaker said, almost no one clapped.[11] Post-election, Santos denied having been a drag performer,[12] and he claimed to people that he hardly ever dressed in drag. It is also no longer possible to go to most of the Santos-era drag institutions in Rio. Some of them have closed due to COVID, that other plague. Phone cameras changed the game.

But there are a few ways to see how Santos might have looked and moved and acted while cross-dressing, either on a stage or off. One is a set of videos posted from the Niterói pride parade in 2007.[13] The videos show a nighttime scene, the *oonce-oonce-oonce* of a techno beat, time kept by the elbows and knees of people dancing. Into each of these videos, at one point or another, comes a person in a red dress. The person stands out, with their bright choker, glittering jewels, bold pose, and low-cut hem betraying the smooth skin of ample thighs.

The videos were two of only ten posted by one of the few accounts followed by @anthonydevolder, and friends of Santos's say the dazzling dress-wearer is indeed him. He has a presence to his motion, a grace, an easy manner of laying his hand on someone's skin. His red lipstick is carefully applied; his hips expertly dip. He smiles professionally, regally, in the sea of gyrating bodies, and his earrings accentuate his teeth. He has learned how to make use of the body he was given. He has transformed.

The other way to clearly see what Santos might have done in drag is to follow his old friend and mentor Rochard, on the infrequent occasions that she dons her finery for a show—as on one evening the spring after Santos won a congressional seat in New York. Far away in a sauna in the neighborhood of Glória, her own glory days long past, Rochard retraced her old steps from Niterói to Rio, trading the view for the energy, taking her outfit out of a dusty plastic cover, and prepared her mind and body to once again take the stage.

It is just before nine p.m. on a Saturday night. A short man with laughably muscled shoulders pushes his way through the door into Club 117. A viewer entering after will pass a skinny bouncer, an unadorned door, and a checkout desk, where he will receive a bracelet and a key. It is only *he*, for women or those who seem to be women in street clothes are not allowed in this space. The viewer is told that it's possible to rent time with a man for $8, and that there is a sauna, and also the show.

Saunas are common places now in Rio to see these styles of drag shows. Different types of pleasure genres are available at Club 117, and the choices make themselves immediately clear. There are the men slowly stroking themselves in the heat of the actual sauna just inside, their white towels fallen to hips or feet. There are the closed rooms where the keys can be used, and the more private consummations therein. There are the bumps at the door, the accidental brushes with hard-ons. And there is the show, which starts right at 9:05, including a Mick Jagger–looking man in a red tie and skimpy blue tank strumming on his air guitar/crotch. A performer dressed as Shiva with extra arms sends beams of laser light into the crowd. Then comes a cowboy with enormous arms, who turns out to be the short man with beach-ball deltoids who entered the club in looser clothing not long before. Now his flannel shirt is cut at the shoulders, his quads nearly break through his jeans, and soon both the shirt and the jeans and a dainty pair of white underpants are off. The underpants travel along with him, patron to patron. All it takes is a small tip to put them back on.

But the experience of watching Rochard is very different—more artistic, emblematic of the kind of exuberant drag Santos once embraced. On this night, Rochard wears a frizzy red wig, a round monk's habit, and crystalline hanging earrings. She is lip-synching to "Big Spender," the striptease song with a Bob Fosse dance from the musical *Sweet Charity*. She is heaving with coquettishness. Playing a game. Within moments, Rochard has pulled off the habit and revealed a shining red singlet, and luscious black locks instead of the red. None of it, of course, is real. But it's dazzling. She has a sense of humor. She is in on the joke, cuddling up to her boa and fake-singing about someone paying to spend some time with her.

Santos's drag mentor owns the stage in red lips and acrobatic eyelashes. She takes careful steps in high heels. The performance is more comedy routine or musical number than sexual display. The room loosens accordingly, as if the high stakes, the one-way conclusion of stripping and petting, can now be relaxed. One can just smile and watch. Rochard is not the most conventionally attractive performer on the stage; she has a pudginess that, as for her pupil, would not have stood up to Miss Rio's unforgiving rigor. For those looking to be seen as gorgeous, in this day and age, in this cruel economy, that means either starving oneself, or embracing your rolls and curves. It's something Santos well knew. There are two manners of changing, either conforming or creating something different. Performing. And isn't there something noble and hopeful about choosing the latter.

––––––––––

*A challenge for Santos throughout* his life has been the tension between his love of beautiful, expensive things, and the need to earn enough money to pay for them. The fun lifestyle and great outfits Santos had when he spent time in Brazil did not come free. Periodically, Santos would need to scrounge up cash.

During a longer stay in his ancestral country, while living with his mother and sister and aging grandmother, he developed a method of mooching off his grandmother, one relative remembers. He'd convince her to give him some reais to go shopping, this senior citizen who went to church every day, a type of quiet devotion remembered years later by doormen in her high-rise building.

Just a few hundred, he'd request. When he returned, there would be the story of how he had been mugged. *What happened was . . .* He did it with others, too. He'd find someone else to borrow money from, and then disappear.

His mother, Fatima, had her own genre of side earning, according to the family member. She always had some sad story or other. She always needed a little helping out. Often it was legitimate. How easy could it have been to raise two kids, going back and forth between continents, no longer together with her husband, working jobs that don't make one rich?

It was who she was. There can be social differences even within a family. It is something that people are attuned to in Brazil. There is a familiar expression that the anthropologist Roberto DaMatta dissects in *Carnivals, Rogues, and Heroes.* The expression goes: "Do you know who you're talking to?" There is a haughtiness to it, a clear indication of a social separation, of an up and a down. It's the idea that, though you might pretend to be someone else, when it comes down to it, economically, societally, you belong there and I belong here.

It is a concept that would not be so foreign to the denizens of certain districts of Manhattan. And it is a distinction that would have been drilled into Santos in Niterói and Rio, in whose favelas lived parents and children who survive, literally survive, off the Bolsa Família government program that offers several hundred reais a month—a crucial cash-transfer program, but still less than what someone can spend on a decent steak dinner in Leblon, one of the continent's most expensive zip codes. And forget about eating at Oro, the kind of place where the food comes parceled in little bites on top of shiny eggs or gargantuan bricks. Be prepared to spend thousands, are you good for it?

*Do you know who you're talking to?*

It feels good to be on the higher end, in the know. The one who should be known, not the one who needs to do the learning. Santos, with all his shouts about becoming rich and anxieties about getting money, must have known this at his core.

For eventually in his time in Brazil, he came across someone who would live on both sides of the divide. Who has been both known and unknown.

Santos and his mother met Adriana Parizzi playing bingo. Years later, she would be the one who moved back to Queens with him, who met his father, Gercino, and even shared New York apartments with Santos, along with her young, shrewd-staring daughter. But it all started in 2008 in Niterói, when Parizzi began giving Fatima money in their bingo games.

This was when Parizzi was on the high side, and Fatima and Santos were on the low. She once told *Patch*'s Jacqueline Sweet that she felt sympathetic toward Fatima since "she didn't have any money."[14] Fatima seemed to be good humored despite her troubles, often laughing. When there were dancing lunches at the bingo halls, Fatima would get up and move her body. It didn't cost much to play, at least one game at a time. But add it all up and Parizzi was laying out thousands of reais a month.

Parizzi and Fatima had a schedule. Their bingo was not just the kind of game you play at a church function, or in an old folks' home, where the cafeteria hosts a round or two to pass the time. No: They might get to one of the bingos on Friday and not stop

until the weekend was through. The games could last fifteen minutes each and could run back-to-back from eleven a.m. to four
a.m. each day.

The bingo hustle, which has operated mostly illegally in Brazil, has been called a gateway drug. Older people and women,
especially, have gotten addicted, but they are not alone. There
are stories of working people losing their livelihoods, and even a
federal judge selling her property and car, to cover losses racked
up at the bingo halls. Still, Parizzi likes to focus on the way the
game and the camaraderie of the halls can fill emptinesses, as
they did for her.

She began playing heavily after her father died. Perhaps that
could be called a turning point in her economic life. Her parents
had done well and saved their money, but they didn't teach her
how to handle the funds herself. She thought, sometimes, that the
money would never end. There were moments, for example, when
she would sit in her home in Teresópolis while her daughter was
in school. She didn't have to work, and so she'd turn on the television and buy the type of jewelry that gets advertised for purchase
by phone call at midday hours. Her bank account dipped, but the
jewelry was beautiful.

Teresópolis is a mountain city on the edge of a waterfall-filled
national park, on a road where it's two ways going up, and one way
going down, so the departure can take forever when you inevitably get stuck behind a truck. The distance to Niterói is therefore
measured in hours and reinforced by the architecture—way up
here, there are homes decorated like Swiss chalets. Yet time after
time, Adriana would take her daughter on the long haul down
to ocean-level Niterói, to stay with a babysitter while she played
bingo with Santos's mother along the elegant shore.

Her life intersected with the Devolder Santoses in various ways. She knew Eula Rochard, Santos's drag performer mentor, and remembered her as a private and withdrawn person offstage. Parizzi's first real boyfriend lived in the same apartment building as Santos's grandmother. She became acquainted with Fatima, others in the family, and, finally, Santos himself, when he plopped down one day at her bingo table around 2009. It was between rounds. Almost immediately, they were friends. The Santos charm rarely fails.

Parizzi is one of many associates who say it's impossible not to like the guy, such is his charisma, or what at first passes for charisma. He had a malleable face, and wasn't afraid to use it. Over the years he struck poses in many pictures for her, in which he grins, mugs, flips off the camera, or jokes. He was good at filling emptiness. He could fill whole rooms. Soon, they were spending a lot of time together.

There was one particular bingo, for example, at a football club next to the ferry terminal. They would park at a car wash where the owner knew who she was. A gas station nearby had a twenty-four-hour ATM machine. A clandestine door brought her and Santos to the second floor, where the bingo was played, and when they came out it could be nighttime, or morning.

There were weekends when she and Santos would stumble out finally when all the gambling was done and get a room in a motel not too far away—something Parizzi paid for, too. It was the type of motel where people maybe go for the bed, not exactly the location, but it was never like this with her and Santos. He was obviously not interested. They were like girlfriends.

In that motel room, surrounded by sighing and climaxing couples, they would enjoy themselves more platonically, ordering steak or potatoes for dinner, which Santos enjoyed. They would take baths. He would shave her, Parizzi remembers. They'd sleep until ten—because the bingo opened at eleven.

And then it would be back to the ATM machine, the football club building, the hidden march to the second floor, the food and drinks and betting, winning and losing, their traditions—throw a little sugar under the table, make things sweeter. In the mornings there would be a line snaking around the inside of the building because the first round was supposed to be free, but Parizzi did not need such freebies; indeed, she dispensed them. When she won, she would sometimes buy the table a round.

She had money. What was the difference? Did you know who she was?

———

*These days, Parizzi lives a* very different life. Essentially all of her income comes from her green-and-yellow Bolsa Família government card. Instead of a washing machine in her favela home, she has a washing bucket. Instead of the motel bed she used to share with Santos, her mattress is a collection of thin mats. She has had to ask her neighbor for beans before, when hungry. She hand-makes clothes for her teenage daughter, weblike tops. And for herself, there is a simple black dress with a knot on one shoulder, one she has had for almost as long as she has known Santos.

She does not let herself entirely off the hook. She did not have a long work history. She has made financial mistakes. She knows she had her problems with gambling, too—just like Fatima. There is a touchiness about having left her daughter to play bingo—it was with a trusted babysitter. The gambling filled the lonely space in her, just like the spending of money.

But she does blame Santos, too. His years of mooching and misleading her. There were all those unreimbursed bingo games and motel nights. So much food. And there were the more direct scams he would attempt, later. And still she would never learn. A low estimate: She would pay 1,000 reais a week for each of them to play bingo, her and Fatima and Santos. They played almost every week. This went on for many months—much of 2010, and some before and after. It amounts to tens of thousands of American dollars, on just the bingo alone.

Parizzi likes to think of herself as an honest person. It is key to her understanding of herself, even in the face of unexpected poverty. Like the time in Scotland, where she had gone traipsing after a man who mistreated her. Once, at a deli where she would buy flowers, they gave her two bouquets while charging for one. She went back later but the deli was closed. When she finally caught up to them, the workers said there was nothing to worry about, since no money had gone missing from the till. It became a nickname for her: "This is the honest Brazilian."

This is what you hold on to when you're on the downside of the economic scale. This is what you want to make clear, very clear, when your friend for so many years was George Santos.

Because Santos's transgressions went far beyond mooching and cadging and experimenting with his outfits and appearances when he was in Brazil. His urge for cash and dissatisfaction with workaday work was too strong. It all led to the little matter of fraud.

That's what it was called when Santos took an old checkbook belonging to an octogenarian his mother had been caring for. The man died, which gave Santos that most valuable thing for paperhangers—a check that looked legitimate because it once was. This was how it seemed, anyway, to the salesclerk at the Salt, a luxury imported-fashion retailer in Niterói. In June 2008, Santos waltzed in and whipped out the old checkbook for his unearned purchase of shoes and clothes, dropping over 2,000 reais. Only later did the salesclerk realize the bank account associated with the checks had been long closed.[15]

The clerk caught a break, though, when a man named Thiago came in trying to return a pair of shoes that had been purchased with those bad checks.

Thiago would later say that the shoes had been a gift from Santos. He knew nothing about any fraud. He and Santos were friends, and he had no reason to suspect anything bad about the guy—Santos seemed to be in good financial condition. He wore nice clothes and went to fancy restaurants and clubs. The kind of guy who, if Santos asked Thiago who he thought he was talking to, Thiago would think he'd know. The salesclerk, too—he thought Santos was a college student, studying radiology. Even then Santos's disguises worked.

This return attempt of a pair of sneakers may go down in history as the most revelatory shoe return anywhere, at any time. It allowed the authorities back then to trace the crime back to Santos, and charge him with check fraud. And it was one of the bombshell toplines in the *New York Times'* explosive 2022 investigation showing newly elected representative Santos was not exactly who he said he was.[16]

What Santos said, back then, in Brazil, was that he was guilty. "I know I messed up but I want to pay," he messaged the aggrieved salesclerk, according to Brazilian court documents from 2009. Santos said he'd used a few checks and then thrown the checkbook in the gutter. He said he'd done the deed. Just before he turned twenty, he'd already been a thief.

In truth, it was not the most serious offense in the world. Ask some defense attorneys in Rio, and they will tell you this: for a first-time offender, someone who doesn't combine the fraud with something more heinous, the client probably won't go to prison. The one irony is that in Brazilian politics, someone who shrugs off a settlement and gets convicted for major crimes and exhausts their appeals can't be eligible for open seats in the national senate and congress for eight years.[17] We don't bother with that kind of backstop in the United States.

But congressional politics was many years away. Santos was formally charged in Brazil in 2011, and became just a kid in some hot water with the law. His scared mother said this to Parizzi, in fact: he was "in a little bit of trouble."[18]

And so it was to Parizzi he turned, once again. What was a few hundred dollars more? She opened her own checkbook. She paid for flights to New York. She didn't have much good going on in Brazil. In fact, she'd leave, too. It was good to be able to escape, to be—for Santos—once again an American. The path to riches was not obvious in Brazil, and people knew who he was too well. He needed a new kind of transformation.

# 4

## Grift City

*I*t could sometimes seem that Greg Morey-Parker's flashy new friend George Santos had an answer for everything.

New to New York, as Morey-Parker was? Santos could show him around. Need a place to stay? He had an open spot in Jackson Heights. Can't seem to find your wallet, including your ID? Don't let that ruin a good night, bouncer be damned. Santos had a solution.

That was a Therapy night, that evening in June 2014. Or maybe it was an Industry night. It could have been both. The clubs were right across the street from each other in Hell's Kitchen, but for those thinking clearly, there was no comparison. Therapy with its two floors, its copious bathrooms, its spacious bar. You could hear yourself think in Therapy. You could drink a Freudian Sip in Therapy. You might see a Broadway star or reality TV show winner at Therapy. You never knew in Therapy. Therapy was fun.

In fact it was what appealed to Morey-Parker about New York City. A gay bar called "Therapy"! Right near all these other gay bars! Accessible by just about any train! Morey-Parker had a soft spot for the MTA, approximately a thousand times better than his native Boston T, even when there was planned work on every line. That was New York. So was the guy Morey-Parker caught downloading porn in a Starbucks. Always something happening. Once he posted a meme, some text over the Statue of Liberty: *A bad day in New York City is still better than a good day anywhere else.* And wasn't it even truer if you were a gay man—indeed, a gay Republican? Looking for another is like "trying to find a needle in a gay stack," Morey-Parker likes to say. But you could find one in New York. They've got all kinds in New York. They've got Santos.

Morey-Parker met Santos at Hombres in Queens, just before Thanksgiving 2013. It was a date, and they had these perfectly similar political backgrounds, but still it didn't start off well. Santos seemed somewhat . . . nouveau riche. Namedroppy. Had a lot of cash and wanted to make sure you knew that. Morey-Parker was a person hungry for companionship, someone who wasn't thrilled to be single, or alone on Valentine's Day. But this was not a date he could stomach. He texted his friend Prince to come save him from the gaudy way Santos was flashing bills.

Maybe the bad beginning was from the clash of cultures. Santos was New York City. Morey-Parker hailed from New England. He likes to say he comes from reserved, careful people; the sort of family who call it "Tax-achussets"; who pay for the check by slowly sliding a card or announcing passively, *Oh, it was taken care of*. These were people who thought a lot about lineage, claiming links all the way back to Captain John Parker of the Lexington Minutemen. There was this long American story.

But American stories can take twists and turns, and Morey-Parker was on the twist side of his, which is to say that he talked a lot about a family trust that he couldn't quite access yet. To outsiders he sure seemed to be broke. Regardless he was very busy, working his way through college, and his lease had just ended. And he and Santos had made up following that misfired date—Santos apologized. He'd been drunk. Morey-Parker accepted his apology. We've all been there. We've all needed a friend. For all these reasons he agreed to take the room that Santos offered.

It was a simple two-bedroom apartment in Queens, on Thirty-Fourth Avenue. The full rent at one point was $1,750. The funny thing was how crowded it became, no matter how the sleeping arrangements shuffled—and they did. The place was home to Santos's mother, Fatima, and his sister, Tiffany; Santos himself; and also a cast of roommates who rotated in or out and sometimes overlapped. There was a pattern with these roommates, Morey-Parker included. They were newcomers to the city who were very excited to be there. They needed something from Santos, the way Morey-Parker needed friendship. And, well, they ended up feeling a little gullible in a way about the guy who had opened his door. Take Wellington Lino, a sixteen-year-old friend of Tiffany's from Brazil who basically didn't speak English. Santos was like a big brother to him, for the first few weeks he was there. Lino mostly stayed in Tiffany's bedroom but sometimes crashed in Santos's room, where he'd be awoken by Santos's sleeptalking. Another roommate for a period was Yasser Rabello, who wanted to be a pharmacist and was thrilled to be in New York. It's fair to say that Morey-Parker had a little crush on Rabello. In fact, it has legal bearing on this story.

This churn of people was pretty chaotic, but it was a clean place, as far as Morey-Parker remembers. Neat despite the lack of furniture. Santos's mother could be anal about tidying up the premises. God forbid he forget to clean out the french press. Good thing it was all sanitary because Morey-Parker, turns out, would be sleeping in the living room. To fall asleep he chugged NyQuil and Benadryl. For the privilege, they charged him $310.

All three of these roommates noticed certain strangenesses about the setup during the periods of their stay. Morey-Parker was never given a key, for example, and sometimes this could lead to chaos. There were the times they were all texting each other to see who could let who in. Once, the family got really angry at Rabello because he was in the apartment when they were all locked out, and though they'd been buzzing the unit, he wasn't answering. The intercom was broken, and no one knew. Lino, just a kid really, spent his days at school, and he thought it was a little weird that Santos was always loafing around the apartment.

The roommates' new friend Santos would sometimes say something that raised eyebrows. Like the fact that he said he went to NYU for a business degree but didn't seem to recognize the name of the school, Stern. Santos talked about having two jobs at what he called the G and G's—Goldman Sachs and Globo, the latter being the flagship Brazilian TV outfit, the type of channel he co-incidentally had tried to sell a few years before when he was at Dish. But now he said he was doing personal-interest pieces for the media company, from here in New York. Once, Morey-Parker messaged him to ask why he was up so early in the morning, and

Santos wrote that he was working: "I'm back on air." He added that he "just did my 1min and 45 sec job lol," and then complained that he'd have to come back later "for the night news."

Then there was the really strange overlap when Morey-Parker once casually invited Santos to a family home in Edgartown sometime. That fungible word *sometime*; it's one you have to have some subtlety to wield. Maybe the time would come, but maybe it wouldn't. The odd part came later when Santos said that actually, his family had this place on Nantucket. Morey-Parker asked where, since he knew some people on the island. Santos became vague. When pinned, he said Meghan Trainor had actually been their camp counselor out there. The famous singer. When Fatima heard exchanges like this, she and her son would start talking sharply in Portuguese.

This all rhymed a little with a similar New England incident that happened when Morey-Parker was back around Boston in 2018, when he asked Santos to come see him and Santos said he was actually going to be in the area. "Tomorrow is my orientation at Harvard," he messaged. "[T]hats exciting," Morey-Parker said. (The university has no record of someone with Santos's name graduating.) They talked on the phone, and Santos said he was getting his PhD in economics. Morey-Parker remembers Santos eventually suggesting it was too stuffy for him, and he didn't like it, and the story faded away.

Eyebrow raising, certainly. But perhaps it came with the territory. New money. Flashy. Ignoring those papers—were they eviction notices?—taped to the door. You don't get to move up in the world as quickly as Santos did, with no money in his rearview, if you weren't pushing the envelope a little bit, moving quick and breaking things, doing things that seemed to not exactly fit. This was one of the roommates' theories anyway. Also, you might not be as fun.

And Santos was. He was a great gossip. He knew how to put together a good crew. He was a great person to know if you wanted to find a niche in the Big Apple. There were times when he'd go out and order $200 bottles of wine. He would flirt. He was cosmopolitan. He could wow a partner, even if it didn't work on Morey-Parker. Take one ex-boyfriend from this period, Jordan, whom Santos met on Grindr in Florida. Jordan was a dishwasher at a surf and turf restaurant and Santos seemed dashing, and very high class: "I was mostly McDonald's and Taco Bell, he was mostly caviar and fancy food."

It was all on display that time in 2014 when Morey-Parker lost his wallet and then went out with Santos to Therapy. It was a nice wallet, a Louis Vuitton Monogram Eclipse. Slim. Morey-Parker had been taught to keep an emergency check in a fold. Not much cash, maybe $40. And credit cards.

Morey-Parker has self-knowledge, even if he was too embarrassed to talk about it out loud. He knows his loneliness gives way to self-esteem issues. He knows he likes a drink, or three. Could he have lost the wallet? Misplaced it? Been messy? What happened to it? And how was he now going to get past the bouncer at Therapy?

Santos had a solution, and this was the essential thing about Santos then—his ability to pull possibilities out of a hat. He was resourceful in the job of life. He had two passports, you see, an American and a Brazilian. He gave Morey-Parker his Brazilian passport. Social media confirms the date, a string of blurry hashtags on Instagram, Morey-Parker reveling in his found community: "#back #of #the #escalade #sittin #in #front #little #drunk #manhattan

#nyc #little #drunk." And then: "#money #dont #last #forver." He was having fun with friends. He could cancel those credit cards. It did not matter.

Pictures of the evening show Morey-Parker with other people, faces almost touching. His white shirt sweaty and open. He even dragged Fatima out with them—he was thrilled about that, a treat. He called her "Mom" in Portuguese sometimes, and was teaching her some English. Here he was, mixing with his new Brazilian crew. Joking about his caipirinha intake. Belonging.

There was a little something floating in the back of his mind that night, though, along with the electronic music, the flashing lights. Morey-Parker would later liken it to a domino just starting to fall. Not that long before the wallet, some checks of Morey-Parker's had gone missing from the apartment, too.

And Santos had an answer: he blamed it on their other room-mate, Rabello.

———

*Rabello had a similar trajectory* with Santos. He fit the pattern. He was an outsider as well, an itinerant Brazilian who had moved east from LA not long before. He bounced from New York to New Jersey, where he'd found work in a restaurant and could live in the basement, but still he was drawn back to the city—he needed something to do.

He met Santos watching the movie *Beautiful Creatures* in Queens in 2013. Santos had been speaking Portuguese in line and they bonded; the gracious native offered to show him around. That's what Rabello wanted, an entrée to the city, someone who knew the nice bars and destinations. Santos had answers.

They went to the High Line, for example, a park on old elevated train tracks that had opened not long before. Santos dressed up for the occasion, a button-down shirt tucked into shorts, though he maintained his air of open, friendly casualness: flip-flops below.

They attended a Halloween parade in Manhattan, right before Santos landed that Jackson Heights apartment, because Rabello remembers they went to Santos's aunt Elma's place to get into their costumes. Santos was living with her at the time, Rabello thinks. Rabello had a little makeup to add for his Sub-Zero costume, mimicking the icy character from *Mortal Kombat*. But Santos was plastered with the stuff. He was a zombie, and seemed thrilled with the chance to look as transformed and hilarious as possible. He had a wild white wig, black paint around his eyes, white across his face, and fake blood dripping down his lips onto a button-down shirt. It was the kind of costume where you take pictures with other people on the subway. Santos took lots. It was fun.

Another time, Santos rented a car and took Rabello to Jones Beach. He wanted to borrow his father's car rather than spend his own money on a rental. But Gercino said no—the car was full of tools. They wouldn't be removed for mere play. The favor was denied, but the young people found their way to the beach anyway. Later, during his political years, Santos would claim he surfed "most of my youth."[1]

He could be flaky, though, and there was a limit to his NYC tour guide–ness. He sometimes promised more than he could actually accomplish—as when he told Rabello about a barbecue and said he'd meet him there, but never showed. It was this kind of obliviousness that drove Rabello to want an actual contract when he agreed to move in with Santos and his family, before Morey-Parker's arrival. Santos had promised a partitioned space in the living room, and when Rabello showed up there was none. He had his contract, though, so they ended up giving him one of the two rooms.

It may seem strange that all these people scrunched into a single apartment, but this is not that different from how many people live in New York City. Roommates cohabitate with other roommates, or sublease rooms to save on rent. Immigrants establishing a foothold often don't mind squeezing in for early years. Even rich people hang on to their rent-stabilized studios. It might seem insane for, say, Peoria, but even a Queens address—far from Central Park West—comes with obscene rent.

Still, Rabello was not quite so high on the apartment as Morey-Parker was. The "quirks" he suffered through at the spot felt less like quirks and more like madness, as when they let the internet cut out. Active internet service was in his contract for the place, but too bad for him—he spent winter days slogging to an internet café to keep up work on his pharmacy studies. He didn't love it. Eventually, things got so miserly between him and the family that the Devolder Santoses cut off access to their cases of water bottles.[2]

Another point on which Rabello and Morey-Parker diverged had to do with Fatima. Rabello's impression of her did not fit the "harmless old lady" trope Morey-Parker believed. Once, he remembered Fatima bad-mouthing some woman who had helped her get cleaning jobs, not realizing that she had at that moment butt-dialed and produced an open line to this very woman. Rabello had the sense that Fatima and Santos were nice to Morey-Parker only because of the story about his looming trust fund. She could be a yeller. In fact that whole clan could, the way they would scream at each other over nothing. Fighting. Drama. Everyone seemed to be on edge.

The roommates in general did begin to notice the myriad oddities of their erstwhile tour guide Santos. His competitiveness. His prolific lies about small things no reasonable person should care to fake, like whether he'd procured a bottle of leftover alcohol or his mother had brought it home from a cleaning job. And his obsession with the lives of wealthy acquaintances he claimed to know.

These were small things in themselves, but with such volume they'd sometimes rise to the surface. It happened with other people too, not just the people under the Santos roof. In a long-running Twitter conversation in Portuguese with a close Brazilian contact, Santos pushed the envelope too much as he goaded the person to bring discounted cigarettes on a future visit to New York. "Cara vc só me procura cuando precisar alguma," the person answered. *You only look for me when you need something.*

———

*There is an essential paradox* at the heart of New York City that has always been present, but has rarely been as well defined as by Mayor Eric Adams, who said not long after winning office in 2021 that he hangs out "with the boys at night" but is "up with the men in the morning." The idea that the ultimate New Yorker is out at Zero Bond or getting up to no good into the wee hours, and then is ready to put on a suit and tie or a name-tagged uniform for the seven a.m. rush, is absurd. Or at least it is absurd if you do it more than once or twice a week, and without chemical assistance of the white, powdered kind.

The mayor's boast was, in fact, not far off from what Santos claimed he was doing at this stage in his life. The all of it. Those who claim to be fully embracing both sides of New York—the hustling, and the workaday working—are basically lying. But this does not always become clear immediately, and certainly not to newcomers like Santos's roommates Morey-Parker and Lino and Rabello.

And like bingo patron Adriana Parizzi and her young daughter, who had played the role of newcomer roommates to the native Santos just a few years before, when they landed in New York from Brazil. It was a different apartment, but Santos exhibited the same roommate patterns. He found a spot that was furnished and comfortable, and Parizzi was, like usual, more than happy to foot the bill. At first Santos was a great friend. He was good to her daughter, waking up in the middle of the night before Easter to hide chocolate and eggs around the apartment so the daughter could find them the next morning. Maybe it would make it feel more like Easter back home for the Parizzis in the mountains of Teresópolis, where piles of chocolate crowd the stores ahead of the season, where the sweets are almost bulging out onto the hilly streets.

But Santos's other . . . pastimes . . . would also come to the fore. Parizzi remembers Santos sometimes going to Atlantic City, and the Tropicana sending vouchers, as his Brazilian interest in bingo became a poker passion in the United States. He also had an affinity for Uno, which they played back in the apartment as a late-night drinking game. It was there, as the cards got warm and the room grew pleasant and laughter-full around them, that you might hear Santos let slip how he really spent his days. What skills and what kind of life he was really developing.

Parizzi recalls him talking, for example, about the help he might provide for someone getting married—in particular, someone getting married in order to get or give citizenship. The US government is serious about such marriages being serious, and so there is a requirement for pictures that show long, actual relationships.

Meaning bona fide relationships that take place over years, not days. So if you need to get these pictures quickly, and not over the course of a lengthy relationship, it helps to hire a photographer, to rent a car, to have people change clothes and be photographed in different settings, under different lights. It helps to have a middleman or mediator for such a thing, and Parizzi says that Santos would talk about helping in that fashion.

Did he get paid for it? "He doesn't shoot blanks," Parizzi says. "Anthony only does things when he can profit from them."

Certainly he talked a lot about different hustles, like his marriage to Uadla, for money, or so Morey-Parker remembers. Morey-Parker says Santos reported the amount to be $30,000. The lonely New Englander really liked Uadla, a sweet, caring person. They'd all go out for dinner sometimes, and when he'd quietly, discreetly, New Englandly pick up the check, she'd jump up to stop him. *No no no no no.* He appreciated that. Yet hers and Santos's was all the more farcical of a union because in 2014, Santos sent out a message to Morey-Parker and a select group of others inviting them to celebrate him and boyfriend Pedro deciding to "join our toothbrushes." This engagement of sorts was to be held at La Bonne Soupe on Fifty-Fifth Street, and Santos encouraged everyone to "be sharp and make it count," though he himself had given people only about a week's notice before the occasion: "Lmao for all of you that know me I can suck on timing!" The boyfriend, Pedro, has said he never accepted the proposal.[3]

There was a mania to some of it, looking back now, as the roommates do. Maybe Morey-Parker should have thought harder about the vanished checks or lost wallet. Maybe he should have pressed on one side or the other when Santos implausibly tried to argue Rabello was to blame for the theft. But Morey-Parker was searching for that matching partner. He had a romantic interest in Rabello. He wasn't going to call the police on a crush. In the end, it was only money.

And maybe it should have been no surprise when Fatima, one night in the Jackson Heights apartment over a quiet beef and noodles dinner, explained that Santos's correspondent gig at Globo had never existed after all. She and Morey-Parker knew each other a little better at this point; they could speak in broken tongues. She also said that she did not have a gaudy Wall Street career, as Santos often claimed.

"No, no," she said. It wasn't true. "I sweep, I mop, I clean cabinets."

She was up with the men, in other words. Santos was just out with the boys.

---

*What do you do when* you've been scammed? Morey-Parker says he moved out in just a few weeks. He did stay friends with Santos, though. He admits this. Whose fault is that? Who gains what from which piece of the relationship? Who is needy, and who offers a missing piece, in different ways, at different moments? Morey-Parker could get depressed. His life was not exactly all together. He was really friends with Santos; it was more than a real estate transaction. And sometimes friends pick up some habits from each other. Morey-Parker, for example, tells people that at the time he knew Santos, he was doing his BA at NYU, the school Santos lied about attending. But NYU has no record of someone with Morey-Parker's name and birthday at the school either. So sometimes, they shared the same story.

Santos's scamming was even more shocking for Lino. That May, he was planning to go back to Brazil and bring some presents along with him. Santos suggested that Lino use Santos's credit card to buy the goods online—it would be cheaper. Lino could just give Santos the cash, and the goods would arrive in time for the trip. It sounded good. The Amazon receipts tell the rest of the story: $399 for a PS4, $39.99 for a FIFA soccer video game, before taxes and shipping. And then a space gray iPad Mini ordered through Apple, for another $554. The goods didn't show up except for the iPad—a beaten up, screen-scratched iPad that was certainly not the brand-new device Lino had ordered. He thinks Santos must have canceled the actual orders right after he made them, and pocketed the money.

Lino went back to Brazil empty handed, and broke. New York City had been a dream of his and he'd loved it; now that was over.

It seemed to be only rarely that Santos hit a speed bump in this era, in this city. He must have been expecting those obstacles on some level; they must have raised his blood pressure at least a little, but fear did not push him to change his ways. Even when he hit up against the cold realities of the metropolis, like housing court, to which he was summoned regarding that Thirty-Fourth Avenue apartment in the summer of 2014. He was being evicted, a failure to pay rent. Despite all that rent or scam money from Rabello and Morey-Parker and Lino, he was thousands of dollars behind.

"Mr. Santos says he mailed a check for $1,500 to my client on the twelfth," said an attorney for the real landlord of record, in a tape unearthed by *Gothamist*. "He didn't."[4]

It was just part of Santos's long history with housing court, a ripe forum for his many excuses, including that he needed to get back into the Jackson Heights apartment to get his fish tank (he did not have a fish tank, Rabello says). But perhaps Santos discovered that you did not exactly "need" to pay rent right at the first of the month. You could hem and haw and go to court and sometimes make a deal. You could speak softly in front of a judge like you'd changed, you really had. You could leave a less encumbered man. You could hop to different apartments. You could get new roommates. You could ignore credit card bills. You could even owe $2,250 in rent and then say you'd been robbed while dropping it off.

Because honestly, the lifestyle kept him busy. He had a lot of scores up in the air. He was juggling. He had a thing going where he'd lose his phone (he didn't really lose it) and then he'd file an insurance claim for it, Morey-Parker remembered. Or he'd just be hawking the devices. Like that one evening when Morey-Parker messaged Santos about getting a drink, and Santos said he was tired and was going to sleep . . . but oh by the way, "I'm selling my phone for 300," he wrote. "If you know anyone who wants it let me know." Even his erstwhile fiancé Pedro is pretty sure Santos pawned his cell.[5]

It didn't work out between him and Pedro, but he was often hawking marriages too. To Morey-Parker ("You could get thirty grand like I did!"), to a different boyfriend, Leandro.[6] To Parizzi— her marrying this guy he knew, who needed a front of sorts for a business of his own.

It was intoxicating for Santos, the illicit earning. "Anthony is moved by money," Parizzi said. It was a culture. It was a world. Like the woman Parizzi remembers Santos befriending who had a car and apartment in Manhattan thanks to an "old friend." Come on, Parizzi says suggestively. You know what that means.

The roommates think Santos could also be simply a small-time thief when the conditions called for it. Like nabbing Morey-Parker's Burberry scarf, rediscovered on television when he saw Santos wearing it, behind a podium, as a political candidate at a "Stop the Steal" rally on January 5, 2021. That was not Morey-Parker's kind of Republicanism. Morey-Parker's New England grandfather had a saying: So-and-so had more shit than a barnyard. Wasn't that true with Santos, here in grift city.

People who knew him then allege a dizzying number of grifts: The one with the exchange rate, when Parizzi had left New York and gone back to Brazil in 2012, was trying to change some money, and Santos pretended it was practically double what it really was. Or the time he promised to safeguard some jewelry for her, and swore to send it her way when she asked. Yet when that ask came, Santos sent her a tracking number that she said didn't exist. Of course Parizzi should have known better. She knew what Santos was. Parizzi got to texting with Santos's cousin Jacqueline, who commiserated with her in Portuguese, agreeing that Santos always contradicted himself. She was ashamed of him, the cousin texted.

His cousin!

He was doing so much scamming at once that the stress showed. When poked, he lashed out. He would curse. He would insult. He and Parizzi texted half a State of the Union to each other about their grievances and mutual innocence: she was (Santos texted in Portuguese) false, a snake, a whale, a big mouth who didn't like to work, a woman with a tongue of evil who should just go look for a man, who had messed with his life, who nobody cares about. It went on.

But that was on the phone. That was not for public consumption. That was not who he was. He was a guy with lots of cash in his pocket, remember? He wanted to show life was perfect, even if he was not exactly up on rent.

Santos's focus was "to get any type of money for free as fast as possible," says Morey-Parker, who professes to hate, just hate talking about money. But that's a privileged position, and not one Santos ever claimed to share. It's a city—a country—of hustling people getting their bag, if we're being honest.

Take the time in the early 2010s when Fatima and Tiffany rented a room in Astoria from Socrates Acevedo. Rent was in the $1,300 neighborhood, and they paid Acevedo around $900. Hey, Acevedo had bills to pay too. Santos came over a lot in those days, and the room filled with cigarette smoke. The kid was good with computers and wouldn't you know it, at one point he offered to get Acevedo and his wife some needed flights to Brazil. He had some connections, the details were never very clear. Around five hundred dollars changed hands, but the flights didn't. So goes the hustle. Notch another one for Santos. And there were so many hustles to do.

# 5

## And Then Came the Dogs

*I*n the same way that a harried dogwalker in a fancy New York neighborhood holds on to a bouquet of leashes, every breed under the sun, so too did George Santos clutch his varieties and mutt mixes of dog scams.

He could get a dog, a really top-notch purebred dog, without paying a dime of his own money. Simply drive a car out to Amish country in Pennsylvania, as he did in 2017. Haggle in the milk house with a harried father of ten kids, fellow with a biblical beard and nineteenth-century hat. Then grab the pups and put them in the car and leave a bad check behind, or a meaningless promise to wire over funds. How else was he supposed to pay? He couldn't be expected to carry so much cash around, could he? By the time the suckers knew for sure they were suckers, Santos was speeding back across state lines.[1]

There was the way he could sell the dogs, sometimes for hundreds of dollars a pop, at puppy-adoption events run by his little charity Friends of Pets United, whose purpose—on paper at least—was to rescue, raise money for, and support the well-being of dogs and other pets. FOPU for short.

That was just the beginning of how he could leverage easy riches from FOPU, which he claimed helped rescue more than two thousand animals between 2013 and 2018.[2] The grift was so good, and his tongue so active, that the pet charity didn't even need pets to rake in funds. In the name of the organization (of which no records have been found to suggest it was actually a registered nonprofit), he could set up an event for, say, a farm in New Jersey trying to build out an abused animal sanctuary. A little display of drinks and barbecue in exchange for $50 tickets. But rather than pass along the money, he could simply get hard to reach.

Santos scouted out fields to romp in, like targeting a big pet-related Facebook community, fertile ground for his fundraising requests and other scams. He knew how to butter up the right people in such a community, like when he sent someone in the eleven-thousand-member "Brazilian Pet Lovers" group a little Hard Rock Café New York dog charm. The recipient posted their praise of the generous Mr. Santos. How much could that advertising have set him back, $3.99?

He could also breed and sell dogs directly. He would arrange for his golden retriever, his beautiful Aurora, to have litters of puppies in rapid succession, something friends and associates of his noticed and thought a little gruesome at the time. To one person, a fellow female golden retriever owner, Santos even advised on the benefits of not neutering. You can make $10,000 per litter, Santos said.

He was quick-moving, fast-dealing. "His tongue waggles," one Amish country farmer told the *Washington Post*. "Smooth talker is how I'm going to explain it." He barked loud and whined when cornered, even wriggling his way out of a theft charge in Pennsylvania for those bad checks he used on dog breeders in 2017. He claimed—and this is rich—that his checkbook had gone missing. He got the charge dismissed, plus his record expunged.[3]

Once, he didn't even bother passing the money raised from a Staten Island charity adoption through his bogus nonprofit. Instead, he simply crossed out the FOPU name on a check and wrote in his own.[4]

His personal behavior with dogs could be characteristically contradictory. A Brazilian social media profile from his teenage years shows Santos claiming he didn't like pets, though by the time he was an adult he would be opening his home to a little kennel of them—eventually, four named Anastacia, Aurora, Electra, and Elsa, names he says he took from Disney and Greek mythology.[5]

A YouTube profile that appears to be his once posted an interminable how-to video about making fresh doggy treats, going through every egg, flax seed, cup of quinoa, and glop of coconut oil. The reason he went to the trouble was that he had a scammer's instinctive skepticism of paying, in this case, for the stuff you buy in pet stores: "They promise you a lot of things and usually there's not half the promises within that." He prescribed fat-free yogurt because he liked his dogs the way he preferred his own and others' bodies: "The leaner the better, you don't want your dog getting obese."[6]

He could sometimes be a little weird about his dog knowledge, as when he told one person on the Long Island campaign trail that he had a degree in dealing with dogs. And the pride of the dog dad could get him into trouble, as when he posted a picture of a beautiful, expensive-looking new designer canine during his second, ultimately successful, congressional campaign. The idea was to poll people on potential names for the new member of his family. Eventually some more optics-observant spirit realized it was a bit too Mitt Romney to advertise your ownership of what appeared to be a money-pit purebred, at a time when so many dogs from animal shelters were looking for homes.

He once made a fool of himself actually about no-kill shelters, going on and on about the need for one in College Point when he was trying to insinuate himself into Queens politics in 2018, ahead of his congressional runs. His big issue—maybe only issue—was animal rights; his best civic experience in a way was the pet charity, which he talked about all the time. Like the night that he showed up to be a volunteer for the campaign operation of Republican Vickie Paladino, when he stayed at her house until one a.m., talking, pitching, not taking the hint from one of Paladino's sons who was cleaning up, stomping around, all but telling the animal lover to get the fuck out and find his own cage to rest his head.

But Santos's crowning canine achievement, his brutal pièce de résistance, the most George Santos dog thing of all the George Santos dog things, was the scam he pulled on Sapphire, the dying pit bull companion of a disabled, then-homeless navy veteran, Rich Osthoff.

---

*Unlike for Santos, dogs have* been 100 percent central to Osthoff's life since the beginning. Osthoff grew up in Howell Township, New Jersey, horse farm country, and when he was three his parents gave him a beagle named Girlie. He had her until high school, and three weeks after she died his firefighter dad brought home a pit bull puppy. Someone had left a whole litter in a basket at the Linden firehouse door, and so all the kids of the smoke eaters got new buddies. That was Emerald, and he had her all through his military years.

Besides his dogs, his navy service might be the thing in Osthoff's life that he treasures most dearly. His grandpa and dad were in the army, and at a certain point he knew he was tired of college, of homework, of working at Six Flags. He was good with his hands; in the navy he could learn how to be an aviation electronics technician. The only problem was that he had to leave his dog behind.

Osthoff has only a few close friends, no wife or kids. His dogs are like his family—there's never been a woman who, when he came home from work, peed on the floor she was so excited to see him. But his pooches have been known to do just that. It sometimes seemed to his neighbor Deb O'Nair that he could communicate with them in a way, like telepathically, and she's one to know, having once been in the fairly well-known band the Fuzztones and schooled in the art of making connections across distance, through space. Osthoff can be gruff or blunt with human fools but always sweet with his four-pawed babies, his hands in a constant state of scratches over the gratified canine bodies.

So, those first nights at boot camp in the Great Lakes sleeping without a dog curled up next to him brought tears to his eyes. Emerald stayed with his mother back in New Jersey, slim comfort for Osthoff. He got his dog back when he was stationed at a command in New Orleans, but his next stop, on the USS *Nimitz*, meant no dogs allowed again.

This was when history first collided with Osthoff and his pets, long before Santos. His first time giving hand signals to a pilot on an aircraft carrier's flight deck was a week after 9/11.

It had been planned as a simple trip from Virginia to San Diego, taking the *Nimitz* for a little bit of a peacetime jaunt. But the terrorist attack on the World Trade Center and the Pentagon changed everything. For weeks, the *Nimitz* floated where it was, off the coast of Brazil—where Santos's mother's visa paperwork said she was at the time, very much not escaping the flames and smoke of Ground Zero on that day, as Santos would later claim. Osthoff and all the other sailors held their breath, waiting to see if they'd be sent to the Gulf.

It was a prime example of how intense military service can be, even when not under fire. A superior asked Osthoff, *You got your cammies and your gun belt?* in case their next stop was Afghanistan. Osthoff was police qualified, essential training for an occupation. He was sweating. That was something to worry about, something to dwell on through the *Groundhog Day* sameness of life onboard. By this time, everyone had memorized what would be in the galley for lunch every Wednesday. Everyone was thinking of what lay ahead. Ultimately it was a different craft and not the *Nimitz* that got orders to churn over to the Middle East, but the stress had been significant. And of course, there were no dogs to provide warm comfort.

Osthoff remembers the anguish of this time in his life, even without being directly on a battlefield. He saw unspeakable bloodiness up close, like the moment a guy's head got blown up by a rotor. Osthoff wore the man's brains on his shoe. Or when he'd just gotten off his shift and grabbed a hot dog in a hangar and some marines doing a maintenance turn tipped over their helicopter.

The rotor got smashed to a million pieces, a marine chopped in half from his right shoulder to his left hip.

It can give you PTSD, as it did to Osthoff, a lifelong challenge.

So even during his much-loved navy time, Osthoff was struggling. It was the stress, the PTSD, and the feeling that something was off in his brain chemistry, something that would be diagnosed as bipolar disorder. Whatever it was, he was self-medicating; he tried counseling; there was an enduring stigma, and eventually he left the service on the kind of "Don't call me, I'll call you" terms that meant he wouldn't be reenlisting again. It was heartbreaking. Guiding those planes on the aircraft carrier roof; flying up in a submarine hunter over the Pacific, ready to fix problems if they occurred—it had been the only job he ever wanted. And just as he was transferring out of the navy, Emerald died.

It was not a good time to be dogless. He was depressed. He was flailing. He was living with his dad in Washington State, way out in the empty woods. Someone at the VA said, *There's a guy in Texas with a litter from a puppy mill. You need a dog in your life.* He did. The dog got flown up to him ASAP. He embraced her. And that was his Sapphire.

Sapphire, the gemlike pit bull that George Santos would eventually condemn to death, was a particularly special companion to Osthoff. She was a sweetheart and a little rambunctious, but she also knew what the hell was going on. She had a big head and a stocky fawn-colored body, and she'd spring into the air to catch droplets from a hose. You couldn't go fishing with her, because she'd splash into the water and return your lure, scaring away any prospective prizes within a nautical mile. At night she claimed her place for some shut-eye next to Osthoff. It was her bed, really; he was just sharing it. Shower too.

When she was a puppy and he just got her, he would walk around with her wrapped up in his coat against the Washington cold, her head popping out of the top of his jacket like she was a newborn. People cooed.

She had a little bit of service training until that ended—her level of rambunctiousness was just a touch too energetic. But she learned enough—or she had always known enough, she was special that way—to be attentive to his moods and feelings. It got to the point where she could recognize a manic phase coming on for him, or a moment of depression. When he had nightmares, she'd do whatever she could to wake him up and cheer him out of it. When the nightmares came while awake, she'd lean against him or climb on his chest and just very physically, with her big dog body, remind him she was there.

If he felt suicidal, she was within reach for a pat or grip or hug or just a warmness, a breathing responsibility that he couldn't leave alone in the world, could he?

He loved her, and could it be that she loved him, more even than your typical man's best friend? When he drove with her across the country to move back to Jersey, his jeans went threadbare on the right thigh because she always had her claws on him there, from her perch on the passenger's side. She didn't want to be in that seat alone.

Osthoff has had some lucky breaks in his life—some good travel, a few solid friends at the right times. His dogs. Once, he saw Bruce Springsteen in a bar and rather than bother him, sent the Boss a drink. The bartender came over after and said to Osthoff, "You're not gonna have to pay for anything here for a long time": Springsteen set him up with a tab as thanks.

But he's also had his share of hard times, and it was often

Sapphire who was there with him. When his history of DUIs and a suspended license caught up with him in the form of some months in lockup, it was Sapphire's welfare he was worried about, the fact that he was forced to leave her out there in the lonely world. One day the Zoloft he'd been taking just crashed on him. It had worked and then suddenly it didn't. He was walking Sapphire out at the Monmouth Battlefield State Park, and the tears started squirting out of his eyes. He didn't have a sad thought in his head. Couple minutes later, he's laughing so uncontrollably his ribs ache. Sapphire came right up to his knee. The leash was loose as a flag in doldrum winds. Usually she strained to run and nose around and explore, but now she just wanted to be close to Osthoff, to help.

He checked himself into the psych ward, and they gave him every mood stabilizer possible. But whatever cocktail it was made him uncomfortable, irritated.

He sometimes bounced between places. He sometimes feuded with friends or family, often not even meaning to. It wasn't really his fault. Through it all, Sapphire was the constant by his side.

One day he noticed the tumor on her left rib cage. At first it was the size of a golf ball, and Osthoff sped her off to his local vet to get it checked out. The vet advised Osthoff to wait and watch—it was too small to take out now, given Sapphire's advancing age. She was around eight years old, and anesthesia had its own dangers. Osthoff agreed, but bad times were ahead. He was out of work and had injured his leg; he became homeless; and the tumor was growing. It was 2016. He set himself and Sapphire up in an abandoned chicken coop on the side of Route 9, pitched a tent inside, and ran some extension cords from the nearby house of a friendly soul, so he could have a phone charger and heater for his suffering companion. Still it was cold and uncomfortable, on their mat on the ground. A cat that was keeping company with Osthoff actually ran off to be semiferal, so primitive were the conditions. But Sapphire would never leave him, of course.

Osthoff brought her back to the vet, and now the vet said yes to operating. The catch was the price, 3,000 bucks, and the imminent closure of the vet's practice, so Osthoff needed to pay in a lump sum and not over time. He was numb. How does a homeless vet find that kind of cash? But a technician in the practice approached him, said she knew this nice guy Santos.

It sounded legitimate and perfectly timed to Osthoff. He looked at some GoFundMe that this heaven-send had put up. The vet tech snapped some pictures of Osthoff and Sapphire right there on the spot, and in a couple days had sent him his own GoFundMe link. There were already—wonderful—$900 dollars. Osthoff felt a kind of relief. People tongue-wag about "thank you for your service," but sometimes they really did give a shit. He put the link on his Facebook page, and his friends and family started tossing in credit card numbers. It wasn't long before the $3,000 mountain was summited, electronically.

Then began the Santos shuffle.

For some reason Santos insisted they patronize a veterinarian in Queens where he had credit, so Osthoff made the trip to the next state over only to be told by the vet there that nothing could be done for the suffering pooch. Now he was worried. The tumor wasn't getting any smaller. And Santos started to be evasive in his communications. Osthoff texted the supposed Friend of Pets in November that he wanted to talk with him directly from now on, not the vet tech, whose political beliefs were becoming annoying. Trump drove Osthoff crazy. Santos replied icily that he and the vet tech "share the same political views" and were "very much alike." He proposed taking Sapphire to another vet to get an ultrasound.

Some cockpit alarm in Osthoff's head was blaring. It's the bullshit meter you develop when you're living foot to neck with the whole sweep of humanity in a boot camp barracks, or in the berths of an aircraft carrier. Osthoff said he felt like he'd been "mined" for his family and friends' donations. Santos came in at 110 percent in endless texts about how reputable FOPU was, and how uncooperative Osthoff was being. Santos reviewed Santos as a "well known and a public person" who had done rescue for many years and in fact was the kind of person who had no reason to—gasp—do anything sketchy with money: "I'm very well off myself," he texted. He sounded downright Trumpian.

Their back-and-forth continued. Santos said he wanted to pick up Sapphire and take her to an appointment sans Osthoff. Osthoff just wanted the funds to go to a local clinic. They got heated. And all the time the lump was growing, Sapphire was getting slower, to the point that she eventually had a hard time lying down.

A fellow veteran tried to step in to help Osthoff. Mike Boll, who ran the New Jersey Veterans Network, floated some solutions to Santos. The money could be returned to the people who'd donated. Or it could be used for a vet in Osthoff's area. It all seemed reasonable. But Boll says Santos suggested he'd use the money however he wanted. The marine and police officer, used to people reacting to his forceful nature, was stunned. He couldn't believe Santos wasn't backing down.

It dawned on Osthoff slowly and then quickly that Santos really wasn't going to provide access to the donated money. A con. Osthoff was embarrassed—perhaps he should have known. Sapphire slowed down even more than she already had. All the youth sapped out of her. The parasite on her rib was the size of a volleyball. To look at it was to wince and feel something heavy on your own stomach. She didn't want to stand up anymore. She died.

Osthoff didn't even have the money to put her down easily. He'd already tapped his network to the bottom with the Santos GoFundMe. He was tapped out. He panhandled some of the death bill outside Home Depot. Everyone was crying at the clinic where they did it, such was Osthoff's already-grief. He put his mouth right near her nose to breathe in her last two or three breaths. He took her remains home with him and slept in bed with the urn for a long time.

He was suicidal. He checked himself back into the VA hospital. He was falling down on his knees in the shower crying. He'd landed a job in a deli making sandwiches, but then he'd find himself weeping over the cold cuts, tears dripping on the meat. He fumed about the guy who'd ripped him off.

Osthoff's distress was obvious after Sapphire, to everyone. Finally a navy buddy of his stepped in. You need a dog, dude, the friend said. The fellow vet was involved in an animal rescue around Virginia Beach. You want another pit bull? the buddy asked. Osthoff told him. Another little female one, reddish, as soon as possible. Like Sapphire.

That was 2017. He would give his new dog, his Ruby, a home. But it was many years before he'd learn more about this Santos character, when he'd understand exactly who he was. Osthoff would learn that he was one in a string of victims, dog owner or otherwise, one of many people who'd been bilked a little, but when you're the bilkee and already low it feels like a lot. Like this: When Osthoff saw pompous Rep. Santos on TV with the inevitable POW-MIA flag somewhere, he wanted to throw something through the smiling screen. The bullshit about honoring service. When Sapphire was alive, those too-brief ten years, she'd watched TV with him too, get excited as all getup when she saw an animal on the tube, a real one or just Brian from *Family Guy*. Osthoff knows she wouldn't have lived forever, but could an operation have given them a few more years? Or better years, before? This was what Santos stole from him, almost blithely, and then snidely, to increase his bank account, it seemed, a little more.

*Part Two*

---

# The Candidate

# 6

## Choosing Politics

*I* sometimes wonder if there was a point in Santos's life when the die was cast, when there was no turning back. When he finally had no choice but to reach for the bigger, scarier scam. When he stepped onto the section of branch after which it would become too thin to hold his weight.

It must have happened somewhere in the middle, after birth but before indictment, a moment that fluttered away entirely unnoticed, in the long progression of scheme after scheme.

It must have been after, certainly, the childhood- and adolescent-era attempts made by his father to urge him to the straight and narrow. He could have accepted one of those pushes. He could have stopped stealing and held on to a regular job. That was, for a long time, a possibility.

It must have been before, just as certainly, the moment heading into the 2022 election when he came to see fellow Queens Republican Stefano Forte. Forte was in his early twenties and running for state senate, and perhaps Santos saw himself as a mentor.

"How old are you?" he asked. Forte told him. Santos looked at the younger man and said, "Wow, well you know, at your age I'd made my first million dollars."

He believed it, Forte is sure of it, something about the tone: "He is one hundred percent buying what he's selling. That's why it's so easy for him."

You get to that point, it's over. There's no getting right with truth when truth doesn't exist in your own mind.

But that moment of last return, when he could have gone clean—it must have come after his time in Brazil, that place of transformation and mutability. It must have come after the Dish Network call center, where he could have settled in. He could have been a midlevel manager by now—a junior executive! No, there was still time then—though certainly it was too late by the time his lie-filled résumé made its way to Nassau County GOP chairman Joe Cairo, a document featuring Goldman Sachs and NYU and a whole set of gobbledygook skills: "Currency and coin counter," "Project and vendor oversight," "Performance monitoring and evaluation," "Forecasting."[1] By then he'd put all the fakery too much in writing.

It's bold to say, but the moment of potential epiphany could still have come after all the scamming of friends and family and roommates. One after another they let him skate, after all, too threatened or loving or implicated to do otherwise. He even could have started over after the incident with a Brazilian man named Gustavo Trelha, whom Santos knew in Florida in 2016. Trelha says that Santos was the mastermind behind a credit card scam, and that the young con artist had a warehouse with all the gear necessary to steal ATM banking information and clone new credit cards. Santos, according to this onetime roommate, knew how to pull off that particular con. The idea was that they'd split the haul fifty-fifty.[2]

This is a serious allegation. This is not pilfering some dollars from someone's wallet. Not jerking around some people who love dogs. But Santos got lucky again. Trelha went to Seattle to put this knowledge to work, and he was caught removing one of the devices from a Pike Street ATM. Then Trelha pled guilty, served time, and was deported back to Brazil, meaning Santos, whatever his involvement—he says he wasn't part of the con—got away scot-free. Right then, he could have changed everything. That kind of proximity to cops and judges could have scared him straight; he might have gratefully enrolled in a nursing program, or found religion. But no. He continued the scamming life.

We are getting closer now, but I wonder how long the last-chance moment came after the death of his mother, in 2016. They had their clashes—great, fiery clashes—but they shared love. As Santos and his sister wrote in Portuguese on his mother's Facebook page after she died: the longing for her hurt, but the memories last a "lifetime." Could not mortality, that ultimate divider, that shocking sledgehammer, have stunned some sense into him? Would not a Catholic think of the afterlife? Sure, he seems to have pocketed money meant for Fatima's funeral. That must have been worth some time in purgatory, but here on earth the funeral director chalked it up to bad business. Once again, the great George Anthony Devolder Santos had escaped.

This could have gone on for a long time. Many years. He still had a lot of rope to give, a lot more pet scams to pull. He probably could have limited himself to a low-grade sleaziness until he became a sad old man. The moment when he could no longer turn back the clock did not come until he made a very fateful and specific decision—the decision to run for elected office.

There are a plethora of reasons why Santos, the longtime liar and scammer, should not have taken a career leap into the public eye.

The rationales he himself has given, even in private, are unsatisfying. He once told his old New Englandish roommate Greg Morey-Parker that he wanted to run for Congress for the stability of the paycheck and pension. Morey-Parker, in fact, remembers Santos specifying that he wanted to get elected to a term of Congress and then he'd get a pension for life. This is not how it works: Members must complete at least five years of service to get the check at age sixty-two, and they need to do more years to receive the pension earlier. And the pension for most members is not even close to a full salary.[3] Regardless, there are more straightforward ways to get a salary and pension, like working for the parks department.

In 2019, Santos texted a family group thread with another rationale for why he'd made the decision to run. He'd done so "after witnessing the invasions of undocumented immigrants," he wrote in Portuguese. This would not actually be a major campaign issue for him, and he had family who were just as undocumented. In the rest of the text he preened about being "the first in the family to get involved in politics but I hope to do honest, clean work that benefits the American people."

Regarding this, let us just quote the way he (with admirable self-awareness) ended the text: "For those who don't have anything nice to say, keep your opinions to yourself :-)"

Santos does have company as a ne'er-do-well who opted for Congress. In the past half century alone, dozens of those distinguished worthies have been indicted for, been accused of, or resigned in the face of misconduct like accepting illegal gifts, lying about military service, embezzling, and having sex with a teenage campaign worker. There is even precedent for the kind of committed congressional lying and scamming that Santos would go on to perfect: former Utah representative Doug Stringfellow told elaborate fantasies about his World War II service in the 1950s, including a secret kidnapping mission for the pre-CIA OSS. In 2006, Randy Cunningham pleaded guilty and was sentenced to eight years and four months in prison on account of $2.4 million in bribes from military contractors. The Californian's haul was luxurious as anything the Ferragamo-loving Santos could imagine: an SUV, resort trips to Oahu, candelabras, and Bijar rugs. And Cunningham's shamelessness, like keeping a "bribe menu," approached Santos's style.[4]

But such retrospectively poor decisions are narrower than the ones Santos chose day in and day out. Stringfellow claimed that he had embellished his war record due to adulation on the campaign trail: "I fell into a trap, which in part had been laid by my own glib tongue."[5] After discovery and dishonor, he quickly ushered himself out of public sight. Cunningham, the bribe caterer, certainly wallowed in the scam, but he wasn't lying about his war record, having been a Vietnam War ace and "Top Gun" instructor. For Santos, the cons and storytelling began long before his first encounter with the hustings, growing to encompass almost every aspect of his life.

And Santos had even more skeletons in his closet than these congressional liars. His past was littered with unsavory characters whose own legal issues make terrible optics for a politician. These characters include the debit-card-skimming friend Trelha, who in 2022 was accused in Brazil of gruesome brutality against the two-year-old child of a girlfriend.[6] Legal filings show a picture of the boy's bruised and injured skull. A lawyer for the boy's family told me in Niterói that Trelha also allegedly beat the dog of an ex-girlfriend, and had similar lying tendencies to Santos: he was a flight attendant but pretended to be a pilot.

Also in this category was Santos's Brazilian lawyer—his own lawyer!—whom Santos at one point directed to handle the old teenage case in which he used fake checks to buy luxury goods in Niterói. This lawyer himself had been convicted and sentenced to eighteen years for his connection to a gang execution. He waited outside on a motorcycle while the killing happened. He started studying law while under house arrest.[7] Second chances should be celebrated, but this kind of connection is not one a congressman typically wants to advertise.

Worst of all for Santos, however, was his connection to J. P. Maroney, who was Santos's boss at the time that he first started running for Congress. The company this boss ran was accused by the Securities and Exchange Commission of being a Ponzi scheme.[8]

Unlike Santos's other motley associates, Maroney was more than just a liability. He is crucial to understanding the budding politician: it was through Harbor City and its alumni network that Santos claims he really got rich, the kind of wealth that he used to convince people he could self-fund a run for office. Harbor City also represented a turning point for him, a sort of finishing school that provided the patina and last skills needed to run for Congress. And there is a direct line between Santos's time at Harbor City and one of the reasons that politics actually was the inevitable place for him, in spite of all the downsides. This glaring reason was that he found politics to be a great place to make money.

———————

*Santos had of course been* trying to make money for a long time, even through legitimate business labor. The places he worked for were not particularly stellar, such as the Turkish-based travel booking company that was a magnet for customer complaints.[9] His most impressive-sounding gig up until Harbor City might have been with a place called LinkBridge Investors, which organized conferences. This was where Santos worked with a former athlete, Pablo Oliveira, who happened to be a six-foot, four-inch actual outside hitter for the Baruch volleyball team, a persona that matched the one Santos would later claim for himself: so the fabulist got a sports story out of his time there, at least. But the job was unsatisfying and not particularly formal—he was merely "an independent contractor, freelancer, sells sponsorships whenever he wishes to," said Oliveira.[10]

Harbor City was another matter—or at least, it sounded like it would be. The point of the company was supposedly to help businesses find new customers through online advertising. Harbor City had developed an exciting way to generate those "leads" to customers effectively and cheaply, and was looking for investors to expand the process. This allowed Harbor City to appear cutting-edge on two fronts: It used allegedly high-end technology like "big data, artificial intelligence, and machine learning" to help companies ensnare the interest of potential customers on the internet.[11] And it was an investment vehicle that promised huge returns.

This all appealed to Santos. He had attached himself to a place where he was not a bossed-around cog in a wheel like at Dish. Now he could make real money—his annual salary at one point was approximately $120,000.[12] And even better, he finally had the imprimatur of serious white-collar finance. Key to the narrative Santos wanted to sell voters—and, really, anyone who would listen—was that he was a successful businessman and Wall Street hotshot. It was the story he told about himself with all those puffed-up pedigreed banking jobs, and also the story he fabricated for his mother, and sometimes even his family more broadly—that they were all wealthy, connected to money, the kind of people with little boutique investment offices and second homes. It was the most polar-opposite life he could imagine compared with his real-life upbringing in Queens, his mother's housecleaning and his father's painting.

He was thrilled to be at Harbor City and anxious about doing well. In a work Zoom recording, Santos said that he felt an urgency to "show J. P. he didn't make a mistake" with him. He needed to close a "big deal."

"I admire him a lot," Santos said.[13]

In truth there was a lot to admire on the level of one scammer to another. What was actually happening, according to the SEC, was that the company's bank accounts accepted more than $17 million in investors' funds, but less than half a million of that went to business expenses. What Maroney allegedly did instead with the money was use it to make payouts to investors—your standard Ponzi scheme—and also to pad his pockets. Much padding: the SEC accused him of spending $1.35 million on his credit card bills, $827,000 on a waterfront home, and $90,000 on a Mercedes-Benz; depositing $394,000 into a joint bank account with his wife; etc., etc.[14] (Maroney has denied the SEC's allegations against him, and the company has not responded in court.)

Maroney was a hustler from a young age, claiming to have had a T-shirt business at age nineteen.[15] He declared bankruptcy not long before starting Harbor City and became a constant purveyor of motivational videos, such as one in 2009 in which he dons a baseball cap and talks into his phone while driving, extolling listeners about the value of not waiting until everything's perfect. Take action. In the folksy words of his grandmother, you shouldn't say that a batch of biscuits failed to pop up. Rather, "they squatted to rise and they got caught in the squat." It's time for the listeners to take action in their business, and they can do so by calling him for a session, in which he'll invest "a thousand dollars of my time and energy." He is, he claims, "Mr. Monetizer."[16]

Really, he was someone who knew how to close a deal. He did so with a former employee, Ajit Kumar, whom Maroney met online and convinced to come aboard in 2016. Kumar told me he remembers the boss "bragging about his past achievements" and seeming "like a flamboyant salesman," even though requests for access to the company books, bank accounts, and other systems "were always promised but never provided." (Kumar eventually quit.)

Maroney knew how to drum up deals even with people who were already skeptical of his shtick, ending one email to an angry investor, "Be sure to JOIN US for this week's Harbor City 'Wealth Watch' for private clients."[17]

Mostly, he knew that people want to make money but not risk it, and so he characterized Harbor City's bond offerings glowingly. They were "safe as a CD," he claimed, basically like "going down to your local bank and purchasing a certificate of deposit."[18] After Santos started working for Maroney in 2020 as the company's New York regional director, he dutifully explained it similarly: "We just give them a better return than a traditional 401(k)."[19]

Wildly better returns: starry-eyed investors big and small were told they could get as high as 18 percent. (The SEC said these returns were very much not legitimate.)

It had long been obvious that something was off about Harbor City. In June 2020, the Alabama Securities Commission put Harbor City on its "Con Watch" website. The company was ordered to cease and desist business within or from the state. Also that month, someone reached out directly to Santos on Twitter to say that Harbor City's standby letter of credit, which is supposed to ensure that a company can pay back investors, "is a complete fraud."

"I'm sorry I'm not following you," Santos responded, asking the Tweeter to email him to talk further. "Our SBLC is 100% legitimate," he claimed.[20] (It wasn't.)

It is not entirely clear what Santos knew about what Maroney was doing behind the scenes at Harbor City. Santos was not named in the SEC complaint—the matter was stayed in 2022 pending a criminal probe involving Maroney—and has claimed publicly that he did not know what was going on. He once said of the form of credit Harbor City used, "I still don't understand it completely," according to a 2020 company Zoom meeting reported by the *Washington Post*. He said he was waiting for Maroney to answer a few questions on that subject.

But Santos learned something essential about dealmaking at Harbor City, and how to profit from the rich people he encountered—skills he would take into politics. He learned how to exaggerate his connections—including lying about a personal relationship with the head of California's mammoth pension fund—and he learned to aim for the big-money people, not even the medium-ranking guys he could only dream of being back at Dish. "I don't target low-level pawns in corporations because I think it takes too long to work up the ladder," he once said in a meeting.[21]

And he learned how to keep asking. "Resilient people make it happen," Santos once said of his service at Harbor City, when he was having a hard time selling. "It doesn't matter how. They just make it happen. And that's what I'm gonna do."[22]

He did exactly that with Andrew Intrater, a donor who was more of a rook than a pawn for Santos in both his Harbor City and his political lives. Intrater was a private equity investor who had a lot of money, enough to toss Santos far more than an iPad's worth or the contents of a GoFundMe account. Intrater had so much money that he gifted over a million dollars to the Shoah Foundation at the University of Southern California.[23] (His family's fleeing of the Holocaust happened to be something he and Santos bonded over, or Intrater thought they did.) Intrater had so much money that he paid a quarter of a million dollars to support Donald Trump's inauguration ceremony, which he attended. He had so much money that his firm also was able to do a million-dollar contract with Michael Cohen, Trump's personal lawyer, in 2018.[24] A lot of his money came from managing the American money of his cousin, Viktor Vekselberg, a Russian oligarch and close ally of Vladimir Putin. Vekselberg also had an unbelievable amount of cash, enough to have a $90 million yacht seized by Spanish authorities after the oligarch was sanctioned by the United States due to Russia's "malign activity around the globe."[25]

The adventures and misadventures of Intrater and Vekselberg are enough to fill a whole book, including special counsel Robert S. Mueller III looking into the payments to Michael Cohen while investigating Russian influence in Trump's election. But as far as Santos was concerned, the rich relatives were important because they had the kind of money Santos has envied since he was a teenager—and because Intrater became such a significant backer of Santos after meeting the young politician and businessman in the run-up to 2020. Intrater and his partner maxed out their contributions to Santos's campaign in his first run, and went way further in his second, pouring in over $200,000 to Santos-related committees.

In between, he and Santos stayed in touch, texting and lunching at Osteria Delbianco in Midtown. His back-and-forths with Santos seem to have endeared the two to each other: "I admired him and fundamentally I thought he's a hard-working guy," Intrater told the *New York Times*. "He's young and he has the ability to win." The admiration apparently also encouraged Intrater to invest with Santos at Harbor City—to the tune of a whopping $625,000.[26]

It was a big deal, for Santos and the firm. It showed that a rich contact could be tapped for multiple of your hustles, not just one.

The coup came in what would turn out to be the twilight of Harbor City, and Santos's time there, too. Intrater's first interest payment from Harbor City arrived in March 2021, but the next month's payment got clawed back. Intrater was perplexed, and reached back out to text his friend Santos, who said things were fine. What was happening behind the scenes, actually, was that Harbor City's assets had been frozen by the SEC, and employees were starting to scatter—including Santos. In May, he started something new: the Devolder Organization.

It was fitting that Santos named this new, shadowy company after himself—his mother's surname—because it was a perfect simulacrum of who he had become and wanted to be. The outfit was the culmination of a dream for him (his own company!) and a repository for all the hustling he'd learned along the way. It could not have existed without Harbor City: he opened the company with the help of a Harbor City alumnus. And the way he described it was that he sought to recruit rich investors, which had been his job at Harbor City. But here, rather than having investors put money in some confusing fund, his business was much simpler and more personal, perfect for his charm and nose for money: he introduced wealthy individuals to other rich people and took a fee for whatever changed hands. Maybe that's a plane. Or a boat. The money for the middleman could be good: "If you're looking at a $20 million yacht, my referral fee there can be anywhere between $200,000 and $400,000," he claimed. He called this "deal building."[27]

He was looking to close deals, just like Maroney. But now, because he had made the jump fully into politics, he could propose those deals to a whole new class of people: the rich donors he was getting to know on his congressional runs.

In fact, Santos was extremely direct about the way he mixed deals with politics. At political fundraisers, he would come up to donors and talk about the good things he could broker with their peers in insurance or pharmaceuticals, "or he would tell them about donors who were seeking to sell businesses or luxury items," according to the *Times*. He once went to a supporter with a Nigerian-prince-seeming scheme about a rich Polish citizen who couldn't access his bank funds to buy cryptocurrency and needed help.[28] He proposed multiple deals to Intrater, who had already come in big for Harbor City and Santos's campaigns. The new deals didn't pan out, Intrater has said. But we do know about one successful donor-related deal that Santos was apparently in the middle of: the transfer of a $19 million yacht called *Namaste*, so luxurious that it had both an infinity pool and waterfall. On either end of the exchange was a big chess piece whose family had donated thousands of dollars to Santos's political efforts. (Santos's lawyer eventually claimed Santos did not broker this transaction, though a person familiar with the exchange told the *Times* he negotiated the payment.) If we take Santos's estimate about his typical cut at face value, he could have made hundreds of thousands of dollars from the yacht's switching hands. That agreement happened just before Election Day 2022.[29]

Deals like this that Santos made as part of his Devolder Organization business are important not only because they show how much money he could earn off politics. The company is also at the heart of another longtime mystery: how Santos was able to loan his 2022 campaign over $700,000.

The way Santos has weaved the story, through his public statements and financial records, is that he loaned his campaign much or all of that money thanks to influxes from the new Devolder Organization, which in 2022 and 2021 paid him $750,000 in salary, plus $1–5 million in dividends. His 2020 disclosures say he had almost nothing the cycle before that: a middling five-figure salary and a bonus.[30]

This story has many holes. One piece of Santos's federal indictment would later allege that he had lied on his financial disclosures: he actually overstated his income and assets, including the supposed $750,000 salary from the Devolder Organization and the million-plus he said he had in the bank. This matches what prosecutors alleged in October 2023 along with the guilty plea of his campaign treasurer Nancy Marks: that the two of them had arranged to inflate his fundraising numbers, including by logging more than $50,000 in bogus donations from relatives, plus a fake $500,000 loan from Santos himself. Santos was indicted for this and other purported grifty behavior later that month, when prosecutors accused him of falsely reporting loans, including the $500,000 sum. The reason to do such an elaborate bookkeeping charade, the prosecutors argued, was to help the Santos outfit look more financially sound than it really was at the time, a common theme for him. A big pot can sometimes convince donors to give more. Also, the scheme was meant to help him qualify for monetary and logistical support from a Republican Party committee program, including help with a poll and access to joint fundraising.

It was something Santos cared a lot about. As one crucial 2022 deadline approached, he texted his treasurer "what did we figure out about the report," and said he was "lost and desperate." He was also thrilled when the scheme paid off: "I GOT [THE PROGRAM],"he messaged her afterward.

Santos's loan shenanigans could increase his bottom line in multiple ways. He could avoid risking his own money but still make it look like his campaign was flush. Or he could improperly repay himself for campaign "loans" not made, as a House Committee on Ethics report would ultimately allege that he did. That report also pointed to evidence of another scheme: that Santos later put real money into his campaign when he got it from a big spender who happened to be a Devolder Organization client. So Santos's company might help his campaign, and the better his campaign looked, the easier it would be to get more Devolder Organization clients.

Indeed, he was now surrounded by rich people. All these marks! Now they were at his fundraisers, or on his call lists. They knew the drill. Some candidate is always asking for money.

Now he could hit them up with a proposition—*Can you max out to my campaign? Can your wife?*—and not only was this not sleazy, it was expected. Every day he was building his rolodex. And so what if he negotiated a little private deal on the side?

This was an enormous draw. Modern politics is often more about meeting very wealthy donors who can cut a check than the old work of organizing and hammering out positions and strategizing on ground games. In other words, modern politics worked just fine for Santos.

---

*But money alone cannot fully* explain Santos's decision to become a politician. There are easier ways to make a buck, even in a sort of gray zone of earning; ways that do not force a con artist to bare his background quite so entirely to the public. No, there was something else attracting Santos into the arena where, as Theodore Roosevelt said, it was possible for a man's face to be "marred by dust and sweat and blood." Something deeper was urging him to the political realm. And there was something particularly gravitational about his moment in American history.

Some researchers argue that delusions are affected by culture or current events—that, for example, people experiencing such conditions in the World War II or Cold War era often believed they were being spied on by Germans or Russians.[31] In later eras delusional people might fear they were being surveilled by corporations or phones. In brain development, science focuses on crucial "sensitive periods" that set our course for better or worse. A similar phenomenon exists for political behavior: the events of early adulthood have an outsize and enduring impact on political values, so that those whose sensitive period came under Nixon voted Obama, while the Reagan cohort stayed red.[32]

Some of the great con artists, particularly those with active imaginations, seem to be similarly susceptible to the zeitgeist. Their cons are in the field of the moment. So Frank Abagnale, the *Catch Me If You Can* faker whose own narrative of shape-shifting has itself been called into question, chose the costume of a Pan Am pilot as his disguise, at a time when the allure of leisurely jet travel was at its height. In the fame-obsessed 1980s, David Hampton hit on the idea of pretending to be Sidney Poitier's son when he was stopped from going into Studio 54 as himself. Anna Delvey dreamed of a hip private club, a perfect fit for the money- and status-obsessed socialite scene nurtured during the Bloomberg years in post-recession, pre-COVID New York City. Elizabeth Holmes embraced the inspirational, founder-worshipping language and ethos of Silicon Valley startups, which celebrated disruptors and college dropouts with singular if punishing visions. This allowed her to gloss over a medical technology that was largely a dream.

There is a selection bias here—the con artists we remember are often the ones whose stories match their time—but sometimes the time can shape the story too.

For George Santos, nurtured by the intense partisanship of Brazil, raised and grown in the Queens of Donald Trump, and tipped into the maelstrom during the insane political cauldron of Trump's win, elected politics was the defining force of his moment. It was the perfect place for a status-conscious person interested in performance, storytelling, money, and messiness.

At first, Santos showed an obsession merely with fashion and pop culture. Throughout his twenties, his now-private or defunct personal social media accounts were littered with mentions of Miley Cyrus, Selena Gomez ("your just perfect i love the fact we share b-days!!!!"), Lady Gaga, Paris Hilton ("RIO MISSES YOU!!!!! LOVE YA!"), *The Walking Dead*, and *The Real Housewives*, particularly Bethenny Frankel, whose own show he would attend, posing with Frankel in a 2014 picture (CNN even unearthed video evidence of Santos peeking under his chair to check if he won a QVC gift card).[33] It is harder to find Santos posts about world events, like "God Bless Japan" after the 2011 tsunami, and "#pray-fororlando" on June 13, 2016, the day after the Pulse nightclub shooting, which he would later go on to dubiously claim he was connected to through dead colleagues.

But by 2016, he had found a new role model who brought celebrity glitz and gossip to civics: Donald Trump.

"I've been on the Trump train, far before Trump was ever president, far before he announced, we're talking *Apprentice* days," Santos explained in a 2019 video promoting a Trump event. "The 'you're fired' slogan to the birth certificate—release of Obama's, you know, shady birth certificate, so on and so forth." These places where Trump intersected with TV culture appealed to Santos, and soon he was pulled into Trump's own political efforts too. He showed up to Trump events in person, including at Trump Tower, where he hoisted a "Gays for Trump" sign featuring rainbow flags. He tweeted his support as Trump headed into his first election, cheering that "we can win the election! Just believe! Gays, Hispanics and blacks do stand with you!" He even toyed with being a leader of his own pro-Trump Facebook group for the 2020 race, trying to raise money for a protest in Buffalo through GoFundMe, because old habits die hard.[34]

It made perfect sense that Santos would follow in the blustery TV star's footsteps. In Trump, Santos saw another Queens native with an outsider chip on his shoulder (warranted or not) who had no political experience but was bluffing and hustling his way to the White House anyway. And it was not such a quantum leap from an obsession with pop stars to one with Trump.

Their shared hometown was part of the attraction, too. Santos's New York was ground zero for Trump and for the political clashes that would take over American society. Politics in the Trump era became identity for many New Yorkers. The stage had been prepped by the mass Occupy movement and Black Lives Matter protests of the preceding decade, nurturing a core group of activists and also poking the kinds of people who tend to get annoyed with activists and protests and a demand for rights in the streets. Trump's run packed everything into an already-crowded subway car. When he won, there was an explosion of action. People running down the avenues again. A women's march. Protest after protest in front of Trump Tower, the soaring visible symbol that drew Santos, as well as the other side.

Every political action has a reaction, and another reaction. When left-wing Democrats including Alexandria Ocasio-Cortez (AOC) rode the anti-Trump wave to power in 2018, Santos became an anti-AOC reply guy, responding to the young progressive NYC icon on Twitter and complaining about her "socialist" politics, including her opposition to the hundreds of millions in incentives for a huge Amazon project that would have brought a new office center to Queens. This "Amazon HQ" project was nightly news fodder in the borough in early 2019, given that the company was promising twenty-five thousand jobs along with the facility. The controversy, which ultimately went national, married politics and business and real estate and people's concerns about new stuff in their backyards. It was perfect TV, and Santos was hooked. Something about AOC in particular piqued his interest, and he sometimes brought her up on the campaign trail when asked what inspired him to run for office. She was just a year younger than him, came from a multilingual household like he did, and had not done much in politics before she ran for Congress. But she staked out bold takes, and leaned into her newness for her party, something Santos realized he could do too. She was a prime example of the cultural cachet he longed for: her New York swagger and take-no-prisoners style had made her cool.

Around this time, Santos dipped his toe into the water, trying for a little party position in Queens, though he didn't end up having the signatures necessary to get on the ballot. But he was going to the political meetings that were happening all over the city, and especially in Queens, which was being painted by the various national medias as this far-left hellscape or utopia overrun with Leninists and immigrants. Those elements were real, but Santos's borough was actually still pretty Archie Bunker when you got out to Maspeth or Whitestone, the suburban-thinking pieces where there were sometimes literal Proud Boys meetings in bars, where people talked about how many Asians were moving into the neighborhood and also the civil war coming. And Santos would go to gatherings in these parts of the city like one Columbus Day dinner for the Queens Village Republican Club. To give a sense of the zeitgeist, consider the woman who asked Santos his position on immigration and let it be known that her own position was that for kids of illegal immigrants, "citizenship should be revoked." Santos, one hand eagerly gripping a microphone, said he didn't think this was possible but agreed about ending the "policy that allows anchor babies." And of course he said all the Trump lines: the wall, coming here the right way, how "if you don't control your borders you don't have a country."

This was in New York, supposedly the country's commie haven. It was impossible to escape Trump-inflamed politics. For a messy person like Santos, for anyone really, it was fascinating. On Twitter, on Facebook, on the news, in the street, the defining conversations weren't about technology or the Yankees or *American Idol* anymore. No: it was politics. Politics touched on everything, and it was the obvious field for someone with delusions of greatness, of fame and fortune, of being something more than an immigrant's son in a basement apartment. Someone more settled and secure than the pudgy kid in ESL. Trump was the archetype of the moment, and he pretended to be rich and powerful, until he was. Why couldn't Santos? If he had gone to San Francisco during the startup bubble, perhaps he would have made a different launching pad for his scam. If he had been more of a peer to Jordan Belfort, he might have used his Harbor City experience to become a true wolf of Wall Street. If he had been alive during Prohibition, maybe he would have been a bootlegger like Gatsby. But politics has always provided cover for alienated people, for those who feel a little like they don't fully belong. That microphone can be a shield, before it is a weapon. And there is an intoxication that comes from the sound of your voice as it commands a total, and respectful, silence.

# 7

## The Excellent Messy Awesomeness of 2020

### Or, How Santos Got COVID and Learned to Stop the Steal

*T*he video posted to Facebook in November 2019 starts with a pair of carefully placed hands, a little dress-shirt sleeve, and widely splayed fingers. The piece of paper that one of the hands is signing is blurry, but the viewer can just make out "U.S. Term Limits Congressional . . ." something. The hands move the paper away before we can read the last word, as the camera pans back to show Santos himself. Almost twenty seconds in, he is still inexplicably signing the piece of paper. Finally, in the manner of a guy sharing something on his irregularly updated vlog, he speaks.

"Hey everybody. Just signed here the US Term Limits for . . . congressional . . . pledge," he says, pausing to look back at the piece of paper in a partially successful bid to refresh his memory about the words written on it.

He is wearing a suit with no tie (and certainly no trim and trademark sweater). He is hunched forward in an overstuffed gray chair, still working on the politician's trick of good posture in front of a camera. His delivery is halting. He stumbles over words and concepts. This is "pretty much common sense for me, running for New York's Third Congressional District," he notes, a belated introduction of the office he wants voters to connect with his name. He says vaguely that it's time to curb career politicians and "start something that makes sense." Finally, with the video almost complete, he builds toward a rousing finish, saying he supports a constitutional amendment of six years in office for members of the House.

"We need to start making people remember that they're there to work, not to build wealth. Uh, so. I urge—"

The video cuts off.[1]

It was part of a not particularly auspicious 2019 beginning to Santos's life as a congressional candidate, his first attempt at the seat. Santos was excited to jump into his new costume, but he was still bumbling through the process, trying thirstily to get press coverage and smooth out some rocky social media posts. Even at this early stage, there were also signs that he was playing fungibly with truth, and blustering to make up for it. A full version of that term limits pledge, by the way, went on a few seconds longer to capture him urging colleagues to sign and "stick to your word" because "it's not that hard."[2]

There were aspects of his run in which he seemed to embrace trial and error, even risking goofiness. One strategy he adopted repeatedly in the lead-up to 2020 was simply uploading shaky

Facebook videos of more famous people talking. That included B-list Trump World denizens like Corey Lewandowski, whom Santos was thrilled to see live at a local Republican club's Lincoln Dinner.[3] When he managed to be in the same room as the commander in chief himself at a September breakfast fundraiser, he pulled up his selfie camera immediately afterward to gush that it was "intimate" and "awesome" and that he was not ashamed to say he'd be saving the lanyard he got there: "Hey, I'm a fanboy, what can I say."[4]

The upside of these clout-chasing gambits was that they could bring him deeper into the fold of the local GOP, which was woefully in need of diverse, fresh candidates. Santos's identity and child-of-immigrants story became a draw to those in the party eager to make inroads into different communities. Heritage could be used as a selling point—Santos has sometimes described himself as the son of a Black man—and Republicans were thrilled that he was already singing their tune. As usual, Santos was a quick study, effortlessly picking up the tone and jargon of his latest field. Early in his 2020 run, for instance, he could speak fluidly on a podcast about the not particularly heralded political career of Chele Farley, a businesswoman and party functionary who had been wiped out by incumbent senator Kirsten Gillibrand in Gillibrand's 2018 reelection campaign.[5] Santos even briefly hosted a Queens public access TV show called *Talking GOP*, on which he interviewed minor lights of the borough's conservative firmament, name-dropping his own efforts on the local level such as being "excessively" against the newly elected Democratic Queens district attorney.[6] He was eager to make his mark.

The show also allowed him to workshop his political pitch, learning what to say to certain audiences and what parts of his background to highlight—or make up. That included his eventually infamous story about Judaism. At this point, it was anything but a clean anecdote. "Quick snippet here," he said in one January 2020 episode, "not trying to claim Jewish heritage or anything, but my family is actually, uh, my, my, my mother's father was Ukrainian. And—I'm sorry, my mother's father's grand— My mother's grandfather was Ukrainian, had his kids in Ukraine. My grandfather grew up Jewish."[7]

He went on to note that he himself was Catholic but "I believe we are all Jewish, at the end, because Jesus Christ is Jewish."

This word salad bears resemblance to the story some of his relatives tell—that the family on the maternal side possibly has Jewish heritage generations back, something that can be difficult to determine conclusively. One researcher, Fábio Koifman, who looked into Santos's family tree, told me he found two entrants from the 1700s—Jacobus and Anna—whose names are Jewish-sounding, at least, though the idea that they might actually have been Jewish is "a guess." Multiple genealogical and historical investigators on both sides of the Amazon have unearthed a wealth of evidence that Santos's maternal grandparents were actually born in Brazil,[8] and Koifman says that Santos's prominent ancestors on that side don't suggest a closeness to Judaism: "All were baptized, married and buried according to Catholic rites and traditions."[9]

However, Santos seemed to recognize early that a Jewish back-story could be a political tool. Later that year, when he was called a Nazi on Twitter by a person with 848 followers, he snapped back with a vengeance: "Wow you pulled the Nazi card on the grandson of Holocaust refugees! Smart move there." It was a reach, but little in George Santos's life hasn't been.

There was also a haphazardness to some of his early campaign actions that were read by party elders as a lack of seriousness. He sported an open collar and no suit, for example, when he made the somewhat requisite pilgrimage to meet Grant Lally at the Carle Place Diner. Lally was a onetime GOP candidate for the seat Santos had in his sights, and was now spending his time lawyering and publishing the *North Shore Leader*, a small Republican-leaning paper on Long Island. Lally was a bit of a macher for the district—he met with another Third Congressional District hopeful at the same diner the next cycle. But Santos didn't seem to have gotten the memo. He was leaning back in his seat, Lally remembers, and "very clunky. He was sort of basking in the attention." When Santos said that he came from a wealthy finance family from Brazil, Lally asked if that meant he was Lebanese, given the number of prominent members of the Brazilian finance class who have Lebanese roots. It was a typical style of question in New York political circles, where ethnicity is used as a matter-of-fact shorthand by both parties. But Santos did not appear to know what Lally was talking about. This struck Lally as odd, because he thought Santos would have been aware of this stock assumption even if it wasn't true: "It's like saying, 'I deal diamonds in Brooklyn, but I don't know anything about any Jews,'" he said. Or you're from a certain part of Pennsylvania and you've "never met anyone Amish."

For the record, Santos was wearing a golden cross around his neck for the meal.

It was a long lunch. The heritage situation raised an eyebrow for Lally, but perhaps not as much as Santos's lack of familiarity with basic elements of policy, as well as his obliviousness about DC totems like the Problem Solvers Caucus: the group of centrist members on both sides of the aisle, of which Tom Suozzi, Santos's Democratic opponent, was vice chair.

In fact, Suozzi was very vocal about his leadership in the bi-partisan, pragmatic, common-sense-for-crying-out-loud Problem Solvers Caucus, something that he would be loath not to mention in basically any political setting, be it a DC fundraiser, a little league opening day, a Glen Cove civic community meeting, or just a handpump at the Great Neck Diner. If you didn't know about the Problem Solvers, then you didn't know Tom Suozzi. And not knowing either of them particularly well was a sign of just how much Santos was in over his head in his first run for Congress.

Unfortunately for Santos, his opponent that year was not just a Problem Solver but also a formidable presence in Nassau County. Suozzi's front-runner-ness was in fact the main reason a more experienced Republican did not jump into the race ahead of Santos. Suozzi had been doing politics since the year Santos was born, volunteering on the presidential campaign of Michael Dukakis. He was the son and nephew and cousin of mayors of Glen Cove, one of the county's two cities, and the younger Suozzi himself was elected mayor in 1993 at the fresh-faced age of thirty-one. He was once a bona fide altar boy, but one with real intensity: his own mother once declined to deny to *Newsday* that her son had a temper.[10] He pulled off a huge upset in 2001 by becoming the first Democrat in thirty years to win a race for Nassau County executive, a peer position of sorts to that of NYC mayor next door. That made him confident enough to launch a shocking primary run for governor against then-superstar attorney general Eliot Spitzer in 2006. He once compared his come-from-behind attempt to that of George Washington before crossing the Delaware. "Anything that has ever happened in history requires sacrifice, particularly when things look bleak," he argued with just the minimum amount of self-aware irony.[11] (He lost.)

Santos had only recently discovered the allure of political

ambitions. Suozzi, in contrast, once acknowledged on a debate stage that he wanted to be president. That was the road the Italian American JFK type plotted for himself. But in 2009, everything came screeching to a halt when he lost reelection for county executive by 386 votes—to a Republican who would go on to serve time in federal prison for corruption, a not-uncommon endpoint for New York politicians.

It was a precursor to the shellacking Democrats would take in the 2010 midterms, a reaction to the heady win of President Barack Obama just before—and a lesson to Suozzi about never taking an election or the political crosscurrents for granted.

His recapture of office would require a return to basics, and door-to-door campaigning, tapping any local knowledge or instincts he still had, to win the fickle yes from a disengaged voting populace. This was a humbling and drawn-out process that Santos knew little about.

Specifically, the road led to places like the North Shore Towers.

———

*Beyond donor call time, beyond* voter contact and photo ops, beyond no-fingerprint media hatchet attacks against unsuspecting opponents, the crucial aspect of a successful congressional campaign might be termed as follows: knowing the territory.

The territory in this cycle's iteration of New York's Third Congressional District included a chunk of the NYC borough of Queens and then a big swathe of Long Island. Geographically, Long Island contains Brooklyn and Queens, but the spiritual and political Island is made up of just two counties—Nassau and Suffolk—and is ribboned by highways that the candidate, even a Queens one, would certainly have to know well.

The candidate must know too about the Northport VA hospital, the only facility of its kind for Long Island's approximately 100,000 veterans, the majority of whom are over sixty-five. The prospective member of Congress will know how in 2016, black particles fell out of air ducts in the VA's operating rooms, and how the HVAC system sucks, and why a veteran committed suicide in the parking lot. And he will have a pitch to make it all right.[12]

He will know about the Bethpage Plume, the miles-long and -wide collection of contaminants that has collected underground on Long Island, due to the chemicals used and tolerated by aerospace behemoth Grumman and its partners and successors for decades and decades. He will know that Grumman was a fundamental anchor of Long Island life in the postwar era, building NASA's lunar space module and employing so many thousands of people in Nassau County that schools staggered dismissals to avoid the traffic jam from the Grumman day shift shutting down. Most of all, he will know that Long Island's only source of drinking water is groundwater, and that the plume of filth underneath the ground is creeping.[13]

He will know the important delis and bakeries, the busy LIRR stations, the traditional Republican areas like Bayville, where, if he's a Democrat, a moderate message will dampen his losses, even as he runs up the score in your Glen Coves or Plainviews. If he's a Republican, vice versa. The little things. He will know the environmental advocates and the precinct commanders, no matter who the Police Benevolent Association will be endorsing. He will know the religious leaders from both the diocese and the storefront churches, and he will know the difference between the reformed and conservative and orthodox temples and be comfortable in their company without needing to pretend he belongs. He will know about the Mets and what traffic is like just before rush hour on the Long Island Expressway. And he will know, in great detail, about the North Shore Towers.

Picture a gated community with all the resort-style, smoke-free elements that suggests. Picture a concierge and doorman and pools and fitness centers and the usual Florida amenities. Now squeeze that gated community into three vertical, thirty-three-story buildings, and place it right on the edge of the Queens–Nassau border overlooking the Grand Central Parkway—"located close to Manhattan," as the community's website haughtily announces. That is the North Shore Towers.

It hosts nearly two thousand residences in self-contained buildings connected by an underground shopping and dining level. Merchants include a fashion boutique and a hair salon. The age of residents leans Social Security. There are snowbirds who spend time in the Sunshine State and others who are fleeing Nassau County property taxes.

Most important, the North Shore Towers are full of so many hundreds of registered voters that the complex has its own polling place. That's been true since 2004. The buildings, in fact, make up an entire election district alone.

Those who know the territory, VA and Grumman and Plume and all, know that they need to campaign inside the North Shore Towers, which means finding a supporter to bring you past the guarded gate. And then the real table-to-table happy hour fun begins.

So it was to the North Shore Towers that Suozzi went in 2016, as part of a bruising five-way congressional primary that was his shot at redemption. In a sign of the spot's electoral importance, it was the scene of the campaign's first debate that March. He won. The next cycle, he was up against a former Navy SEAL and businessman who looked great on paper, and so it was back to the North Shore Towers for a debate touching on the federal tax bill and whether or not New York gets screwed monetarily by the federal government. And Suozzi knocked it out of the park, his opponent not able to match his long political experience, drive, incumbency, and attention to what the North Shore Tower–type voter wants to hear.

So by 2020, Suozzi had put in his time in the trenches in the never-ending campaign world of Congress, not just winning a seat but defending it, via constant and repeat handstroking of the veterans' groups and environmental advocates and North Shore Towers of the land. Coming into New Year's, he was focused on getting through another tricky primary, which this time included a fiery progressive hammering his carefully-honed Problem Solver stances. In other words, Suozzi was not thinking much about this Santos, who was new and untested, and didn't know the territory.

It sometimes appeared that Santos didn't even have a map, the way he was muddling his way through the lead-up to the general. He didn't have a primary opponent, yet he was still struggling to get fully in with the local Republican leaders. The Third Congressional District at that time spanned three counties—Queens, Nassau, and Suffolk—and even though Santos was most tied to Queens, he felt insecure about the level of support he was getting from his local party chair, Joann Ariola. After the holidays, his old diner date Grant Lally ran into him at a tony gathering of the New York Republican world, held at the New York Athletic Club in Manhattan. Like many of these kinds of old-school GOP productions, it was a high-class and boozy affair. At first Santos just gave Lally a wave, but then he came over to vent. He was in a snit because he hadn't officially gotten the nomination yet. And Lally remembers him being particularly harsh about Ariola, whom Santos had spent months buttering up with nice clout-chasing Facebook posts and pictures, talking about what a phenomenal party she could throw, etc., etc. But tonight, Santos kept referring to her as a "bitch."

This surprised Lally, perhaps even more than the Lebanese situation or Santos's lack of DC know-how back at the Carle Place eatery. Santos hardly knew him, and yet here he was complaining in vulgar terms about a party leader over a perceived slight.

That felt novicey. And there were other challenges ahead. It was a cold winter in New York. Still, the event circuit was hopping. Does it only seem so now in light of what was coming? First the virus in China was only on the news, and then it was here a little, but in a seemingly isolated way. People in the political world touched elbows or feet to say hello and scoffed, showing off their knowledge of foreign and scientific affairs but also not taking the threat too seriously. Santos showed up at another gathering, for an outfit that mashes up Israel and US relations with the oil and gas industries. Steve Israel, who used to run the Democratic Congressional Campaign Committee and who once held the House seat Santos wanted, showed up as a favor to a former colleague, and one of the many bipartisan hands he shook that day was Santos's. One shakes many hands at functions like this, and the Long Island power broker wouldn't have remembered clasping palms with Santos if it wasn't for two things he learned later. One was that Santos would claim on a local radio show that Israel had announced at this event that Santos was going to be the first Republican he ever voted for in his life.[14] It was not true. But the second element of the handshake was more potentially life-changing. It was a warning that the old political territory was shifting. Because Israel learned a day later that someone at the gathering had tested positive for the thing called COVID-19, and it was Santos.

---

*Santos has spoken about his* early bout with COVID in different ways at different times. He has, for example, claimed to some people that he ended up in an iron lung. He has said he was ambulanced into the hospital,[15] something that carries special weight in New York City, where the moan of sirens marked the unceasing toll of the early weeks of the pandemic. He has provided shifting timelines, one of which would have made him one of the very first people to get sick in New York—right around when the world was shutting down. Santos has said he caught the virus at the Conservative Political Action Conference in late February in DC.[16] He even suggested to aides later on that he, himself, was the "patient zero" down there.

Some of this may have been speculation or exaggerated, and his reputed bout with COVID certainly provided a great press opportunity for him: he looked not particularly worse for the wear in a March 18 Fox Business appearance that gave the novice candidate great free exposure.[17] But he also fought hard against skepticism of his COVID survivor story, providing pictures of himself in a hospital bed and an image of a lab test.[18] Videos of him at the time show him taking the health scare seriously: on March 24, he shared selfie footage on social media that showed him walking carefully back to the hospital to get retested, wearing a blue puffer and a surgical mask molded assiduously under his eyeglasses, trying to keep his distance from people on the street. Admirably, at that time, given the lack of knowledge about the disease, he said he wanted to walk rather than endanger people on public transit. Even driving would have meant engaging a valet at the hospital, he said, and he didn't want to take that risk.[19]

It was an example of the health-conscious side of Santos that doesn't come out much in public, the way he frets about his respiratory system and hygiene, how he promotes handwashing and doesn't like when dogs bring gross things inside and rub themselves on your couch.[20] He seems to have been scarred by his COVID experience. Lally, the Nassau County macher, remembers him looking terrible the first time he ran into Santos post-illness. And for his part, Santos told the *Newsday* editorial board that cycle that he had been delirious for a couple of days during the ordeal, screaming and yelling for his mom.

"Mom, mom, I don't feel good," he said, though his beloved mother had been dead for years.

He called it the worst two weeks of his adult life, and something of that experience can be seen in the video he posted on Facebook upon his release from quarantine—the jaunty freedom of escape, the renewed joy at being outside, even if it was just the old and typical streets and stores and crosswalks of Queens. "Life's already short," he would say sincerely about shutdown in another video.[21] Wouldn't you too walk for miles, many miles, after being stuck indoors so long? The video has the kind of infectious and apparent honesty lacking in his obsequious fanboy shots of Republican bigwigs, missing in the stilted signing of a House term limits pledge.

A week after his first negative test, he took to Facebook to report a return to the campaign trail, yet he was forced to make some changes to his plans. "We've canceled all in-person fundraising events, and taking the candidate out of commission certainly hasn't helped our fundraising numbers," he wrote.

It was a tricky situation. He would later recall that there was a period after his sickness, in those early, scary days, when he was a free man but nobody really wanted to risk seeing him. Lots of prospective voters didn't want to come out and chat, and that limited his chance to make a dent in his opponent's name recognition. Then there was the problem of the shift that was happening in the Republican Party at the time. While some elements of the GOP—including Trump—were already tired of shutdowns and waiting for a vaccine, Santos continued to walk a fine line between COVID caution and carpe diem. He once posted an exasperated Venn diagram of the different takes on COVID that could be at the same time true—including caution and economic fear about business closures. Such uncommon nuance forced him into some tortured positions, such as his 170-word written explanation in May of why he had skipped a rally: "I'd like to remind everyone that my absence was greatly due to the fear of becoming reinfected with the virus due to my personal vulnerability to respiratory infections," he said in part. "Please stay safe out there and keep voicing your rights safely and responsibly while thinking about thy neighbor."[22]

He was a big promoter of masks and social distancing back then, two years before he flipped to what became the standard-issue GOP complacency and vaccine hesitancy. By at first respecting the instructions of health experts and doing appearances virtually, he ironically was kept off the physical campaign trail for months—and it hurt him.

It was the last nail in the coffin for a campaign that never really climbed above six feet under. Santos was already facing stiff odds: He was running in a presidential year, during which Democrats in moderate suburban districts were eager to throw out Trump. There was a blue registration advantage. He was facing a now-established congressional incumbent with decades of New York political experience and knowledge of the North Shore Towers of it all, something Santos was far behind in learning. And while the campaign was largely pushed online, Suozzi could use the power of incumbency and being a sort of essential government worker, turning his congressional office into an unemployment center, agitating for federal money for pandemic-epicenter New York, and dropping off personal protective equipment to Sikh community leaders and VFW halls and more—including, of course, three thousand pieces in June for the North Shore Towers.

And there was one more thing going against Santos: The candidate. Santos himself.

There was something off about him, remembers Suozzi's long-serving former chief of staff, Mike Florio. Despite talking about his big-business career, he had essentially no money that would allow him to introduce himself to the public. By April, the filings said he'd spent little more than $30,000. He seemed to be checking all these different boxes that didn't typically go together, Florio recalls. He was gay, he was Jewish, he was Catholic, he was a finance guy. In a clubby New York political world where politicians mostly came from town dynasties, ethnic strongholds, ideological cul-de-sacs, or the local party hierarchy, he was an enigma.

There was, for example, his home address. His original statement of candidacy claimed he lived in Elmhurst, practically on the opposite side of the borough from the westernmost points of the district. You don't have to technically live in-district to serve, but it sure is advisable. Florio remembers looking up the address and being stunned: "Is he moving?"

There were other weird moments. Santos was liable to stumble through lines like "there's nothing to sneeze on" or "it's good to renovate the blood."[23] He would give these bizarre interviews, as in the fall when two radio interlocutors pointed out a seemingly innocuous line from his campaign biography: "In his spare time George Anthony enjoys volleyball and tennis and has entered numerous amateur tournaments across the Tri-state area." The daughters of the interviewers happened to play those sports. Rather than just remarking on the nice coincidence, Santos riffed, "I actually went to school on a volleyball scholarship." He went on: "When I was in Baruch, we were the number one volleyball team." He explained that he played against Harvard and Yale and "slayed them" en route to be champions "across the entire Northeast Corridor."

This was all a remarkably disprovable lie—a big story he decided to weave. Yale didn't even have a men's varsity volleyball team. But still Santos couldn't drop the thread. He claimed that every school that Baruch came up against was "shaking" from the encounter; he evoked images of nonexistent teammates of his who were six foot seven, six foot eight, "just stretching their arms up in the air" rather than jumping; and he concluded by saying that he took the game so seriously that he "sacrificed both my knees and got very nice knee replacements."[24]

Yarns like this—so colorful, so elaborate—perhaps should have been eyebrow raising for those who heard them. But there is science behind Santos's ability to go undetected. People tend to be biased toward thinking statements they hear are true as opposed to false, a consistent finding in research on the subject.[25] Hypotheses for this truth bias include that it would be too chaotic to go through life always suspicious of everything you're told. We think we'll know when someone's lying to our face, but that's not the case. Even experts who are supposed to be good at sniffing out liars often perform like novices when put to the detection test. In a 2004 study in which 121 Spanish police officers and 146 undergraduates were tested on their detection abilities, for example, the cops performed worse than the students.[26] Serial liars—who are not incredibly common across the human population—benefit from these loopholes. And Santos was finding that even in the rough-and-tumble world of politics, where voters anecdotally expect lies, a truth bias still exists. This, too, is borne out in research from 2023 in which participants watched videos of politicians who might be lying. Even in that setting, the researchers found evidence that people were more likely to think statements were veracious.[27]

So Santos skated along, raising few suspicions. It wasn't enough to let him win, of course. Suozzi's campaign logged a twenty-point poll lead in October, confirming what the Democrat had known all along: he was cruising to victory. At one point, in a September email exchange, Suozzi's camp raised the idea of and then decided not to pursue opposition research on Santos. Why would they use it? Negative attacks could just boost his name recognition.

In one of the few times the candidates were together on-screen, Santos's Zoom background for the civic association debate was a grainy picture of his campaign poster, while Suozzi opted for a gravitas-inducing bookshelf, which was par for the course for the high-end elements of the district. This was territory, after all, that covered wealthy enclaves like Great Neck and the Gold Coast. Gatsby country. Prominent on Suozzi's shelf, one could spot his *Power Broker*.

Santos just didn't seem to know the territory, the little ins and outs. He seemed shocked when Lally's newspaper, the GOP-leaning *North Shore Leader*, ended up endorsing Suozzi. But this was the clubby world he was trying to barge into: turns out an old Lally staffer had once been Suozzi's babysitter. Incumbency helps. Santos's anger about the non-endorsement seemed a bit odd to Lally: the publisher told me years later that the newcomer didn't submit press releases and hadn't taken ads out with the paper either. Among Long Island's smaller, politically affiliated outlets, there are sometimes frank acknowledgments of media business realities like this.

Santos tried his bumbling best. He roared as loud as he could about the need to stop socialism, using the AOC byword from an election ago that was still emblazoned on his brain. When George Floyd was killed by a Minneapolis police officer in late spring, he jumped on the Blue Lives Matter bandwagon. Now he had a real subject; now he had a theme. He could rail against antifa and the "riots" in Manhattan and the way NYC mayor Bill DeBlasio (*sic*) was encouraging the murder of NYPD officers, including those cops in Shake Shack who seemed to have been poisoned by angry fast-food workers (they weren't, but plenty of people who weren't George Santos believed that yarn too). He jumped up on a truck bed in a blue polo and white shorts to address a huge cop-friendly outdoor rally in Eisenhower Park in July, when it was already clear how potent the law enforcement issue was becoming in ring suburbs like Nassau. He was in the right place, on an island that is home to more NYPD officers than any other jurisdiction outside the city,[28] a place where blue lives have always mattered, where the city always seemed a little faraway and dark skinned and dangerous. It was a place whose political DNA has white flight embedded in it, where in 2020 a fierce debate raged over state-level criminal justice measures. By the end of the campaign, "bail reform" was on its way from an overdue liberal idea to a conservative talking point. These were fertile issues, and soon, the reaction to the social justice uprising that engulfed the country after Floyd's death would translate into a red wave for the GOP in New York. But it hadn't quite crystallized yet. The backlash hadn't slammed Long Island.

So it was that Santos headed into November 3 with essentially no chance of pulling off a win. This became clear on election night, as the returns came in—Suozzi was just barely behind Santos in the in-person votes done on a voting machine, but there were around 100,000 absentee ballots out, and way more had been requested by Democrats than Republicans. This meant Santos was certain to lose. But, at the time, due to quirks in New York's byzantine election law, you couldn't start counting absentee ballots until long after the election. So Suozzi—who would ultimately win comfortably by more than 12 percentage points—appeared to be "down" on election night, if you counted only the in-person tally.

It was mathematically nonsense, the same "red mirage" that took place all around the country, given how much the party of Trump had denigrated voting by mail during COVID—an unnecessary self-own. But now Trump was also sending a message that the election was rigged, and Santos—who was thrilled to model himself off his fellow Queens schemer—followed suit.

Overnight after polls had closed, he was quick to suggest on Facebook that he had won with "72% ballots reported." Soon he was tapping into the same #StopTheSteal rhetoric that Trump was using on the national level, complaining darkly that "ballots just keep pouring in" and that "this just smells rotten," without providing any evidence of wrongdoing. The day after national outlets called the election for Biden, and Rudy Giuliani held a wild lie-filled press conference about ballot challenging at Four Seasons Total Landscaping in Philadelphia, Santos took the vibe to the local level, saying his campaign had been "flooded" with reports of irregularities in the district. Like Trump, he made noises about the process being a threat to democracy, and it culminated for him as it did for his mentor from afar in DC in early January, when Santos claimed in a January 5 rally that "they did to me what they did to Donald J. Trump. They stole my election."[29] He later claimed he was at the Ellipse for the pro-Trump festivities on the fateful next day, just before the violence broke out. Until then, "that was the most amazing crowd and the president was at his full awesomeness that day," Santos said in a TV interview in 2021.[30]

This is what everything was building toward back in November, when his team barged into the offices where bipartisan election workers were carefully counting absentee votes. Election officials told Santos's people that they could take part in whatever part of the process they wanted. Grab a mask, social distance, check out the count. There was nothing to hide.

But there was, it turned out, something for Santos to gain.

_____

*There has always been something* of a *Producers*-style quality to Santos's political career, a similarity to the Mel Brooks farce in which two losers purposefully stage a terrible Broadway play with the expectation that it'll close on opening night, they won't have to pay back their investors, and they can escape to Rio de Janeiro, then and now a place of reinvention. Santos was not actively trying to lose, but he did dabble in win-by-losing financials one day after the 2020 election, when he opened the Devolder Santos for Congress Recount committee.

This was essentially a fundraising mechanism to pay for the inevitable legal and associated expenses of a recount needed for a nail-biter race—or that's the supposed case for such committees. The strategy of using recount committees has legal backing from a 2006 Federal Election Commission advisory opinion on the subject. Two of the candidates who made prominent use of such outfits are Santos and Lee Zeldin, both of whom share a campaign treasurer, Nancy Marks.

There can be method to the madness of starting a new campaign outfit in the frenzied aftermath of Election Day, even if a recount never happens: the donation limits for the new committee reset, meaning that donors who had maxed out to Santos during the campaign cycle could give thousands of dollars once again.

There was no need for a recount in Santos's race, and there would not be. It was not even close. By November 15, a sheet of talking points from Suozzi's team logged 79 percent of the counted absentees as going for Suozzi. The talking points suggested Suozzi would win by more than twenty thousand votes, underestimating by more than half his actual win margin. Yet immediately, in the days after the election, Santos started raising money. He ended up getting lots of it—over $256,000—and quickly. And it came from all over the country.

The recount gambit reaped big benefits for Santos. Much of the money he raised was recorded as being spent on fundraising, which helped establish connections that would pay dividends in his next run. There were other eye-catching expenses, and bizarre bookkeeping—such as dual payments made by his two different committees to an election observer who said he got only one such payment. Or the double charges for a $2,000 laptop from Best Buy. Or the $500 bill at Il Bacco Ristorante, paid a day after Santos held a business—not campaign—meeting at the same spot.[31]

The money was coming in easily, and going out nicely, even though Santos had mathematically lost.

Committing to the bit, Santos decided to go down to new-member orientation in DC, as if he expected to truly win once the paper ballots were finalized.

New-member orientation can be a heady time. "They roll out the red carpet for you," said Florio, who went in 2016 as part of Suozzi's team. There are dinners. There are sweaty parties. People dress up and show off. It has long been thus. In 1988, New York newcomer Eliot Engel sported a "charcoal, Italian-cut suit and a red paisley tie and matching pocket handkerchief," according to *Newsday*.[32] You start getting access to the trappings of power and prestige. They show you how to vote. Everything is historic, even the box from which the freshmen draw their numbers to determine office space. The mahogany container is over one hundred years old and dates back to the tradition of a blindfolded House page pulling out marbles for lawmakers. Even journeymen get a tingle.

Then there's the big dinner under the dome in Statuary Hall, with its pilasters and gallery walls made of sandstone, its white marble carved in Carrara, Italy, its shape of an ancient amphitheater and all the acoustics of shock and awe. In this room with its figures of history staring down at you, the Marquis de Lafayette himself addressed the Congress. Now you are in his and their company, by virtue of your election (or in Santos's case, not at all election), and the tables are draped and white, and you are very far from Elmhurst or Niterói or the Dish Network call center. When Florio had his

Statuary Hall moment with Suozzi, he remembers leaning over to his right to talk to Charlie Crist, himself an incoming member of Congress, the latest move in a long political career. Florio asked him how this was different from being governor of Florida. Crist goes, Look where we are. Look up. Isn't this wonderful?

It was.

In 2020, the setting seemed to reach something in Santos, too. During his "orientation," he toured the Lincoln Memorial, pondered Abe's "energy," as he posted on Facebook; checked out the Washington Monument, found its history "stunning"; experienced the "awesomeness" of a fellow Republican's race getting called while he wandered the #redroom of the #westwing. And of course he gleefully posted about it all to his growing number of followers, and indeed he was getting better at the posting, better at being part of the in-club. As when he expertly records himself asking for donations for his almost-colleague Kelly Loeffler, who is fighting to maintain her lead and keep her Senate seat. "Send in as little as five dollars today," he says.[33] He is a long way from the clout-chasing videos of last year, little watched and thank goodness for that. Now he's stopping the steal, and glorified for it. He has become, and is treated as, a voice of the party.

Then the culmination, his own Statuary Hall dinner, which was not the same as usual due to COVID precautions, but Santos got a moment in the hallowed space anyway, when Kevin McCarthy addressed the Republican newbies—Santos among them. He's filming. And then McCarthy lifts up his phone to the microphone, and who could it be but the one and only—Donald Trump. The man who'd changed politics and paved the way. Speaking to him. To Santos. "We're very proud of you," Trump says over the phone McCarthy holds. And it sure sounds like in response, Santos shouts

"Wooooooo!" Certainly he sees that moment as the highlight of his time in DC, he breathlessly posts later.

"This country is just so amazing it allows the most amazing opportunities to everyone who works hard to achieve their dreams," he writes.[34] A kid from Jackson Heights has now met two presidents, he says (he doesn't specify the second). Later he'll say on the *America's Mom* podcast that when he put that badge around his neck at orientation, it gave him "chills."[35] His tone is bursting.

He had spent his life pretending to be a bigger deal than he was. Now there were other people calling him a person of substance. That was the message of the dinners, the parties, the palm-to-palm business cards, the backslapping, the telling of war stories here. We made it. Santos, with all his lying and exaggerating and bumbling and scheming, had made it. Or faked it. But if you squint, how different was he really from his peers, after all? He had become, or nearly become, part of "that handful of insiders who invent, year in and year out, the narrative of public life," as Joan Didion described it in *Political Fictions*.

It has been posited about Santos's half countryman, the steelworker Brazilian president Lula, that he did not get fully interested in politics until he visited that nation's congress for the first time, and saw that there were only two people from the working class there.[36] In his own politically opposite way, could it be that Santos's electoral ambitions were stoked to an explosion in this November moment, once he saw the Potomac and the capital up close, when he got a taste of what winning could feel like, and what national attention he could get from the MAGA crew? Without all of this, he might not have ever tried again. By the same token, without his fakery about almost winning this election, and the attention that wrought, political leaders might have never given him a second chance.

Regardless, he made a decision pretty quickly. He was not going to disappear into history, quit while he was ahead (not exposed), and go back to petty scamming. He still didn't know the local territory and had little interest in the North Shore Towers grind. But he had found a social media shortcut. And when you throw your hat into the ring, you never know what might happen. You might catch fire. And so he was already promising another run. We know because he told me so, in a phone call two weeks after the election when he finally publicly conceded to the obviously victorious Tom Suozzi.

"It's been an interesting journey," he said, before claiming he was heading back to New York by train. In keeping with his postinfection level of COVID seriousness at the time, he said he planned to quarantine for fourteen days once he arrived. He also said he had other, bigger plans.

"I am running again in two years."

# 8

## The Coattail Candidate

*T*eodora Choolfaian met George Santos in the fall of 2021 at a cocktail party at Westbury Manor, home to gazebos and garden acres and other expensive backdrops for wedding pictures. They were on their way out together, hitting the fragrant air in formal dress, chatting about Vladimir Putin.

It was the lead-up to the Russia-Ukraine war, and Choolfaian, a Bulgarian immigrant, noted that the Russian autocrat was a cold-blooded, conniving figure, not somebody to be provoked. Santos tried to follow along.

"Oh, Vladimir Putin, this little man, this little unhappy, unsatisfied, man," he said, leeringly. "Why can't anyone satisfy him?"

It had a sexual edge to it somehow, and clearly Santos thought it was a good joke. He was laughing.

It was not the insight of the sharpest geopolitical mind, but Choolfaian, a naturalized citizen, chalked it up to the usual American naivete and also the fact that to be fair, Santos did not seem invested in the actual particulars of their conversation. Mostly, he was just interested in pleasing her.

It was not a foregone conclusion that Santos would be trying to flatter and curry favor with this civilian, this busy mom of three. It was equally unlikely that either of them would be at this glitzy GOP event, if you rolled the clock back a few years. But their intersection was a sign of the tailwind social and political forces that would soon boost Santos, even if he didn't know it.

Both had been city people who were not exactly habitual voters. They swam in the business of New York, which is business, and only occasionally brushed up against politics. Choolfaian had even been a Democrat, and the political talk she tended to encounter was typical for that side of the aisle—environmentalism, immigration, the sense that Republicans were old-fashioned and out of touch. Where she and Santos diverged for a period was in Choolfaian taking a time-honored path: she started to have children. You go into a snug little den then where everything about the outside world is outside. You go looking for a bigger place to live. You move to Long Island.

In Nassau County, the newcomer will find backyards and cul-de-sacs and beautiful seascapes and old-money mansions, and also a world of local politics like a hardened web of tree roots, gnarled and only sometimes poking aboveground but underlying everything—your taxes, your garbage pickup, the little speeches before certain concerts at Jones Beach. But it was easy to step around the roots or not notice them much, unless it came about that you tripped.

The tripping came for Choolfaian with COVID. At first, she thought the government was doing the right thing with the pandemic restrictions. In the beginning, the masks and all made sense. She got the Pfizer vaccine, because she thought it was going to stop the madness. But as the chaos of 2020 turned to the monotony of 2021, and once Delta was over and spring made its butter-melt into summer, she expected things would be different when her three children went back to school. They had already endured months of closures or restrictions to their desks. The six-foot diameters. The haphazardly worn masks. Surely that had to end in September.

But she was wrong. And she became angry.

She was a parent. She was deeply invested in her children's lives, yes. She sometimes felt that she was a secretary for playdates. So she could not avoid thinking about the lives of her kids and the other schoolchildren, masks rubbing their noses raw, sweating and uncomfortable, told to stay separate from other students when that is the most unnatural thing for a child. So knows any parent who has been on a playdate. Taxes are high in Nassau County, and this means that taxpayers—parents—want some ownership over their product.

This was how Choolfaian found herself in front of the Port Washington train station one day, holding a homemade sign, protesting the COVID measures. It was striking; it was new. She says she had not really done something like this before. But there was a tactile thrill to it. She was poking the world. She began going to school board meetings, being theatrical. Crying, ripping off her mask. She organized a meeting of parents with an assemblywoman to ask about "the long-term consequences of wearing face coverings for children in early childhood education settings." She held more signs: UNMASK THE KIDS. THIS IS CHILD ABUSE. She began to realize a strange thing: people were listening to her.

All around there were troops willing to be rallied to her cause. Everywhere she went in town, there was another person who could be convinced of the craziness of all (*waves hands*) this. She could be relentless, really; it's true that some people said this. But here her relentlessness was sowed on a fertile field, her organizing capacity reaping something larger than playdates. Such as the protest by the Greenvale T. J. Maxx in January when piles of snow on the ground did not deter people coming out and making their argument—about unmasking kids and letting them "breathe"—to the passing cars and the odd camera phone. These people were angry. And so was George Santos, when he showed up to that unmasking protest at the beginning of his second campaign, poised to take flight.[1]

He was there right with her, in the snow, wearing tight jeans, shouting into a megaphone. Because Choolfaian could offer something he wanted—door-knocking, phone-banking, grassroots activism. She was good at it. And that could be useful for him. And he knew that there were so many more angry, engaged people like her.

---

*One way to think about* George Santos's second run for elected office is that this time around he wasn't the raw-material novice offered up as tribute in an unwinnable race. Instead, he was a coattail candidate, the happy recipient of a lot of accidental forces of history that he did not create but deftly rode. The coat he was clinging to was less a garment and more a kite: Nassau County and Long Island in general had become a seething hurricane of angry and annoyed citizens primed to vote red no matter whose name was on the ballot line.

First on the list of grievances was COVID-19, and the reaction to that pandemic two years into it. New York was ground zero for this international disaster, served by three metro-area international airports, some of the nation's first confirmed cases, and over eighty thousand deaths. At first, many New Yorkers were like Choolfaian, vocal about their solidarity with essential workers, and willing to mask up and social distance to #StopTheSpread. The virus's danger, as it rampaged visibly across the state, was too real to act otherwise. And though Manhattan offered the nation its visuals of an empty Times Square and people banging pots and pans, Long Island was just as central to the COVID story. It was host to the powerful Northwell hospital network, whose leader, Michael Dowling, became a sort of unelected COVID czar in New York. Long Island also was home to huge percentages of the first responders, from police to fire to EMTs, who were suddenly getting plaudits for their service on this new and invisible front line. The first nurse to get the official vaccine in the whole United States, at least according to Northwell, was a Northwell employee and Long Islander, Sandra Lindsay, a Jamaican immigrant who herself lost an aunt and uncle to the virus. She lived alone, and once made a pact with a health care friend of hers that if one of them caught it bad, the other one would come over, move to the basement, and quarantine. Lindsay hoped the jab, as she called it, would be the beginning of the end.[2]

But as the vaccines rolled out across the region, a restiveness took hold. The shots were amazing and practically without side effects, and it was supposed to be a summer of fun. Then people started to get sick anyway. It was all still happening. And the messaging from the highest levels was neither consistent nor airtight.

There was, for example, Andrew M. Cuomo, the prickly and man-of-action governor of New York. Though he was slow in the crucial early days to shut down the state in the face of the health threat, he soon did an about-face and became the nation's reigning governmental pandemic fighter, turning his daily COVID briefings into must-see (and sometimes hammy) TV as he auditioned for the presidency or at least a great book deal. He charmed the MSNBC voter and sold posters featuring his cute pandemic catchphrases, urging New Yorkers all the while to stay the course. This message remained firm and insistent even as some of his constituents began to tire of the disruptions. They did not like the limits on how many people could be in their own homes; the requirements to mask up everywhere; the constant push toward vaccines; and all this while Cuomo was fighting the charge that his administration's early policies on nursing homes had resulted in thousands more avoidable deaths.

The rebellion percolated on Long Island. In May of that first pandemic summer, cops gathered in Southold without masks for the retirement celebration of a town police sergeant, and there was an outcry about the hypocrisy, then an outcry about the outcry in return. This cycle repeated weekly. So-called patriot groups began to hold wildly successful political meetings when they tailored the subject to annoyance at masking. It helped that there was not much else to do. Might as well grab a case of beer and head to the protest in Commack and see all your friends, Cuomo be damned.

Looking around at the state of things and grinning was the antivax movement, alive and well on Long Island. That movement has flexed its power periodically in history, not least in 1904 Rio de Janeiro about a hundred years before Santos got there, when people angry about compulsory smallpox vaccination, instituted by a devotee of Louis Pasteur, decided to wreck and burn the city for days.[3] In New York, the movement got a foothold in 2019 by rallying behind the religious exemption that allowed broad swathes of people to skip childhood vaccines. Democrats, who had just taken over the state senate for the first time in a decade, got rid of the exemption. This was in response to the country's biggest measles outbreak in twenty-seven years, one centered in New York's ultra-Orthodox Jewish communities, where the religious exemption had been heavily exploited.[4]

The closed loophole did not mandate forced vaccination. It just required shots for kids to attend school. Fears of childhood vaccines causing autism or other serious problems have been long studied and discredited. But a warning sign of the misinformation-filled craziness to come was visible at the state capitol during the exemption fight, when antivax protesters carried signs and chanted about illnesses like measles, mumps, and chickenpox being good actually because they "keep you healthy" and "fight cancer."[5]

Still, for the next few years the antivaccine push was mostly relegated to the unproofread corners of the internet and social media, pushed by single-issue ideologues and a tragic cohort of parents whose kids developed autism around the same time they got their vaccinations.

Long Islander John Gilmore was right there with them. He is the executive director of the Autism Action Network, one of the groups most committed to promoting the—again—discredited idea that vaccines cause autism. He says the group has a mighty 100,000-member email list, including some 30,000 or 35,000 from New York. But at base, he's the father of a child in his twenties who needs assistance in most aspects of daily life, who can't be left alone, and who has been that way, Gilmore says, since his first round of childhood vaccines. No amount of scientific evidence will convince Gilmore that this truly despair-inducing situation is not the result of needles. And so he has become a warrior for a deeply personal cause that has led him to distrust numbers, established information sources, and mainstream leadership.

Many allies and sympathizers approach the antivax orbit in the same way—even Santos. Gilmore says he met the political hopeful at an event for the Whitestone Republican Club, ahead of his first campaign. Santos was open, friendly, happy to chat, and familiar with vaccine issues. "He said he had a niece who has autism," Gilmore says. Santos once said the same on social media.

For a long time, it was a lonely road for families who sought to connect their experience with autism to vaccines. But when COVID hit and authorities started pushing these new, still-emergency-authorized shots, the antivaccine forces found a new audience. Especially in New York, where government leaders were strenuously promoting the jab, including by making it hard or at least annoying to live without one. During a significant stretch of months, particularly in New York City, you'd have to flash your vaccine card or a picture of it to get into a much-anticipated restaurant or music venue. It all came on top of the intense legal rules and new social norms about the size of gatherings and mask usage, which lingered even during pandemic lulls.

The masking, and then the vaccine mandates for workers across the economic spectrum, functioned as a sort of gateway drug to the wider antivax movement: the pot that led to heroin, as Gilmore puts it. He saw the annoyance at pandemic restrictions as a reaction to governmental overreach. And he was happy to collect email addresses.

He also noticed something geographically interesting about the provenance of his emails. If you mapped them, the patterns would look like suburban donuts around big cities in blue states. In his own backyard, he thinks, a major ingredient in that donut is the prototype of the Long Island mom, who is "sort of notorious" for looking out for her kids and not being deferential to authority, Gilmore says.

It is a well-trodden path, one worn into existence years before Choolfaian and other parents began complaining about masks in schools. Long Island parents had already been at the heart of the opt-out movement, in which thousands of mothers and fathers pulled their kids out of school in the 2010s rather than have them sit for statewide exams. One of the national leaders of that effort was Jeanette Deutermann, a Nassau County mom of a fourth grader, who got angry about Obama-era moves to standardize school curriculums and tie teacher evaluations to tests.

The bureaucracy of it all raised hackles for parents like Deutermann, who remembers her elementary schooler coming home in 2013 with a notice that he'd been "selected" for "Sunrise Academy." Students who had been both high- and low-achieving on the recent benchmark tests got the call, and it meant the kids had to come in at seven thirty a.m. twice a week for test prep. That was how Deutermann came to found a Long Island Opt Out Facebook group, which soon drew thousands of members. The movement, percolating in other suburban areas too, spread around New York and beyond.[6] And it has remained potent through the present, with large swathes of Long Island students continuing to skip mandated standardized tests.[7]

---

*Some of Long Island's penchant* for middle-aged activism like this can be explained by the comfortable socioeconomic status of many of its residents, who have time for the kind of nonoccupational labor it takes to rally peers for a cause. The giant land mass features merely the population of the single borough of Queens, but its residents are represented by scores of units of local government, including more than one hundred hotly contested school boards, providing many open slots for civic input. And the region's proximity to the media capital of the world keeps it close to the national conversation: see the ink spilled in 2021 over Smithtown, a vast majority-white place where the school board became a culture war battleground after such indignities as a Broadway actress invited to read for a literacy night having in the past tweeted critically about cops.

But the litany of controversies and fights can sometimes make it feel like there really is something in the water on Long Island, and not just its nerve-racking pollutants. That possibility struck Congressman Steve Israel not long before he began serving as the chair of the Democratic Congressional Campaign Committee. In June 2009, he got a call from a neighboring Democratic congressman who had faced a shockingly escalatory protest about health care the night before at an expected-to-be-sleepy Setauket town hall. The congressman had to be escorted to his car by police officers. Israel hadn't heard that from any of his colleagues around the country—yet.

It turned out that Long Island was not an outlier but an early landing spot for the Tea Party movement about to sweep the nation.

"There's something about Long Island's culture," Israel mused years later, in the wake of Santos's victory and the local red wave around it. There is, for example, the list of local traumas. When terrorists struck the Twin Towers in 2001, everybody on Long Island knew somebody who was affected, whether they were a police officer, a firefighter, or trader with Cantor Fitzgerald. A few years later, as the 2008 economic meltdown exploded, everyone in this region of overextended homeowners knew someone whose house was in foreclosure. It made Nassau and Suffolk counties "fertile for the politics of anger and resentment," says Israel, who represented much of the territory Santos would later win.

Santos himself was attracted to the Tea Party–style rhetoric that has been a potent weapon for challengers in recent years. One of very few authors he has referenced publicly is KrisAnne Hall, a fringe antigovernment activist and self-described constitutional attorney who, Santos said on a podcast, helped him gain "clarity" on the Constitution, which he said was written in "very elaborate and quite obsessively formal language."[8] Hall's books, one of which aims to "refute the notion that the Constitution is a living, breathing document which must be interpreted and reinterpreted according to the changing needs of society," often rail against government overreach and executive orders. She calls Obama "kingly" and argues for the primacy of state power. The intellectual framework is one of reembracing American exceptionalism and resisting the federal government—a mood that continues to percolate for some voters on Long Island.

Modern Long Island is neither firmly red nor firmly blue, but rather acts as a kind of swinging bellwether and microcosm of national political currents. The local ebb and flow of the anger and resentment reached a high point in 2016 with Trump, who won the island on Election Day, and soon stoked the national flames with another charged Long Island issue: the gruesome violence perpetrated by MS-13, a gang with roots in El Salvador and Los Angeles. The string of killings the gang committed on Long Island horrified residents, but also became part of Trump's anti-immigrant arsenal due to the gang's membership being

Hispanic (as well as its victims). Anger about criminals morphed into nativist sentiment, even in a metropolitan area where newcomers were all around, working at Dish Network or restaurants or office parks next door.

Israel, a longtime incumbent, could feel the shift in the last years of his congressional tenure. People in Huntington diners used to smile and want to shake hands when he walked in. "Now they're staring grumpily at their menus, they didn't want to make eye contact," he said.

It is this kind of environment, he suggests, in which someone like Santos could thrive.

———————

*There was another cultural issue* that took hold of the minds and popular imaginations of Long Islanders in the years leading up to Santos's win, one that fertilized the soil of the GOP political root system perhaps more than any other. This was the set of changes to New York's criminal justice system that came to be called "bail reform."

In 2019, Democrats in Albany finally tackled what they saw as an unacceptable and enduring unfairness: that many New Yorkers accused of minor offenses were able to get out of jail and prepare for trial at home only if they had thousands of dollars to pay bail. Those who didn't—often Black or Hispanic residents—were stuck behind bars without having been convicted of a crime. The reforms eliminated the use of cash bail for most misdemeanors and nonviolent crimes, using less onerous means to ensure a return to court. It was a sea change to the New York legal system, and it went into effect in January 2020. Within months, American society would be rocked by the pandemic and a racial reckoning after a

Minneapolis police officer killed a father and sometime security guard named George Floyd.

That is the context for the great debate over bail that dominated the next three years. Republicans leapt at some increases in New York crime statistics, even though they were generally on par with jumps in other jurisdictions that made no changes to bail. Democratic infighting meant the bail changes were done in a messy patchwork way that resulted in some glaring loopholes, but the legislators' repeated tweaks to the legislation and entreaties to wait for more data didn't make the GOP howl any less. And a wave of exaggerated political advertisements swept through the Empire State like the second coming of Willie Horton. A test case came in the open 2021 race for Nassau district attorney, where one of the Democratic state senators who helped negotiate bail reform was going up against Anne Donnelly, who would later become one of the people investigating Representative Santos. A mild-mannered career prosecutor who had worked under both Republican and Democratic administrations, Donnelly ran grimly on bail. One of her ads included a picture of a dreadlocked Black man below ominous red lettering: "Is your family safer with this thug released back on the street?" (He was incarcerated when the ad ran.)

Another featured a testimonial from the victim of an alleged antisemitic assault in Manhattan—a heinous attack, but one that had only a pretty tenuous link to the bail changes, which allowed those accused of less serious crimes to get out pretrial without posting bail. These attackers, in contrast, had bail set for them as usual after the incident.[9] That didn't stop the victim from saying the bail changes were setting "thugs" free on the street.

This was the gist of the antireformers' strategy, focusing on harrowing anecdotes while tying all sorts of mayhem to bail. Candidate after candidate took the same tack, and it worked in race after race in 2021: painting the state as a dangerous and apocalyptic place, using examples helpfully provided by the front page of the conservative tabloid *New York Post*. Often, as with the antisemitic assault ad, those examples of violence were pulled from the streets and subways of New York City. And helping to push this issue was the Nassau GOP.

It was not a new position. The suburban wing of the Republican party had been using its neighbor as a foil for generations, long before Santos came on the scene to run in his city-and-suburbia-straddling district.

The very creation of Nassau County was in some sense an early reaction to the Big Apple. "During the consolidation of the five counties in and around Manhattan into the new municipality that became the City of New York, local residents on Long Island lobbied the state legislature to establish a new county independent from the city," writes Nassau native and GOP political guru Michael Kaplan in an unpublished manuscript detailing the local party's prehistory. "Albany lawmakers acceded to their demands and on January 1, 1899, Nassau County was created."

For the next hundred years, the county would be reliably Republican, particularly in local elections, instinctively positioning itself against the behemoth next door. The mantra changed over the generations—sometimes it was "protecting the suburban character of Nassau County," as GOP chair Joseph Margiotta said in the 1980s, years after he fought the construction of affordable high-rise apartments.[10] Sometimes the "sixth borough" was invoked, as in, residents wouldn't want Nassau to become that. Or, in the early twentieth century, the prayer to "keep the Tammany tiger out of Nassau," referring to the tightly controlled party boss system that had thrived in the city for decades.

The irony was that the Nassau GOP was pioneering something of a Tammany system of its own out in the suburbs, where patronage was the way of the world and locals knew to talk to partisan leaders for even seemingly civic problems. The system's initial architect, J. Russell Sprague, was so tightly controlling that he is known for his somewhat-legendary instruction, "Always know how a meeting is coming out before you call it." Sprague's great coup was assimilating the newcomers who flocked to Long Island as the suburban age of America dawned. Levittown, and its government-subsidized cookie-cutter houses, was the center of that story. The newcomers were often white ethnic Democrats, notes Marjorie Freeman Harrison in a 2005 thesis on Nassau politics. But the Republicans were relentless: "GOP representatives were tipped off by letter carriers when a new family arrived, and the party, in the person of a friendly neighbor, arrived at the doorstep to assist with the details like making sure garbage was picked up and broken sidewalks fixed."[11]

This partisan centrality to daily life had its legal pitfalls when political leaders overstepped—say, with the kickback scheme that ensnared party chair Margiotta in the early 1980s. But even a seriously shocking scandal or six wasn't enough to shake up the strong GOP machine, which at that time was still the place to go whether you wanted to become a top county official or a summer lifeguard.[12] Ronald Reagan himself once acknowledged how fertile Nassau's territory was for the GOP, claiming that when a Republican goes to heaven, it looks a lot like Nassau County.

The party was also rigorous about where it got its candidates (from within) and how it sculpted them (almost to a mold). For some time, there used to be what was called "charm school" for candidates, current GOP chair Joe Cairo told me. Cairo is a happy warrior and sports fan who went to the only out-of-state university New York politicians of a certain type are allowed to attend (Notre Dame). Cairo himself attended charm school in '75, after he was appointed to fill a death-related vacancy on the Hempstead town council. To get ready to face the voters, he first had to go see an etiquette expert in Manhattan, every Friday afternoon for around ten weeks. There were moments of culture clash in the expert's doorman building overlooking Central Park. Cairo didn't like her advice about overpronouncing words: "Thursday," say, with a nearly r-less flourish. You'd get laughed outta town back home for talking like that. But there were useful lessons about decorum, and how to be taken seriously. To this day he still wears over-the-calf socks on the off chance that he crosses his legs at a meeting and the suit pants ride up. And he learned how to address a crowd, how to fight through nervousness—pick out one person, just one person in the room. And speak to them.

The political situation in Nassau County is different than it used to be in the charm school days. Former US senator Al D'Amato, who jumped from town office in Nassau to the Capitol in 1981 and stayed there for eighteen years, is now a pot lobbyist and name on a federal courthouse, as well as the last Republican to win a US Senate seat in New York. Locally, Democrats have made inroads, so much so that they now outnumber Republicans by party registration, if not voting inclination. There is no more charm school, and the party's candidates are less afraid to break the old mold. It used to be said that there was such a thing as "Republican hair"—straight, coiffed, and combed back, probably white, certainly Caucasian. There had never been—or at least Cairo cannot remember—an openly gay member of Congress from the party in Nassau.

Which is where George Santos fits in, at a moment of flux for the party. The machine does a kind of vetting through lifelong knowledge of candidates, being warned if so-and-so drinks too much, has a gambling issue, or a girlfriend or two on the side. But Santos was not a party person, not among the Nassau farm team, Cairo wants to make that very clear. He was not a former baseball coach or town trustee or village mayor before he made the leap to Congress. He was not a committeeman who spent years walking the petitions necessary to get candidates onto the ballot. He was a Queens guy, not even recommended very highly by the Queens party chair at the time, frankly, but in 2020, who else was going to run for what was sure to be a losing race against a longtime Democratic incumbent?

There are a few things that stuck out to Cairo about his encounters with this newcomer. Of course there was the time Santos came into Cairo's office at GOP headquarters and launched into his fantastical volleyball story. That he'd been sort of a star at Baruch (where by the way he'd graduated summa), and had actually been a "champion." That was a word that Cairo did not take lightly. He had all kinds of memorabilia in his office—a picture of him as a high school football official, and a piece signed by the legendary Fighting Irish coach Lou Holtz that sat right in Santos's eyeline, and it said "Play like a champion today." *Champion.* It does make you think.

But mostly, Santos seemed like someone the party could run and basically ignore. The newcomer intimated as much, portraying himself as a wealthy Wall Street type with the ability to tap his network and easily fund his campaign without much help from the party coffers. He once told Cairo offhandedly that he'd been looking at expensive houses on Long Island and had even made an offer in the $2.5 to $3 million range. At one point he confided that he was "handling finances" for Linda McMahon, the former Trump official and wrestling mogul. He said he was going to call her up and get a big check from her (his filings do not show such largesse).

Cairo is no dummy. He must not have hated the fact that wherever the money came from, Santos-affiliated accounts gave over $180,000 to Nassau Republican Party committees alone. (The committees refunded large portions of that money after Santos imploded.) It's a stretch for him and the Nassau Republicans to mostly blame the Queens GOP for Santos, given that Nassau made up the majority of the Third Congressional District during both of the fabulist's runs. In 2022, Nassau had nearly 80 percent of the district's registered voters. Queens certainly wasn't strong enough to boss around the storied Nassau machine here. Santos would have been an also-ran if Cairo and his party decided to block him.

But there were signs that the kid understood the program, or what the world was like in Nassau, even if he was an outsider with a strange résumé. Coming into the 2020 campaign, Cairo said, Santos shared that he had been using his mother's name because he had been close to her and his father wasn't a big part of his life. But he planned to use his father's name—Santos—now because "politically that might be more advantageous than Devolder." Cairo's assumption was that the up-and-comer felt it was more ethnic. If you squinted, it was almost Italian.

In this way, a party that had once forced candidates through the grinder of charm school now shrugged and said "go ahead" to someone unvetted. They didn't even require years of service and servitude before allowing him to run. New party.

Santos's success was not, however, a sign that the party machine was dead. Cairo himself had come up through the machine's heyday, and like other top Nassau politicos he'd experienced a little legal issue in the past, misusing a few hundred thousand dollars in client funds, after which he'd parted ways with his law license for a while.[13] Then he came back to keep the system humming. In 2022, the well-oiled machine and its army of committeemen was pumping on all cylinders, fresh off a monster cycle that saw them win big on the county level, not just for district attorney but also triumphing in the race for county executive, a huge focus for the party. It was non-national races like these, plus town races and more, from which the real and low-show jobs flowed, and patronage was still key to the Nassau system. Members of Congress could get their names in the papers, but how much actual employment could they provide—a handful of modestly paid staff salaries? This was not where the Nassau GOP typically focused its attention. Rather, in 2022, the party saw an even bigger opportunity with the governor's race, in which Republican standard-bearer Lee Zeldin was nipping at the heels of incumbent Kathy Hochul. Governor is where it's at. There are administration jobs galore, plus all sorts of contracts and funds. New York is a Democratic state, but from time to time a Republican can break through the blue.

That seemed possible in 2022, and so the Nassau GOP threw its significant weight behind Zeldin, a Long Islander from neighboring Suffolk County. The push included door-knocking, funding—hundreds of thousands of dollars directly to Zeldin's campaign in the fall of 2022—plus mail and social media homing in on the bail situation and the general prognosis of New

York City as a crime-ridden place. This message, that the city was full of mayhem, illegal guns, and criminals using them, was amplified by county party regulars as well as the *New York Post*, whose cover or headlines inevitably seemed to feature someone being pushed into the subway tracks or shot to death. It was a message that was also pushed hard in tight state senate races and was equally good for every Republican, including Santos, the somewhat accidental congressional nominee.

Was this maelstrom of bail and crime a message that danced, just a little, around race? This was the Nassau of Levittown, one of the birthplaces of suburbia, home to restrictive covenants that kept out almost all nonwhites for a generation. The county is becoming more and more diverse, but that doesn't stop the new generation of newcomers from looking disdainfully over their shoulders. A radio interviewer once told Santos that suburban housewives should be rising up against "radicals" due to the Left's attempts to install low-income housing in places like his district. "Suburban housewives love me," Santos said,[14] and went on to highlight his fight against using an empty hotel to temporarily house homeless families.[15]

That particular fight was in the town of Jericho, but the impulse has often been present in other parts of Long Island. The freshly arrived have for decades been escaping something: Crowds. Schools. Poverty. Crime.

"People who want to move to the suburbs, they don't want to live in the city," Cairo once told me.

That ancient urge, given new resonance, was ready to boost Santos, too.

---

*Across Long Island, GOP candidates* from town council to statewide office had good feelings about the 2022 midterm election to come. Every once in a while, even in a supposedly blue state like New York, the voters decided to throw out the bums, counter the always-present power of the five boroughs for a while. The Long Island Republicans were familiar with this cycle. It had benefited them before. It smelled like it was coming again, that whiff of "don't tread on me" among the voting body and a little bit of Democratic desperation.

Many candidates began bowing to one or another of these powerful cultural forces. It was sometimes awkward, as when a vaccinated lawmaker would have to argue why actually it wasn't all that important to get the COVID shot; or a sober and careful GOP lawyer would go tongue tied when asked what changes would actually improve the bail system. This was not a problem for Santos. He could make pivots, even about-face. He could enthusiastically—wholeheartedly—embrace every single cultural impulse percolating on Long Island. A lifetime of lying had prepared him to harness this moment. His tall tales and never-ending stories were now more than a colorful habit; they were a tool.

So it was that the man who took the whole COVID thing so seriously he walked to the hospital in a tightly fitting mask to get tested, also called masks "face diapers" and, elsewhere, lambasted Cuomo's "tyrannical ruthless thirst for power" for closing restaurants.[16] He poked fun at Kamala Harris and Kathy Hochul for wearing masks at a speech and a cemetery;[17] he warned about the "cordon" that could descend on the city, keeping everyone in.[18] He spoke darkly about what Democrats were doing regarding masking—"I feel like our entire country is stuck in a nightmare and can't wake up," he once posted—and people loved it all.[19]

He knew the buttons to press, the grassroots issues to absolutely run with. He posted about the efforts of Florida governor Ron DeSantis to block classroom talk about sexual orientation, which Santos said had his "full-blown support" and shouldn't be called the "don't say gay" bill, actually: "The Left is hell-bent on creating a false narrative because they want to groom our kids."[20] Though he was nowhere close to having a child in any school, let alone in the Half Hollow Hills School District, he also showed up at a school board meeting to decry a pro-mask video he'd seen online, supposedly posted by a district teacher. He did not even do the politician thing of arriving seconds before a speech and cutting the line. No: he waited his turn with other angry members of the public, said his piece, affirmed his name.[21]

He spoke at a school board training course, where civilians were encouraged to run for that most local of offices. He knew the language—"Refuse to co-parent with the Government!" he posted in March 2022. He knew the stereotype, maybe the truism, that mothers could be a potent political force especially when rallied to the Republican side. The way he put it was that "waking up the mama bears will be the worst thing the Left ever did to themselves."[22] He had spoken to Choolfaian, the Port Washington mom, after all, and he had a sense that he was right. He said he'd "rather battle Antifa than a group of moms protecting their cubs!" He found that this amped-up register suited him. He did not sound as if he were pandering or making things up.

And always, always, there was the threat of bail reform and Black Lives Matter, the movement that had exploded once again around the world after George Floyd was killed. It became a Santos touchstone. He blasted the New York City mayor for painting a BLM mural in front of Trump Tower;[23] he claimed the movement—all of it—was an "existential threat to my district" and also Marxist, one of his favorite campaign words, one that worked better when used to slander racial justice protesters. He screamed about looting and disruption, and ungrammatically mixed COVID in with the crime angle: "Good morning to all except Kathy Hochul who fights harder to mask children than our out-of-control crime rates."[24] He ran a campaign ad with the tagline "Safer with Santos" and shared that a poll of his had found public safety and law and order and the "threat of Antifa and Black Lives Matter marching down their suburban area neighborhood" as a top issue in his district. He went on: he sensed a fear among voters who live "very peacefully" out there in the 'burbs, where they allow their kids to play on the front lawn and not be attended.[25] He painted a picture of chaos emanating out toward Long Island's lush pastures.

Santos saw that you could say anything on the political stage and they hardly fact-check it. It's part of the culture. Everyone expects a little exaggeration. He felt right at home. Sometimes he would return to his old habit of taking a pebble of truth for his politically advantageous stories—after Russia invaded Ukraine in early 2022, Santos went back to his familial-root yarn and said his Ukrainian ties were "very vague," but here he was talking about them anyway. In other times, he verged into unadulterated misinformation. Claiming a vague and not super mathematical "spillage" of city crime into the suburbs[26] is one thing, very different from saying (he found himself saying) that Jeffrey Epstein (who he'd "met") was murdered, and there was something to the theory that Trump, his much-loved Trump, was facing a giant conspiracy of enemies: "They tried to shame him, they tried impeachment, nothing worked," he said on a podcast. "They tried Russia Ukraine blah blah blah." Then came the next plan: they "called their best friends China and say, 'Release the kraken,' and that's essentially the coronavirus."[27]

In the Trump era, not only was there little penalty for conspiracy-mongering or outright lying—it could actually be a draw. Election misinformation was just part of showing your colors, as Santos had done quite publicly at the pre-January 6 rally in Freedom Plaza when he shouted to the crowd about his election getting stolen.[28] It became one of his favorite canards, this habitual liar. There were many flavors. He could be flippant about supposedly almost winning, or he might be very dire, as when he claimed that he beat his 2020 opponent on "election night for fourteen days until the ballots never stopped coming in." He said it on podcasts and in public. He even touched on it to people posing as Republicans, as when he told an undercover Democratic tracker that yes, he "wrote a nice check for a law firm" to help out some of the "January 6 patriots."[29] Was it real? Who cares. Democrats clutched their pearls, but the right wing loved it. The crazier he talked, the more he aligned himself with MAGA World. And there were supporters to be found there.

He was seen hanging out at a red-white-and-blue-bedecked clubhouse in Ronkonkoma called the America First Warehouse. This event space, which opened in 2019, was like Colonial Williamsburg for Trump diehards, packed with diner-style furniture and depictions of the former president as Thor, glamour shots of his family, and flags screaming TRUMP WON and AUDIT THE VOTE. Being angry with liberal pieties was gospel in this hangar-size room, which featured posters that said ILLEGALS DESERVE NOTHING and I MISS THE GOOD OLD DAYS WHEN EVERYBODY WASN'T AN OVERLY SENSITIVE PUSSY. There was a display of ballot boxes labeled DEAD PEOPLE VOTE HERE and SPONSORED BY G. SOROS. One time at the warehouse I watched a prayer circle join hands in support of outsider Republican candidates. A speaker vowed to make the space "the home of the antiestablishment party," and that vision occurred—the warehouse opened its doors to school board activists, antivax Long Islanders, and Trump World luminaries. Here at the warehouse, Santos, who once claimed "I am no right-winger,"[30] could now cultivate ties with the far-right—including groups like the Long Island Loud Majority, an outfit classed by the Southern Poverty Law Center as "antigovernment," whose leadership has called all-gender bathrooms "disgusting," who say the nation's future is "on the line," who think the election, of course, was stolen, who believe that prominent transgender women are "still men" and that "a Communist was in charge of the CIA," meaning John Brennan.[31] Santos was close with this outfit, which got its start selling T-shirts saying DEPLORABLE and WE THE PEOPLE to people hopping in their vehicles for pro-Trump car parades. Within one political cycle, Loud Majority had established a podcast, a recording studio, and a "Patriot Consultants" corporation, and had scalps to boast in school board elections. Of course, they showed up in force to the January 6 festivities.[32] And naturally they opposed COVID mitigation strategies too. One of the group's active associates—Dave Lipsky—became a Santos donor. His daughter Gabrielle would go on to serve as Santos's press secretary.

Santos went where the energy was. In 2022, that included seeking out the crypto evangelists. Despite being a party-endorsed candidate and benefiting from their machine operation, he quietly aided some of the loudest primary challengers also running for Congress on Long Island, such as Michelle Bond, the then-head of a cryptocurrency trade group whose partner was Ryan Salame, one of the top executives at FTX. In the months before that ill-fated and lie-boosted crypto exchange imploded, Salame became a Santos donor, too.

The political class paid and got paid. Alliances were struck and abandoned and reforged. And all the while, lies consumed the discourse. Good-faith civilians could turn disillusioned after trying to get involved. Their Facebook groups burned feverish, and then insane. Misinformation swirled on the various social media since nobody trusted—or hell, received—a newspaper anymore. The outlets that did exist were paywalled, woebegone, stodgy, or late to the game. Still people believed what they read, when it was typed up on a cell phone by who can say who. Were there going to be quarantine camps? Did an MS-13 witness get murdered because of criminal justice reform? Nobody saw the no's. Why was the top issue in a congressional race the entirely state-level battle over bail anyway? Who cares. It was in the water. And Santos was ready for a swim.

# 9

## *The Producers*, Part 2

*T*here was another benefit that Santos came to appreciate about politics as he charged into his second run for office: all the money he could spend.

He spent a Dionysian amount of money on hotels and airfare, flinging $917 to the W Hotel in South Beach, Miami, and $732 at the Soho Grand in NYC. He dropped hundreds at the Trump International Hotel and Hyatt Regency in Washington. He flew all over the place, including Kansas and Memphis, burning through over $42,000 on flights during his second campaign, which is more than double what his fellow Long Island GOP freshmen spent that cycle—combined.

Meals and things to eat tend to be the most common expense on federal campaign finance reports—a campaign army marches on its stomach-filling pizza and donuts, or something. But this time around, Santos took the eating to new heights. He logged more than ten trips to the Manhasset Cipollini, a place housed in "Long Island's most impressive shopping destination," a.k.a. the Americana shopping center. He dropped $300 at an internet-viral Miami steakhouse.[1] All this was nothing compared with the tens of thousands of dollars that his and his sister's political campaign committees munched through at the red-sauce, white-tablecloth spot Il Bacco Ristorante in Little Neck, Queens.

A quick visit to the ristorante is necessary to get a sense of just how great this political money situation was for Santos. Santos was a big fan of the spot: he has called the family that owns it "very good friends,"[2] including Joe Oppedisano, the subject of tabloid ink in 2020 when he crashed his Cessna into the water near the Throgs Neck Bridge. He broke sixteen ribs, and his passenger died. Santos welcomed both Oppedisano and his daughter Tina to his "Small Businesses for Santos Coalition." The Oppedisanos also were good for some contributions to Santos's campaign, as was the owner's brother Rocco, who has had various encounters with the law, including losing his permanent resident status in 2009 and being caught by the Coast Guard ten years later steering a sixty-three-foot yacht from the Bahamas toward Florida. The yacht had "14 undocumented Chinese migrants and a Bahamian national aboard—plus more than $200,000 in currency stuffed into the bedroom walls," according to the *Daily Beast*.[3]

Santos clearly felt at home at the restaurant, which hosted the Whitestone Republican Club and their very boozy and very maskless conga line during the prevaccinated December 2020 COVID uptick. He showed up "all the time," according to a valet, who noted to a reporter that Santos's partner was the tipper.[4]

Once, in November 2020, Santos brought a potential investment client to the spot, part of a charm offensive in which restaurant staff took coats at the door, whisked the guests up to a private dining room, and Santos ordered "dish after dish," as described in a juicy *Washington Post* piece.[5] The potential client smelled a rotten branzino and kept his money in his pocket, and Santos was later sauced that he'd put out for the dinner, even though he claimed it was on his company card: the client's lawyer, Santos's former friend Tiffany Bogosian, estimated to me that he'd shelled out around 1,000 bucks.

It is difficult to tell exactly what Santos was doing financially at Il Bacco and elsewhere due to the sloppiness of his filings. But there were at least a few potential hustles in the pasta e fagioli: one was simply that Santos could have been using political donors' money to pay for nice meals. Was a certain sit-down more of a campaign meeting, or a personal expense? This is a gray area that is always ripe for exploitation.

There is also the uncomfortable coincidence that Santos's favorite restaurant people happened to be donating money to him. Campaign finance lawyer Brett Kappel frames it this way: "You are giving money to the restaurant for a meal, and then magically the same money gets contributed to your campaign." It has a hint of "contribution in the name of another," which Kappel describes as potentially being "the FEC version of money laundering." (The restaurant owners have not been implicated in wrongdoing.)

Noteworthy too were the seven payments Santos says he made to Il Bacco during the 2022 cycle that were in the very specific increment of $199.99. Coincidentally, if he had happened to spend two pennies more, he would have had to keep some form of documentation like a receipt. What would an all-seeing security camera at the restaurant have shown about each of those $199.99 visits? Could he have received food and wine worth much more than that, and paid far below market price? Could he have been using campaign money for some other purpose while saying it was going (receipt-less) to Il Bacco? The possibilities abound. And Santos's filings eventually said that he used this $199.99 trick dozens of times in total, including for expenses where it seems impossible to spend that amount, like at a JFK parking facility where no combination of fees ends in $.99.[6]

He logged expenses of exactly this figure more times than any other candidate running in the entire United States that cycle, when *Politico* checked in January. It was a gimmick that concealed his outflow and hinted that all was not exactly scrupulously outlined in the books.[7]

Santos's financial outlays in general were brazen. He spent so much on fundraising that it actually shooed off one prospective donor, who told me about glancing at Santos's filings after being asked to contribute and being shocked at the sum sent to fundraising consultants. "I think there's something weird here," the donor thought. This was a pattern. For disciplined political campaigns that are focused on winning at all costs, it would be essentially insane to spend only about a third of their budget, as Santos did, on commercials and ads. That fraction is even more out of the ordinary in New York, where media buys and everything else are so exorbitantly priced. Rick Lazio, a former Republican congressman from Long Island, tells a story about blowing a fuse regarding his campaign sending fruit baskets to his hotel rooms: "This is not how we're supposed to be spending this money," he told *Newsday*.[8] Santos, in contrast, had these really swanky finance-bro style vests for his team. One veteran from his Democratic opponent's 2022 campaign was a little jealous about the cool merch. A colleague of this envious aide explained the obvious: "You realize how much a Patagonia vest costs," the colleague said. "It's crazy they're spending this much money on Patagonia vests."

The vests looked name-brand, though the campaign finance filings don't confirm. In fact, there were lots of problems or at the very least irregularities with the filings, including multiple revisions, contributions that were not accounted for, and unitemized payments totaling hundreds of thousands of dollars. At one point, hundreds of $199.99 disbursements to "Anonymous" were revised away in an amended filing. The paperwork also shows more than $10,000 spent with a company called Cleaner 123 for "apartment rental for staff," though the New York Times was told by a neighbor that Santos, the candidate, had been living there himself for months.[9]

The irregularities extended to the fact that there were filings for so many political campaign committees started by Santos or his associates. There was, for example, the brand-new state-level group Rise NY, which was funded by Santos's donors, logged payments to Santos's younger sister, Tiffany, for running it, and was supposed to promote voter enrollment to help build "a Republican skyline" in New York. Of course, the group mostly helped Santos, including with payments to a Queens landlord that exactly matched the cost of his rent for the location, plus $1,800 to go with two guests to a fancy gala for the Liberty Education Forum, featuring guest of honor Melania Trump. (Tiffany was not named in her brother's federal indictment.)[10]

The money accrued by fundraising—dollars donated by people who were supposedly hoping to boost Santos's political run— allowed Santos to fund a fun lifestyle, to eat and travel well, and even to act like the wealthy macher he always pretended he already was. He could, for example, use his campaign haul to give thousands of dollars to more than two dozen candidates for Congress. He could even make a big deal about promising to give the money that was not his, and then never give it anyway. That was the case when he set up a joint fundraising committee with Texas Republican Beth Van Duyne, did an event with her that pulled in $11,600 from two Long Island donors, and proceeded to not send any of that money her way, she alleged.[11]

It was all so easy, and profitable, operating within the rules or bending them. Santos had found a field through which streams of money flowed. It was almost shockingly easy to divert some of that money. In the preceding years, he had built a career of small-time hustling, the kind that gets you slapped down by the law eventually when you grab for too much. But here was an untapped resource, one where everyone laughed at the watchdogs. Campaign finance regulators? A joke. Particularly when you had someone who could help you navigate through the ooze.

---

*George Santos's navigator—his campaign treasurer*—was a Suffolk County entrepreneur and widow named Nancy Marks.

Treasurers are crucial to campaigns: no expenditure can go out and no contribution come in before a candidate names a treasurer. Campaign treasurers put the candidate's money in the bank, authorize and keep records of receipts and disbursements, and file all official committee reports and statements. It is a significant responsibility, and a potentially precarious one—treasurers can be found liable for their actions on a campaign.

There are different kinds of treasurers, across political levels. There are the groomed, fancy ones who operate perhaps out of New York City or DC, hired guns who can do this stuff in their sleep but charge a premium for it and have no sense of what's going on in Glen Cove or Forest Hills. There are the small operators who are a little shabbier but know the territory and have a personal touch. And there are the treasurers who are volunteers, friends or family of the candidates, who are maybe an accountant or just very assiduous with paperwork. Consider the LaValle cousins in Suffolk County, whose impressive political careers have ranged from the Port Jefferson mayoralty to Trump surrogacy and their name (Kenneth's) on a college football stadium. Yet John Jay LaValle says that both simply used his father and then his sister for the treasurer role. The key thing was having someone you could trust, and John's father was no joke. Sometimes John would ask for reimbursement for dinner and dad would say no. It had to be completely and perfectly within the bounds of the rules.

This kind of rigidity is not exactly what Nancy Marks became known for in Suffolk County. One way to put it might be that she was ready to do what she could to help a candidate—that she wanted to solve problems. She wanted to be part of the solution on a campaign, not the schoolmarm who always warned about the letter of the law. This kind of loyalty, flexibility, and helpfulness endeared her to candidates, many of whom stayed with her for years, and it allowed her to combine the most enviable traits of the different types of campaign treasurers. She eventually grew to have the client list of much more polished, nationally well-known treasurers; yet she remained a popular local operator working out of a home office. And while she did not exactly volunteer her services, at least not to Santos, she did see him as special. Her ticket to the big time. Even, almost, family.

"She had, I thought, a motherly love for him," is how one of her customers, the Bronx GOP chairman, explained it to the *Times* in 2023. "That was 'her George.'"[12]

It was a loyalty that ran deep. One person from Santos's campaign suggested that "if he told her to jump off a cliff, she probably would have done so."

She traveled with him, even out of the state. She became deeply invested in his success. She featured prominently in meetings, showing up on weekly planning calls and serving more of a kitchen cabinet role than simply that of someone who enforces the financial rules. Emails sent back and forth by people on the campaign show her name in bold, a sign of her importance. She was part of the Santos family in a way that other political people weren't, those who come and go; and family was central to her life.

She was a very "family-oriented person," says Neil Foley, who hired Marks as treasurer for a few of his early runs for Brookhaven town council starting in 2014. Foley would sometimes go to Marks's longtime home in Shirley to drop off paperwork, sometimes meeting her husband or a daughter at the door. Shirley is part of a little area on the southern coast of Long Island that comes just before the Hamptons start, which is not to say that this working- or middle-class area is anything like the summer-season Hamptons. Rather, its end is how you know that the Hamptons have begun. Marks's house was modest, with a small lawn guarded by a Virgin Mary statue. Foley would say hi and goodbye to Marks's kids, and then head to the home office to take care of political business. The converted garage matched Marks's mom-and-pop style: a cohort of middle-aged women worked gamely through the chaos, smoking cigarettes and drinking Pepsis and Cokes. One visitor remembered thinking of the sloppy piles of paper, and how there were potentially millions of dollars in checks and credit card information there in the open. A surprising disconnect existed between the modest room and its groaning copiers, and the prestige of the political clients whose paper detritus cycled through. It meant that the family home's address was stamped on the paperwork of people who moved and shook in Albany and New York City and Washington, who pushed the levers of the world.

Marks's husband, Peter, was a former correctional officer who loved camping, fishing, and hunting, and who battled cancer for years. He would do heavy lifting for her when she needed it, like hoisting boxes of printed campaign materials in and out of the office. But there were weighty monetary and health problems that he couldn't overcome. In 2018, Marks shared a GoFundMe organized by her husband in which Peter talked about his long road of treatment, including surgeries to take out his gall bladder and 15 percent of his liver. Stunned with the brutal force of a Stage 4 diagnosis anyway, he was prepping for a drug trial at Sloan Kettering. Money was tight, including the costs of staying in the city for treatment. The GoFundMe included a description of the teenage kids at home, two of whom also had medical issues.[13]

Peter died in 2019, and the loss for Marks was enduring. In April, she posted on Facebook the simple phrase, "Miss you everyday." The next summer, she took the family on an RV trip, a way perhaps to cope and remember. To some who worked with her politically, it was also a sign of how committed she was to her family, that she would disappear for a stretch of family vacation in the middle of filing season.

It became an inflection moment in Marks's professional career.

Her economic needs were significant, an escalation of bills as her husband got sicker and sicker. For some years she had been looking to expand her business. It was around this time that she began working with George Santos.

To understand how perfectly matched she and Santos were for the moment of their meeting, one has to go back to Marks's beginning, to her political education and how her scrappy form of political service was learned.

Her life in politics began modestly, when she volunteered for a failed congressional campaign in 1992. During the '90s, she did part-time work for local campaigns, a few hundred dollars a pop. It was in 1996 that she started working with Suffolk County legislator Fred Towle, whom she eventually served as campaign treasurer.[14]

Towle is exhibit A of the fact that George Santos did not create the political swamp on Long Island—he merely marveled at it, and then borrowed from a long tradition. Of Towle let us just say that he pleaded guilty to accepting bribes in 2003, and then pleaded guilty again to tax evasion in 2018. The Shirley power broker is said to have fairly serious medical issues, including the threat of right-leg amputation, which force him to wear a walking boot cast more or less continuously in public.[15] But there is an off-color joke around the county that the cast might be covering something, given his history of dealings with law enforcement, including supervised release and wearing a wire to help in other corruption cases. The joke goes, "What if there's an ankle monitor under there?"

Towle and Santos share a predilection for hustling. As one Shirley civic leader describes Towle's work in business and politics, some of which has happened to turn out nicely for the neighborhood, "The table is always tilted toward him and the money rolls his way." He has long been the guiding force behind the *South Shore Press*, a small weekly newspaper sometimes described as a "Republican rag" that nevertheless is one of few very-local media outlets in the area. Republican political hopefuls therefore often find themselves reluctantly groveling at Towle's doorstep for good coverage. It goes beyond networking. One Suffolk elected official recently endured multiple overtures from Towle himself about advertising with the paper, at the same time as an endorsement consideration proceeded.

Nancy Marks has had different levels of connection to her old boss Towle over the years. In 2015, when she was serving as campaign treasurer for a district court candidate, she hosted a meeting at her home with both the candidate and Towle. The candidate was hoping to get the Conservative Party's ballot line for the race, and Towle offered his services as a consultant (with a $10,000 price tag) and a little advice about donating $2,000 to the party, according to a *Newsday* investigation. The candidate left the meeting thinking the suggestion was that if she paid Towle and the Conservatives, she'd have a better shot at the line. It is illegal to sell a ballot line. But Towle told the candidate that everything was copacetic, as he'd be doing the consulting through Marks's company, Campaigns Unlimited.[16]

Marks has denied that Towle made an explicit offer of a party line for money. The offer garnered some attention from prosecutors, but did not result in charges for Marks or Towle. Yet the incident is indicative of the way politics works in Suffolk County. It is a place where a few power brokers run fiefdoms, which require courting. And it is a place where politics can be good business.

Marks would come to learn that she could take a piece of different parts of the political game, just like Towle. Someone is going to get paid to fundraise, and someone is going to get paid to print campaign literature. And someone is going to get paid to do the lawn signs, and the mailers, and also the campaign consulting. Why shouldn't she be that person, especially for the contenders in her own backyard? She was already good with the books. Her treasurer work had connected her to lots of donors, and the centrality of the role meant that she saw all different pieces of a political campaign. All she needed was a company—several companies—that someone could hire to do this work.

She also learned that she could make a little extra on the top. Or this is what some people have claimed about their interactions with her over the years.

That includes Peter Zinno, a former college track coach and East Meadow school district social studies teacher who threw his hat in the ring for Congress in the 2010 cycle.

At first, Zinno was thrilled to find Marks, since he didn't have the money to hire someone fancy. He got a recommendation for Marks from Lee Zeldin, the young conservative firebrand who would go on to be a Trump World denizen and come close to winning the governor's mansion. Zeldin and Marks were both from the little hamlet of Shirley, and their daughters were friends at school. Zinno made the pilgrimage to Marks's home office and hit it off with the down-to-earth campaign operative.

Nancy's work with this early candidate offered her some of the same benefits her Santos association would later provide. She didn't know the players in Zinno's neck of the Long Island woods, and it didn't hurt to make new contacts. Zinno had an admiring network—he had been a school administrator, coached

Olympians—and his political future looked promising. When he held fundraisers, she attended them, and she handled everything including the checks and writing the thank-you cards later. She even once told him that she would be starting a political action committee down the road and that she could help him more with fundraising then—something she did end up doing with Santos. It all meant more business for her.

Unlike for Santos, however, things didn't go Zinno's way with the nomination. When he was ready to wrap things up with his political adventure, he told Nancy to keep the account open so he could make donations to charities and such later on. One day he reached out about making a donation like that, and she said he had no more money.

He was perplexed. He'd used some bucks but not that much. He looked over his filings and realized: she had been wrongly billing him for things, he later claimed in court papers.

When he confronted her, she had excuses. "I need to get paid for my services," she said. "This is what I do, I'm not going to do stuff for you for nothing." She claimed she deserved every penny. He took her to court, saying in the complaint that she "billed me in an inappropriate, excessive, and unauthorized manner over the past three years."[17]

It wasn't even that much money, a few thousand dollars. But he felt that she had taken advantage of him; that she squeezed money because it had been easy. He said in the court documents that the services she'd billed were potentially "never rendered," even.

Zinno ended up losing his little case, with the arbitrator noting he'd waited a long time to object to Marks's behavior and had failed to provide supporting evidence. But it was behavior like this that drew the scrutiny of Marks from federal prosecutors, who came to at least one client to make the case that she had overpaid herself.[18]

It can be easy to play small tricks with the books—candidates are often taking a leap of faith when they hire a treasurer, delegating their financial life on trust. And people trusted Nancy, the family woman, the hard worker, the home office queen. Even if there were whispers about whether there may have been a sort of "Nancy tax."

She was not charged then, but she always seemed to be close to ruin, as when a printing business successfully sued her for breach of contract for some $5,221 worth of printing work, mere documents and envelopes. She fought against foreclosure. In truth, being a treasurer is a thankless job. The hours are long and the work is tedious, and at the end of the day you need to churn through clients to make a middle-class existence. Even in Shirley. Particularly as she tried to support her family, alone. She built that client list and squeezed as much money out of it as she could, but the contracts she scrounged for rarely paid all that much at once. In this way she was very like Santos, who was also chasing opportunity after opportunity to get his next buck, forced to push a little further every moment, a little more recklessly, in search of the next payday. It is not necessarily comfortable to scheme.

---

*Among George Santos's voluminous campaign* filings is a July 2022 payment to an address-less company called ECM Marketing for $3,825, covering digital marketing and advertising services, for the primary.

This exact bland company name doesn't show up any other time in federal filings in recent years, though it pops up in state-level races with a Shirley post office box address.

That address is associated with the similarly opaque ECM Consulting and Marketing Inc., but if you shell out five dollars for the New York State business incorporation records of that outfit, you will find who organized this company, and who therefore appears to be connected to Santos: Fred Towle, the convicted felon and political hustler from Suffolk County. The person listed as filing the company's incorporation paperwork is one Nancy Marks.

The origins of the company are interesting. The paperwork was filed on August 10, 2018, which happens to be nine days after Towle pleaded guilty for forgetting to declare approximately $1.2 million in income from businesses that included one called East Coast Marketing, which did political consulting and permit expediting with governmental entities.

The initials of the new company, you will notice, match the old one. Nothing really changes in Suffolk County business or politics.

Nancy Marks has denied that she had a financial interest in this ECM outfit, even though one Long Island elected official who contracted with the company multiple times in the last few years told me that Marks was the point of contact. Her exact overlap with which iteration of Towle's business is not particularly important in the grand scheme of things, but this through line is a good example of a few truths Marks learned from the Fred Towles of the world and brought down to her work with Santos: There are lots of small contracts to be had quite easily in politics. These contracts go to people with political relationships. And someone at the center of a web of businesses pulls contracts (and therefore political money) his or her way, even if the ownership of those businesses is opaque.

In May 2021, Nancy Marks and George Santos would double down on this principle even further by literally going into business together. This is not a common occurrence for a campaign treasurer and her boss, especially one who is actively running for federal office. Yet that spring the two colleagues joined forces as part of the formation of something called Red Strategies USA. Along for the ride, incidentally, were also alumni of the Harbor City Capital alleged-Ponzi scheme that Santos was receiving payments from at least as late as April 2021.[19]

Red Strategies became very good at sponging money off Republican candidates for various political services, whether or not that candidate had any real chance of winning office. That included Tina Forte, a QAnon-slogan-spreading hopeful who wanted to run against congressional shoo-in Alexandria Ocasio-Cortez in 2022. Red Strategies charged her over $100,000 during her no-chance effort.[20]

Marks and Santos, through their separate and joined businesses, went on the hunt for political contracts. Marks has done work for anti-AOC candidates no less than four times, benefiting from the nationwide donations that have come from GOP obsession with the young lefty firebrand. (Clearly Santos was not alone in his love-hate relationship with Ocasio-Cortez.) Santos would pitch the services of Red Strategies while on the campaign trail himself. He could be wildly insincere about the company—while on a Google Meet call with Red Strategies workers and some candidates, he once pretended to be just facilitating the meeting and having so nonexistent of a connection to Red Strategies that he introduced himself to their side.[21] He would sometimes try to nab a contract from a candidate whom he knew to be flush. Or he'd get his claws into someone young and new to the political scene.

That was the case with Jordan Hafizi, a Staten Island twenty-one-year-old who might as well have been an advertisement for the kind of young voice that old pundits are always urging into the fray. He covered breaking news, police, and crime for his local newspaper while attending the city's public universities, and with the ambition of youth, he considered running for mayor in 2021 to get his name in the public sphere. When he settled for a city council run instead, he gave his old newspaper a list of issues on his mind: the need for more express buses; the urgency of safeguarding Staten Island from another Sandy-like storm; and the problem of wild turkeys, which he had heard a lot about while door-knocking. "We need to trap these turkeys and relocate them to different parts of the state," he said.[22]

His research was admirable; his sense of what really mattered to voters was spot on. Now he just had to carry out his run. To do so, according to a campaign source, he turned to Santos, on whose congressional campaign Hafizi had volunteered.

Santos seemed to be a mentor. In perhaps his best bit of advice, according to the campaign source, he was the one who encouraged Hafizi to run for council rather than mayor. He also introduced Hafizi to Nancy Marks, and he guided him toward a political consultant shop called Red Strategies.

Hafizi had been looking at a different, more targeted company. But Santos persuaded Hafizi to go with Red Strategies because—in the grand Nancy Marks tradition—it did everything. It was one-stop shopping. Santos suggested he had a connection there but not that it was literally his company—one that his personal LLC had been authorized to manage and control.

The recommendations of Hafizi's mentor were far from flawless. Marks was professional in her treasurer work but very busy and, sometimes, hard for Hafizi to reach, even as crucial deadlines approached, according to a campaign source. And the brief, basic video ad made and shared by Red Strategies turned out to be expensive: $22,450. When Hafizi had a little money left over at the end of the campaign, Santos urged him once again to dump the dollars into Red Strategies.

The kid was the first person eliminated in the primary's ranked-choice voting, but Red Strategies, whoever they were, had already been paid.

———————

*It could be argued that* there is a subtle but significant difference between hustling a little on some political contracts and committing outright, large-scale theft. Marks has many defenders in Long Island politics who have worked with her for years or found her to be a loyal friend.

"Nancy Marks is one of the most honest people you'll ever meet," says Robert Cornicelli, a radio personality and military veteran who ran a right-flank GOP primary for Congress in a district adjacent to Santos's in 2022. Another thing Suffolk GOPers sometimes say about Marks is that she seemed different with Santos.

Just how different became clear in October 2023 when Marks pleaded guilty to conspiring with Santos, admitting to an unmade $500,000 loan and inflating his numbers with fake donations.

It was brazen bookkeeping magic from a treasurer who prided herself on aiding clients. Doing what needed to be done. Her filings could be sloppy—one campaign would take a fine-toothed comb to her materials. At least once, she had been found to bulk expenses under that $200 receipt limit, and mark them anonymous, a tactic she would later appear to use for Santos. But with Santos, her work in general seems to have branched into his more unapologetic style of whole-cloth fictionalizing.

Santos for his part has tried to distance himself from Marks, calling her a mere fiduciary, laying the blame for messy filings on her. Marks has not commented to reporters about the whole saga. But her attorney claimed that Santos had "mentally seduced" his client, according to the AP, and Marks herself argued to other people that she had been duped by Santos as much as anyone. One story people heard from her was that, not long before publication of the climactic *Times* piece, Santos claimed that the brain cancer he'd supposedly once had was back. He would have to go radio silent for a little while to deal with it.

Marks was upset, according to a person to whom she related this story. It brought back memories of her husband's painful death from cancer, which had launched her family into crisis, which she had worked so hard financially and otherwise to escape. She told Santos she had the best doctor. He promised to call. Later, when she reached out to the doctor herself, she learned that Santos had never gotten in touch.

He had been lying to her all along, she claims.

With or without her help, however, Santos had certainly learned enough political business tricks to really make a bundle. In November 2021, half a year after he and Marks and some Harbor City Capital alumni formed Red Strategies, Santos was listed as part of a new company in Florida called Redstone Strategies LLC. This time, just he and one of the Harbor City people, Jayson Benoit, were involved in the creation. The new outfit purported to do very similar work to the similarly named Red Strategies, even using very similar contracts. As with the other new business, Santos hawked it to clients. As before, he was not always clear on his involvement in the company. Once again, the work could appear shoddy. A state senate contender named Stefano Forte told the *Daily Beast* that "they did do some fundraising for me, but ultimately I was unhappy with their work and decided to part ways with them." That was after he'd shelled out more than $14,000.[23] Another Redstone patron was Robert Cornicelli, the congressional candidate and veteran. He found Santos to be a "charming guy" and once asked him how the hell he was raising so much money; Cornicelli's outsider campaign could use some of that. Santos said he had these great people Redstone, to whom Cornicelli forked over $4,320 in the spring of 2022. But it was only a brief engagement, because soon Cornicelli's campaign guns realized these Redstone folks weren't actually raising any significant money.

It turned out that Santos's company had another side to it beyond janky political work, which served as an even straighter funnel for cash. It started with a similar pitch: in the fall of 2022, for example, Santos had an associate tell supporters that he needed money for TV advertising. And the money—say, $25,000—could be sent to a Florida-based company whose particulars happen to match this new joint, Redstone.[24]

A funny thing about big donors is that sums of that sort are practically meaningless. Such people are always looking for ways to get around the strict four-digit limits on what can be sent to federal candidates. The spigot hasn't even been turned on unless it's spitting five. Because this money is basically not real to such donors, they do not really even have to understand where it's going, or the fact that the business they were patronizing was not actually an independent expenditure committee set up to support Santos's run. It was set up as Santos's pocket, according to prosecutors.

Here, there wasn't even a facade that Redstone did some political work. Redstone became just a vehicle for him to keep cash.

This became the top-ticket scam in Santos's May 2023 indictment. It was straightforward: a "fraud scheme." Federal prosecutors alleged that Santos used the bulk of the tens of thousands of dollars from two campaign donors for his entirely personal benefit: including payments for a car, personal debt, and luxury designer clothing. The money went to bank accounts controlled by Santos, even though he'd personally texted one of the contributors, who appears to have been the gullible investor Andrew Intrater, that the money would be spent on TV advertising.[25] It was, arguably, a beautiful scam.

That was at the end of October 2022. Santos had learned the byways of the Suffolk swamp and cultivated them in his own grifty, special way—a way that relied less on paperwork shell games, and more on bald-faced lying. It worked. He had pulled in thousands. But now the financial games were over and his second election day was at hand. And a strange wind was blowing.

# 10

## The Perfect-Storm Election

*T*he idea was that George Santos was not messing around in 2022. Not for him the random, faceless consultants; the drab guys from DC who didn't have a feel for the candidate or the district. Not for him the separate crews of quarreling, catty specialists, focused on their own lane and not pulling together. He was going to build a close-knit, winning team.

That was why he'd be hosting a weekend field trip at a donor's very large Sag Harbor mansion. The plan was to lock everyone up inside the house and really team-build, hone a fighting machine and all that, or so he said during his first meeting with Campaign Strategy & Consulting.

"Sounds wonderful," founder Karin Murphy told him, but she wanted to know when. She runs a business, has kids. She'd have to get the date on her calendar.

Once he had the team together, Santos promised. Soon.

That also sounded good to Tracey Alvino, a partner in Murphy's firm. She told Santos she knew some places in Sag. But he didn't seem familiar with the area.

"It's gonna be offseason," he said, brushing off her overture. "There's nothing to do out there."

It took a while to finish signing the contracts and cross the *t*'s on exactly what Campaign Strategy & Consulting would do for Santos—ultimately, it was social media, coalition building, and community relations. But a few weeks into their partnership he stopped mentioning the Sag Harbor weekend, and even though the team grew to include other political professionals and outside cowboys, there never was that team-building.

Ah well. Nevertheless. It was just the beginning of the Santos weirdness for Campaign Strategy & Consulting.

For example, he seemed to care acutely about his team's appearances. He liked having put-together, conventionally attractive people on his arm. This is a man after all who once felt the need to come to the defense of the attractiveness of his old obsession Alexandria Ocasio-Cortez, noting that she "takes care of herself" and "if you're gonna compliment her on her looks I won't go after you."[1]

It was to Alvino that he made repeat phone calls about all the work he was getting done to sculpt his body with liposuction and lip injections, and who recalled his campaign trail remarks about Ozempic. The new client could also be demeaning, making comments about Murphy's clothing, suggesting that she dress perhaps a little more revealingly. It was the way someone needles you to distract from their own insecurities, but it still felt like needling. Finally one time Murphy snapped back at him about fashion.

"George, you just want to go through my closet, but it would take you five years to get through," she said.

Murphy speaks softly and has a Cheshire cat smile. She makes the kind of confident eye contact that shows she knows how to size up the other person and perhaps wring advantage from the situation. She is a political survivor and savvy operator, with business interests that include some real estate as well as politics. She also hosts the *Long Island Patriots Radio* show on WRCN 103.9 FM with Alvino and another one of their Campaign Strategy & Consulting colleagues, Jack Cutrone, called "Dependable Jack" on the show.

They all have a talent for radio jockeying. But listening to Murphy's smooth and sharp patter on that program, you might wonder why it's Santos and not her on the ballot as a candidate. Her life away from the cameras makes sense, however, if you flip through some news clippings from 2016 regarding a purported sexting exchange involving her and then–Nassau County executive Ed Mangano. The fiasco featured a message supposedly from "Ed M" that started "I'd lay you down," according to CBS2, which deemed the rest too X-rated to repeat.[2] Murphy's marketing firm had received two contracts from the county that were just below the amount that would have to have been reviewed by county lawmakers. This is the stuff of tabloid dreams. Both parties vehemently denied the impropriety as well as the messages—Murphy called them a "fabrication"—and a Nassau police probe later said that the messages were a "hoax."[3] Yet that was after Murphy, who was going through a divorce, had been the "wife" in the *New York Post* headline "My Wife Was Having an Affair—But Not with Nassau Exec."[4] Typically, it's not great to be in the *Post* unless you're a major-league athlete or have "Hon." in front of your name. These days, Murphy describes that time in her life as "harrowing," a brutal encounter with a political battleground that caused her "months of anguish."

In sum, Santos was not Murphy's first brush with Long Island political craziness.

But the Santos gig certainly got crazy.

Though it was his second run for office, he would sometimes do bizarre, neophyte things. He'd say he had done a poll that came back really good, in his favor, but he wouldn't show the numbers to Murphy, though she asked repeatedly. He would sometimes show up late or want to leave early from events her team had planned for him, like one at the end of January 2022 to encourage people to run for local school boards. It was an issue the consultants and Santos were shrewd to focus on, but on this night he showed up to the American Legion in Rockville Centre looking like a slob, in skinny blue jeans, sneakers, and a gray zip-up sweater. He told the team that he had to leave early because he had a donor opportunity in Head of the Harbor. Everyone in the world of Long Island politics knows that there's one really opportune donor family in Head of the Harbor, and that's the Mercers, whose patriarch Robert and next-gen leader Rebekah have spread their billions to Donald Trump and other Republicans. Their estate is named "Owl's Nest" and is both secretive and gaudy, famed for a $2.7 million train set and an annual costume ball, the "villains and heroes" edition of which was attended by the former president in 2016. A previous iteration was World War II–themed and featured a tank. Mercer pere is prickly, once telling a prospective diner that "I do not enjoy eating at restaurants because I do not hear well in that type of environment."[5] Political supplicants tend not to dash off unprepared to see these donors while wearing a zip-up sweater. But when the Campaign Strategy & Consulting crew asked if Santos's supposed Head of the Harbor trip was to see the Mercers, he said "actually, yes." He said he was going to meet Rebekah, who had been a member of Trump's transition team.

The consultants thought he was lying. The traffic alone at that time would've been terrible. (Rebekah said through a spokesman that she never met with Santos and called the idea "ridiculous.")

He would sometimes play mind games. The team held a call with him in which he asked for different ways to get into the news. They suggested putting out some policy positions, like something on the always-evergreen concept of road congestion. Soon after, he called Murphy with a different way to get attention: "It can't get out," he said, "but Trump is going to endorse me."

More and more, Trump was a model for Santos.

"It's coming out tomorrow," he went on, "so don't say anything."

When tomorrow came, sans endorsement, he called back. "This woman on Twitter wrote something about me getting the endorsement from Trump," he said.

Murphy asked, "Did Trump support you?"

"Not yet," Santos said, once again making future promises. "He's going to."

It didn't happen afterward either. It occurred to Murphy that what Santos was trying to do was see if she'd call up a reporter and leak the supposedly looming endorsement, perhaps willing it into existence.

Other members of the Santos crew—who never did assemble for that luxurious Sag Harbor team-building weekend—had their own questions about the campaign. It sometimes seemed to be an effort built just around spending money and fundraising.

"Money money money," was how one former strategist put it.

The candidate would spend in eyebrow-raising ways, even beyond those hotel stays and restaurant stops. He loved personal shopping, sometimes pausing in Great Neck to pick up a new pair of Ferragamo shoes that can go for $350 to $1,000 a pop.

He also cycled through political vendors. In 2021, Santos had allowed his campaign to commission a look into his own background, a "vulnerability" study that is common practice in politics and allows candidates to prepare for their opponents' attacks. At first Santos was OK with the process, but then started to get cold feet and wanted to cancel it. When the nearly $17,000 report finally came back in late fall, the results were shocking. This flamboyant, wealthy candidate, a confident voice for the party, had faced multiple evictions and was once married to a woman. The report found a suspended driver's license and no record of his supposed college degrees. Who lies so openly, so repeatedly, about where he went to college? Some of his vendors got on an emergency conference call and told him he should drop out. Santos instead pushed back on the findings and said he wasn't going anywhere, bluffing his way through as usual. He promised to show diplomas (and never did). In response, members of his team left.[6]

So by the time the Campaign Strategy & Consulting people came on board, there had been plenty of chaos already, more than enough to sink a typical campaign.

But they would soon see that they might be sitting on a pot of gold. Santos had been expecting to run in a pretty Democratic district, one that had been tweaked since 2020 to become even bluer. As in 2020, the early perception that this race would be unwinnable for a Republican helped pave the way for the outsider, Santos. But in the spring, things took a turn for the better for Santos and his spanking-new campaign crew, when a state court declared the new district lines unconstitutional, requiring new maps. Under the court order, the updated, less partisan map was to be drawn by a congressional mapping expert, a postdoctoral fellow named Jonathan Cervas. This young man ended up with significant power to make or break congressional candidates in New York. His fairer map enraged Democrats and ended up tightening the Long Island districts, giving Santos a fighting chance.

This was news. This was fairly unexpected—Republicans saved by the courts, in an overwhelmingly blue state. It could even make the difference in control of the entire House of Representatives. Suddenly this race was not so much of a joke. There was no incumbent on the Democratic side: Santos's previous opponent, Tom Suozzi, was making a quixotic bid for governor. And the thing that even the skeptical staffers had to admit was that Santos was indeed getting kind of good at this campaigning business. He'd been doing it for three years, after all. He always did have a knack for sensing what a crowd wanted to hear at the right moment. He could figure out the right language on, say, veterans' issues, and discuss those issues passably well. He had learned just enough of the territory. He could clean his clothes up when necessary; his "look" was improving, his charming preppy costume getting fleshed out. The Jewish line was something he could always try. Indeed, the stories about Judaism came hot and thick now, growing wilder and wilder, as he made the lies serve him. In a position paper sent to pro-Israel leaders, he claimed he was a "proud American Jew."[7] In November 2022, speaking to *Jewish Insider*, he revealed just how transactional he was being with this fabrication: "The way I look at this is, I'm going to represent one of the most Jewish-rich districts in the country, with the most population of Jews," he said. To appeal to that population, he basically donned a new religion, pointing to "my mother's Jewish background beliefs, which are mine," as well as "my father's Roman Catholic beliefs, which are also mine." The outlet said he described himself as a nonobservant Jew. For good measure, he added that he'd made four visits to Israel.[8]

He wasn't exactly wearing out the leather on those Ferragamo shoes by doing every single community event—there was a joke among the interns on the opposite-side campaign that they never saw him in the field, which is why they once went nuts when they set eyes on a guy that looked maybe like him at the Manhasset Sephora. But Santos's donor calls were surprisingly effective. He spoke the language of money, whether it was chatting about the family office he ran or the way he managed the trust of his sister after getting an inheritance from their mother. What might be called the Hampton Jitney circuit between Manhattan and the splendid Long Island coast was becoming overloaded with brash crypto millionaires and others who were newly rich. He blended in.

It was a strange situation for Santos and the consultants. He still bumbled, but also showed flashes of crucial excellence. His district still leaned blue, but it was shaping up to be a red year. It was not too clear what might happen in the churn of the actual vote. Santos's Democratic opponent Robert Zimmerman was polling, and it was true that the final new district map made it a plus-8 Biden region. But that was data from a presidential year, which this certainly wasn't. And the alarming thing was that for the general election, even though Zimmerman often found himself ahead of Santos or tied, it was always within the margin of error.

---

*Screenwriters could not have found* an opponent for George Santos more different than Robert Zimmerman.

He was twice Santos's age and long familiar with money. He was silver haired, always perfectly coiffed, and seemed to live in a suit in public. He had already run once for Congress and twice for state assembly, and also started a thriving communications business on Long Island, all before Santos turned two. Far from a faker, he was as much a member in good standing with the establishment as you can get, familiar with the Clintons, friends with various congressmen and -women, and a hobnobber with the brat pack novelist Jay McInerney and Hamptons doyennes like Candace Bushnell, whose newspaper columns became *Sex and the City*. He was a well-known political donor and bundler whose various civic positions included serving as a national committeeman for the Democratic Party.

Where Santos was a Long Island outsider, Zimmerman had spent a career rubbing shoulders with the power brokers of the region, Democrat and Republican. He served as a pallbearer for the funeral of Nassau GOP chair Joe Mondello, and his communications and strategy firm has done work for Long Island school boards, water districts, businesses, nonprofits, and Nassau Off-Track Betting, a political patronage shop now run by the current Nassau GOP chairman. Zimmerman is careful to say when that gig is discussed that the contract was won under a Democratic administration.

Santos had to try weird scams like the fake Trump endorsement to get media attention, while Zimmerman was a literal PR pro with a thick rolodex of contacts among local and national reporters, with whom he practices his passion for sentences that start with "Speaking off the record," followed by a short pause. Santos had no political experience and few allies in any party. Zimmerman had worked for two New York members of Congress and could point to a host of political causes he'd championed over the years, including having traveled to the Soviet Union in the 1980s in support of detained actual Jews. (He's actually Jewish, too.) He is the kind of guy who even if he wasn't invited to a wedding, would make sure to send something nice off the registry. Even in the crowded Democratic primary in 2022, his list of endorsements from leading lights like Hillary Clinton was laughably strong, while Santos was still introducing himself to GOP functionaries.

There was, however, one big similarity between Zimmerman and Santos, and it naturally became the main takeaway recycled in every dial-up profile about the race. Both general election candidates, it just so happened, were openly gay men, perhaps the first time such a race had ever been run in these United States. Santos's identity, not exceptionally common among GOP federal candidates, once again became a draw.

This angle disgruntled Zimmerman, given his feeling that though Santos was gay he was no friend to gay Americans. On the campaign trail, the communications executive was often happy to launch into this line of attack, pointing to his opponent's positions on trans issues, the occasional drag queen story hour, and other hot-button LGBTQ+ topics of the moment.

It was less often that he would wax personal about what it was like growing up as a gay teen on Long Island long before Santos came of age. He once called it "very isolating" and noted that he used to "hang out at the diner on Friday night. I didn't want to tip my parents I didn't have a date, or a date for the school dance." This was in Great Neck, the place he still calls home. A teacher once suggested that conversion therapy could be an option. "I knew I wasn't going to do that, but that was a mindset in those days," he says.[9]

In some ways, he was like his ally Hillary, who had to wait to become the establishment before having a chance at her historic run. By 2017, Zimmerman was being lauded at a gala by the LGBT Network, his sexual identity no longer something that provoked discrimination. And there was no incumbent in his district. It was his turn.

But unfortunately for Zimmerman, the weather was changing. "It was a perfect storm," says Isaac Goldberg, who was a direct mail consultant and campaign strategist for Zimmerman.

The first sign of trouble on the horizon was the whole redistricting fiasco. Zimmerman had thought he would be competing in territory stretching all the way up to wealthy Democratic corners of Westchester, in which Biden's share of the vote was more than 14 percentage points higher than Trump's. Instead, the new district hit areas that were tough for Democrats, such as the famous Levittown, or Massapequa, with its Irish and Italian American cops and firefighters, and, perhaps, financial professionals, but not the kinds that had been living easy for three generations. Put it this way: when veteran Republican representative Pete King (and son of an NYPD officer) had what he calls essentially his toughest race for Congress, in 2006, his vote total in Massapequa alone made up for losing no less than six other communities. It is a "tremendous Republican stronghold," King put it somewhat gleefully from retirement, and now it was Zimmerman's to deal with.

Doubly frustrating for Zimmerman, much of the national media and donor class did not see the Third Congressional District in this competitive way, focusing instead on the presidential-year numbers, the voter anger about abortion and January 6 extremism, and overcounting the sense that suburbs like Long Island were becoming more diverse and Democratic. Besides, Zimmerman was not able to spend his time talking general election quite yet, because he was in the middle of a very competitive five-person primary, and because that primary was pushed back from June to the end of August due to the delayed final approval of the new district maps.

The smart money was divided on whether Zimmerman, for all his experience and establishment strengths, would even get out of that primary, which featured five contenders including a young hustling county legislator who once tweeted "I believe strongly that #crypto is a positive force for good in the world" and won the support of the Democratic Party's newest megadonor, the crypto king Sam Bankman-Fried. Zimmerman and Santos both knew well that you need to court and defend against big money in modern politics. While Santos had no primary and coasted the summer, Zimmerman had to wring his campaign's bank account and his endorsement list to fend off this and other primary offensives.

So it was not until late August that Zimmerman emerged from the rigors of intraparty conflict and turned his attention fully on this Santos character. There were barely more than two months to go—this is a district that takes Labor Day parties seriously, and also all the Jewish holidays. It was August, but November 8 was knocking on the door like an overeager canvasser. And this was the moment when a certain opposition-research report from the Democratic Congressional Campaign Committee finally found its way to Zimmerman.

---

*The barstool opinion of the* whole George Santos saga could probably be boiled down to: "I don't know though, don't they vet these guys anymore?" The vagueness of *they* is useful here. Clearly somebody should be vetting America's candidates, but who? After Santos's full debunking in December 2022, the finger-pointing began. New York and national Republicans blamed different internal factions. The state Democratic Party said opposition research wasn't its job. The two individual Democrats who had run against Santos thought they had plenty of ammunition to waste the guy. And news organizations pleaded about being stretched thin, meaning that the true story of the talented Mr. Santos leaked out in dribs and drabs, with his full fraudulence emerging only after the election. Each explanation was plausible but added up to systemic failure.

The most dumped on, though, the most scrutinized body, was the Democratic Congressional Campaign Committee (DCCC), which did in fact do some vetting of Santos and put together a report on his convoluted life.

This eighty-seven-page document was filled with all sorts of goodies about Santos, including statements showing just how closely tied Santos was to the January 6 movement, and comments about abortion that many in the district would see as extreme. That included his support for states to be able to ban abortion without exceptions for rape or incest, as well as being "in favor of criminal charges" for doctors who performed the procedures. The downside of being a liar in politics is that you sometimes say crazy things for one room that will play terribly in another. The report caught Santos saying the kind of wacky stuff that even raised eyebrows among his own staff, like the idea that Biden's "corporate string masters" were preventing a cure for AIDS.[10]

There was evidence of his ties to the sketchy firm Harbor City, his history of evictions and civil judgments, his evasiveness about his finances, and even the first unraveling of his supposed charity Friends of Pets United, which did not appear to be one of the IRS's tax-exempt organizations.

The report tossed in some red flags that seem almost mild in comparison to the above, such as the note reading, "As Of July 2022, Santos Had No Issues Page On His Website." But the document implored its readers to look further, labeling this "preliminary research," concluding with the warning that "further research will be necessary on George Santos."

One obvious criticism of this first draft of Santos's real story concerns how much the research team missed. It did not, for example, turn up the fact that Santos didn't actually go to NYU or Baruch, nor did it alert readers to his years-old check fraud case in Brazil. The vulnerability study that Santos greenlit for himself, on the other hand, was able to secretly get some more of that material. The way the DCCC prioritized information also obscured some Santos craziness: the document led largely with Santos's extremism regarding abortion and January 6.

One rationale for the misses has to do with research practices. A DCCC staffer who was involved with the campaign told me that the group's opposition researchers are instructed to rely on public records, partially so that there will be a clear citation for whatever damaging information researchers find. That citation helps when you want someone else to create an ad or run an article about the issue. The DCCC researchers didn't go to Brazil or look through Brazilian public records, according to this staffer.

School attendance, however, might have been easier to track down. Though there are sometimes barriers to such information, the researchers might have simply asked. When I asked an NYU spokesperson about the institution's protocol in such cases, the spokesperson said that "an individual's attendance and degree are considered 'directory information' at NYU" and that it is "customary" for the university to answer queries about whether or not someone has a degree.

Another factor affecting what opposition researchers find are the different strategies used by different teams. Some political combatants on both sides have the impression that Democratic detectives focus more on the embarrassing issue-based gaffe than on, say, a personal attack that might be perceived as gossipy or dirty. Hence, perhaps, the missing information on Santos's previous marriage. Republicans also seem to have a better sense of how to go in for the kill—including by forming their oppo into clear narratives and trying to use it to tie up a candidate in frivolous lawsuits, for example. The sense of Democratic primness was on display in 2012, when the political publication *Roll Call* embedded with the DCCC's twenty-five-person research team for a day, during which time one twenty-two-year-old analyst somewhat generously said of his targets: "My research humanizes them to me . . . Call it Stockholm Syndrome or call it what you want, but either way, I don't walk away from at least any of the research books I've done thinking they're a bad person."[11]

Killer instinct or not, the DCCC does a lot of research. During the 2022 cycle, there was a book for every potential GOP freshman on Long Island as well as other competitive candidates across New York. The Santos packet opens by noting that the research within it was completed in little over a month, just ahead of the primary. And it certainly included an embarrassment of riches for any opponent to use or probe.

It was left to Zimmerman, then, to make use of it—a fateful moment.

Zimmerman's defenders argue that opposition research was

the DCCC's role here, and that there was not time to complete and deploy more research that could have crystallized Santos's con. First Zimmerman would have had to engage the services of another researcher, or find someone on staff, and let them loose on the particularly flimsy pieces of Santos's story. Then the campaign would have to design a tracking poll and put it into the field to see which pieces of the research were most effective to the only people who actually mattered—voters. Follow that with the ad-making process, laying out a big capital investment to get the story of Santos's quackery or alleged corruption on TV. And in the expensive New York media market, to make and air a single ad can cost hundreds of thousands of dollars.

Worse, one ad is not enough. There is a reason candidates repeat the same darkly ominous one-minute spiel in the interim between baseball innings so often that it becomes a joke. That's the only way to penetrate the consciousness of a content-overwhelmed audience. And the TV commercials should be paired with the same message in pieces of direct physical mail to voters, and digital ads next to their Google searches and social media scrolls. One-off or muddled shots in the dark rarely work: look no further than the anti-Santos press release the DCCC itself blasted out in late August, which included lots of the research team's best hits, and labeled Santos the "epitome" of a "shady Wall Street bro" with a "history of shady finances."[12]

Needless to say, it did not break through the murk.

The Zimmerman team did some delving into Santos's wealth of wacky past quotes, but did not unearth the big biographical nuggets. They focused their campaign efforts on some of the top lines in that research document, attempting to paint Santos as beyond the pale on abortion and aligned with Trump's insurrectionary efforts. It was the same message that his fellow Democrats around the country were using for their big midterm push, after the Supreme Court overturned *Roe v. Wade* in June. Gallup reported a month later that the percentage of people who considered abortion to be the country's most important problem was at its highest since the pollsters started tracking abortion mentions in 1984.[13] The abortion issue helped Democrats from Virginia to Michigan and beyond, and GOP election deniers imploded across the country, leading to a historical anomaly of a midterm season for Democrats in which the party of the new president, Joe Biden, barely lost ground. But something different was happening in New York, where abortion wasn't threatened and suburban voters were obsessed with crime coverage, fed up with Democratic leadership on COVID and culture wars and preparing to buck the trend.

Hindsight is twenty-twenty. At one point, the Zimmerman campaign considered taking on the issue of crime and bail reform more straightforwardly by alerting people to the fact that Zimmerman had been an auxiliary police officer in Jericho. There was talk of running an ad with him in uniform. But he already had been boasting about his endorsement from former NYPD commissioner Bill Bratton. This was true and sounds great in campaign literature, yet it doesn't exactly strum the souls of the beat cops heading home to Massapequa after their day tour.

Some forces were largely out of Zimmerman's control. One was the powerhouse gubernatorial campaign of Republican Lee Zeldin, who came within approximately 6.5 percentage points of the incumbent Democrat, Kathy Hochul, in a state where Democrats more than double Republicans in voter registration. Zeldin is a sharp tactician and former army lawyer who rode into Congress with the Tea Party wave, a movement whose deep conservatism and prickliness he shared. But he continued moving even further right in the Trump years, becoming one of the former president's top allies and defenders, culminating in his vote not to certify the 2020 election results. This was a far cry from the moderate Republicanism of Nelson Rockefeller and George Pataki that had long been the hallmark of the New York GOP. But Zeldin had his ear to the ground in a way that his more centrist colleagues did not, and his campaign tapped into many voters' frustrations with crime, COVID, and shifts in American culture. His popularity at the top of the ticket gave a boost to some middling members of his party downballot, and it also coaxed an unusual amount of outside spending from GOP donors like the cosmetics mogul Ron Lauder, leading to a blanket of anti-Democrat TV commercials.

There was very little that Zimmerman could do about the unprecedentedly close gubernatorial race other than be angry. And certainly there were many Democratic campaign operatives on downballot New York races that cycle who found themselves wishing for more of a show of force from Hochul, or more of an attempt to protect their side's flank on crime and bail. More than one distressed operative made grim jokes along the lines of the following: if former governor Andrew M. Cuomo had been running for another term rather than stewing in retirement after accusations of sexual harassment, he would have mobilized the national guard to individually protect the subway ride of any commuter who wanted that.

And there was another force that was just as much out of Zimmerman's control, much to his surprise and frustration: the media.

The Democrat encountered all sorts of problems as he tried to get media outlets to cover Santos. There were reporters who essentially responded "Snooze" when asked to take a look at a potentially sketchy but certainly random newcomer candidate. One responded "Is there an emoji for Ambien?" when prodded to look into Santos's missing financial disclosures. Some of those reporters were legitimately busy with the Zeldin run or big races all around the country that seemed much tighter. They didn't think Santos had a chance, anyway. "Guys my editor kiboshed this," one reporter texted the campaign. "Too much uncertainty and I have a full docket. I'm sorry."

Another problem was that some reporters did in fact cover Santos critically, but no single critique cohered before the election and cut through the noise. The *North Shore Leader*, the *Daily Beast*, and my own *Newsday* stories highlighted his fake mansions, Ponzi-accused employers, questionable recount fundraising after 2020, confusing home address situation, and more.[14] These articles did not capture the whole breadth of Santos's shenanigans and did not connect the dots into a kill shot. But plenty of skeptical, even damning stories were published about the Republican before he won.

The surfeit was almost overwhelming, giving the impression that this clown had no chance of winning and energy could be better spent on other targets. It was the same sense of information overload that helped Donald Trump skate by with impunity during his runs for the presidency. Every day brought another Trump scandal. People tuned it out, distrusted a fractured media that had grievously diminished in influence, or baked it into their political calculations. In such a partisan environment, people so inclined were voting red almost no matter what, particularly in restive places like Long Island. Meanwhile, Democrats missed the urgency. Zimmerman would go on to get 51 percent of Democrats to the polls. In order for him to have matched the GOP wave and beaten Santos, he would have had to mobilize almost 71 percent of Democrats, according to a party analysis. And that's assuming every single one voted for him—two hypotheticals that are surpassingly unlikely in a nonpresidential year.

For a sign of just how red Santos's district was feeling, Santos aside, Robert Zimmerman and Kathy Hochul were not the only ones who lost the environs. US Senate Majority Leader Chuck Schumer lost in the district to a basically unknown sacrificial candidate who barely raised half a million dollars. Schumer won statewide but got the scare of his life in places like CD3. This is a politician so attentive to regular voters that he tours every county in the state annually; who holds press conferences every Sunday about regular-Joe issues like the size of airplane seats; who literally wrote a book about an everyman Long Island family named the Baileys, arguing that Democrats must pay attention to the proverbial them. The Baileys went red with a vengeance in 2022.

Despite all the alarms blinking scarlet for New York Democrats, there was a bizarre sense of optimism from the Smart Establishment. Some of this was surely coming from Democratic approval of all the energy that had been unleashed by the Supreme Court's ruling on abortion, an energy that was particularly powerful in red areas where abortion rights were in legitimate danger. But the Smart Establishment did not factor in the degree to which abortion was well protected—at least for a little while longer—in blue states like New York, which were instead going through different political paroxysms that threatened a jolt to the right. Exhibit A for the overconfidence might have been the late-summer event at the Hamptons home of Bernard Schwartz, the investor and Democratic megadonor. The muckety-mucks in attendance included House Speaker Nancy Pelosi, former New York lieutenant governor Richard Ravitch, legendary Watergate reporter Carl Bernstein, former DCCC chair Steve Israel, and Zimmerman, who was just gearing up for his fateful general election.

"There was a sense of inevitability in the room," says Israel, who says he was not so certain the race was actually in the bag at all.

Even muckety-mucks can blunder. On the way into the event, one attendee had been excited to show other guests how Teslas can be turned into boom boxes. But the Tesla driver couldn't figure out the trick on demand. The watchers gave up and headed out of the parking lot toward the house—this is the kind of house with a parking lot, of course—when suddenly the Tesla behind them exploded in ear-splitting rap music.

_____

*It did not seem to* matter what weird or eyebrow-raising thing Santos did on the campaign trail. He was keeping and gaining momentum.

In an October forum with the League of Women Voters he talked about how he opposed floodgates near the Throgs Neck Bridge on account of possible flooding elsewhere, a fairly anodyne position he shared with others in the local GOP. But then he couldn't stop himself.

"Climate is a cycle," he went on. "We've gone through numerous ice ages and we have been able to come back as a planet. It's a fact."

It was one of the few forums at which Zimmerman and Santos actually appeared together, in person, and Zimmerman cast a skeptical expression.

"You can look at me all you want, Robert," Santos said. "It's a fact."[15]

What was basically an example of sotto voce climate denialism did not make a blip.

Why would it? He made similar antienvironmental arguments on other stages. And there were so many other strange things that Santos said.

When he came onto Marcia Kramer's CBS2 show for a short debate with Zimmerman, the two threw the usual talking points back and forth about crime and inflation and defunding the police ("You've got three positions on every issue," Zimmerman zinged). During a break in the show Santos told Zimmerman an elaborate story about a mansion he was building in Oyster Bay, how the permitting process was so exhausting and how he was probably going to sell the property. It seemed like he was trying to ingratiate himself to his dapper, wealthy opponent. He also claimed that he'd been on this particular TV set before, because he knew the *Real Housewives of New York City.*

"Bethenny's a friend of mine," he claimed.

"Well that's nice," said Zimmerman.

At the end, the candidates were asked who they'd want for a dinner partner. Zimmerman gave the boring if predictable answers of Lincoln and Eleanor Roosevelt, while Santos said Marilyn Monroe. It was a surprising reference, not even particularly current, but indicative of Santos's obsession with looks, class, and fame.

For another softball query about favorite family traditions, Zimmerman pointed to New Year's Eve, watching a holiday movie and getting together with family in "sweats." Häagen-Dazs "is always a staple."

A routine-enough answer, which became bizarre only when Santos followed up for his response to the same question by citing family time, in which people would also wear sweatpants. And—

what a coincidence—he added that there would also be "pints of Häagen-Dazs all over the place."[16]

It was as if the fabulist's tick of borrowing other people's stories went into overdrive and Santos forgot to wait half a minute for a separate audience.

Things were zany, but the world was spinning toward Santos's particular brand of zaniness. Did he sound too conservative? Not for this election! Were his different Jewish heritage stories weird? Not to the donors at Mo's Bagels & Deli in South Florida, who heard Santos use the pretty Talmudic term "halachically Jewish" and saw it as a clever nod to Jewish law from someone in the know. (He showed up an hour and a half late that day, but the Jewish banter helped smooth things over.)[17] Did he cross clear lines of civic tradition with wild abandon? His January 6 stuff only got him more MAGA cred.

To his campaign staff, he was a weather vane. He sometimes seemed to care about work-life balance, not wanting people to feel beaten down and giving them nights off here and there. On the other hand, his erratic behavior and snide comments encouraged the departure of team members, a chaotic stream of whom became "formers" long before a single 2022 vote was cast. That ultimately became the case for the women at Campaign Strategy & Consulting, too. They had vamoosed over the summer, growing irritated about being bossed around and marginalized, frustrated with Santos's frivolous spending and lack of engagement with community issues. The ride had gotten not worth the weird. Santos had seemed something like a funny "gay husband" to Alvino at the high points, but there were also all the little demeaning put-downs. Like Santos asking Murphy, for example, *What's up with your hair, that little flip, what's that about? Why do you drive an*

*Audi, what's so good about it?* He poked and poked and poked, as if it might keep questions or critiques of himself at bay.

It could be exhausting to live within his house of cards. But voters saw only the exterior.

And they were focused on other themes. On Election Day Eve, I watched Hakeem Jeffries—powerful, House Speaker-in-waiting Brooklyn Democrat Hakeem Jeffries—show up to suburban Queens for a last-minute get-out-the-vote event with a businesslike Zimmerman and the American Federation of Teachers leader Randi Weingarten. The gathering was a disaster—few who weren't paid to show up did—and there was a very vocal counterprotest from people lugging signs like VIRUSES DON'T EXIST and shouting, "You're gonna end up in a quarantine camp!" Weingarten, who by her position would typically be seen as a huge asset for a Democrat in a tight race, had for months been rocked by demonstrators and critics. The school board issues of diversity, equity, and inclusion (DEI) and COVID were national, too.

"We are not gonna allow disinformation to prevail," said a tieless Jeffries, but it already had. The Long Island tide was red and rising. On the way home, I had to pull over on the side of the road to tap out a little item about the size of Long Island's red-leaning early-vote turnout, already dwarfing that of Kathy Hochul's home turf of Erie County.

Santos's race ended up not even being close. By more than 7 percentage points, the lying, ethically challenged newcomer was the victor. It was so clear so early that Zimmerman conceded within hours from his party at the Inn at Great Neck. Santos missed the call—at that very moment, he was giving his victory speech at Il Bacco, his preferred Italian restaurant in Queens, just across the county line.

There were multiple plausible reasons to choose the red-sauce spot, including Santos's connections to the owner, a donor; and the many times he'd already spent money there, in or out of $199.99 increments. But another was the fact that the restaurant was in Queens, within the NYC border—a way to highlight that this Republican here had won in the land of blue. And that was a triumph in truth. The room was pulsing with energy, a dawning sense that this squad had pulled off a huge and exhilarating victory, in one of the districts that would move the House majority back into the GOP's column. This random, wacky congressional race—it had become meaningful. Santos floated around the room and took pictures with people, just the beginning of being sought out.

As for Zimmerman, in the Great Neck hotel, he gave his own sad speech in the ballroom space. He said goodbye to friends and family, did some mutual consoling, and then he went home. It wasn't his time.

But the topsy-turviness didn't end. Later, almost morning, a vehicle pulled up outside that very hotel, and out climbed George Santos. It turned out that his campaign had taken a room at the same hotel earlier in the day, a place to prep for election night, and now he was here to pick up a car left behind when his team departed for Il Bacco. It was a surreal and almost symbolic coincidence, that the two opponents would use the same establishment out of all the possibilities in the district, and also that they would be in such totally separate echo chambers that they'd landed on the same place and hadn't known. Zimmerman's party was certainly well advertised. But the overlap was of a piece with the race's abnormal portents. Outside the inn, Santos appeared to one observer to be ebullient from his victory. He could also be heard speaking with the valet about the big sad political party that had taken place at the hotel earlier. Santos explained to the surprised late-night employee that he—yes, him, right there, his carefully sculpted appearance, his perfectly contoured story—was the guy who had won that race.

# 11

## Keep Posting

*T*he post-election *New York Times* article that December started with a standard description of Santos's campaign biography, the "storybook journey" that took a son of Brazilian immigrants to the House. Then a note of caution.

"But a *New York Times* review of public documents and court filings from the United States and Brazil, as well as various attempts to verify claims that Mr. Santos, 34, made on the campaign trail, calls into question key parts of the résumé that he sold to voters," wrote Grace Ashford and Michael Gold.[1]

It was a careful beginning to a devastating takedown of Santos's life. The piece was full of embarrassments for the congressman-elect, the first threads of a significant unraveling—the pet scams and the fake college degrees and made-up employment at Goldman and Citi Group, the brazen check fraud case from Brazil a decade and a half before. In three thousand words, one after another supposed biographical fact was exposed as fiction.

The glow from Santos's surprise victory did not last long. A little more than a month, to be precise.

The response from a shocked public was immediate and scathing. But of course the hit on Santos himself was like the word of God. Con men always know on a certain level how their stories will end, but only in the way that we're aware death comes for us all. When the curtain is pulled, astonishment still pounces. Santos went dark. He said nothing. He did not get in touch with his party chair, Joe Cairo, for more than a day—days! He had experienced a full unveiling, the likes of which he had never suffered, having been for so long protected by his parents, his friends, getting lucky again and again when he touched up against the powers of the law. Here was the fulfillment of the prophecy written in his nervousness, his sweaty palms, his discomfort in his own life. Something bad was coming. Here it was.

But soon Santos committed to an enduring strategy: post through it.

It's what he had prepared to do all his life. It was what he learned from Donald Trump, from America's Teflon culture of second chance. Everyone could have a spin-off, even O. J. Simpson, as long as they could be shameless, and keep moving, and stay famous. Never let your Twitter account go gently into that good night. Keep posting.

It's what he did, metaphorically speaking, in private, where he was telling some campaign veterans and incoming government staffers that this was all just a misunderstanding. It's what he did when he finally did connect with Nassau GOP chair Cairo after the bombshell article. What was the deal with all this lying, Cairo wanted to know. Santos had excuses ready. He actually had graduated from Baruch College, but someone must have searched under the wrong name. Mix-ups. He was going to have a press conference and set things straight.

He didn't have that press conference.

It was surprising to Cairo that Santos would continue to stand by such a flimsy lie, even as he was supposedly coming clean about some of the fables to national party leaders. Like, he'd keep lying on one call and say the opposite story on another.

It was something of a hot seat moment, or it should have been. The article came out before Santos was even sworn in. And Santos did bow in some deference to that, wielding his beloved Twitter merely to say just before Christmas, "I have my story to tell and it will be told next week."

It was always the same with him. Anthony and his stories.

But the big reveal, the big explanation for it all, never came, just a reversion to form. In interviews here and there he admitted to some embellishment, or "bad judgment calls," perhaps a "poor choice of words."[2] The Republicans in Congress had only a slim majority and needed his vote. So they swore him in, and he was off to the races, sparring with Adam Kinzinger, posting a picture of the Illinois Republican apparently crying, tweeting that he wouldn't be resigning, and generally being a noodge.

The posting continued off social media, in public, where he carried on a defiant show that nobody could shame him, least of all himself. He was spotted in the bars in and around Capitol Hill and Georgetown and Connecticut Avenue, moving with an entourage. Observers reported that he was partying. He was kicked out of the group text threads for both the New York GOP members and the New York Republican freshmen, the millennial version of excommunication, but that didn't matter to him. He took whatever microphone he could. The House Republicans have a regular conference every week to go over the agenda for the next few days, and there's an open mic period for people to get up and say whatever's on their mind. Pete King, the stalwart Massapequa vote-getter and onetime dean of the Long Island congressional delegation, remembers speaking maybe twice in his twenty-eight years. Santos was said to address the assembled a lot at the beginning of his term. People were shocked he was raising his head to talk at all. "He's not being defensive really," King noticed, "he's actually on offense."

That was a small showing, sort of, just a room of his peers, but when the State of the Union came around, America in general got a chance to see Santos's choices. People were surprised, or the talking heads were, that the freshman had angled his way down into the aisle right as Biden walked by. Usually it is eager members of the president's party who will line up hours early so their constituents see them shaking hands with the big dog, but why would Santos want the freeze-frame with a Democratic president? Biden, not his first rodeo, avoided the controversial New Yorker, but Santos watched him pass while everyone else watched him watching. For a moment he looked just like the anonymous celebrity hound he so recently had been, drawn by glamour and power. Later, as the group of honorables shuffled and mingled, cameras also caught a little testy exchange between Santos and one of the Wise Men of his party, Mitt Romney, onetime presidential candidate and current very senatorial senator, who told Santos, "You don't belong here." *Go sit in the back row and shut up* was the implication. Santos appraised him coolly, a duck-faced grin, and, according to Santos anyway, called him an asshole.[3]

So he wasn't getting any love from Romney, but he had his apologists, and this was really confirmation that something was shifting or broken in America. "Look, there's a lot of frauds in Congress," said Texas representative Tony Gonzales. "I mean, George Santos is the least of this country's worries."[4] Kevin McCarthy, who had spent years tacking hither and thither in the Trump winds, needed Santos's support to firm up his Speaker vote and bolster his majority. Hence he pushed aside all the talk about a Santos fundraising aide impersonating McCarthy's own chief of staff while trying to raise money, something that would later result in a federal indictment for that aide;[5] he let Santos take his seat and launched a slow procedural investigation. Compare this to the Republican speaker before him, John Boehner, who in 2011 applauded the quick exit of a different New York congressman who sent a shirtless photo of himself to a woman he met on Craigslist. But that was before the House GOP caucus was taken over by the likes of Marjorie Taylor Greene, whose embrace of conspiracy included a 2018 post suggesting a Rothschild-connected space laser had started California forest fires. She and Santos became friends, and their merry band included other members willing to say anything and make McCarthy's life miserable. Like Paul Gosar of Arizona, who was the first representative to cosponsor a Santos bill and once put up an anime video that showed him killing a fellow member of Congress—the inundated and fetishized Alexandria Ocasio-Cortez, of course. This was the fringe but vocal cohort that closed ranks around Santos.

If he really felt undefended he could always turn attention to the people he felt were against him. They were helpful to lash out about. Like the young woman in an orange dress and heels and the guy with a button-down shirt, who—the audacity—took a picture of him while he was in public in April. Santos tweeted a picture of them, and his director of operations, Vish Burra, responded, "Strong clearance rack vibes on that dress." Nice! A few months later, as his fellow Republicans sharpened their knives, he joked menacingly about outing people: "Funny thing about the NY GOP apparatus, it's filled with closeted Gays that play a hard pretend game." Or, when this book was announced in February, Santos called it my "latest grift" and said he was "hopeful that the reporter I've had blocked for over a year, @mjchiusano has a great imagination."

I was not the only person and, eventually, reporter he blocked. Blocking was a favorite tactic of his. It is the flip side of forever posting. On his personal (as opposed to congressional) account, he could stop anyone he wanted from looking. Elon Musk says it's a free country. By the time he was fully exposed as a fabulist and fraud, he was interested only in preaching to the choir anyway. And there was plenty of choir, a big bubble, a decent portion of the American population who didn't trust what the mainstream media was saying, figuring this kid must be doing something right if the Elite Powers That Be were so panty bunched about his every move. He rubbed shoulders with chaos agents like Roger Stone, Trump's and Nixon's political trickster. He had a home with the "Young Republican" outfits, like the one in New York whose gala he once attended along with Marjorie Taylor Greene and Jack Posobiec, who helped advance the very bizarre Pizzagate dream. Santos also showed up at a similar gathering in DC where he was celebrated by people identified as anarchocapitalist, feudalist, and paleoconservative.[6] The choir was big enough for his brand.

The paranoid style of American politics is not a new feature, and Santos benefited from the long tail. I once called a phone number that I thought might be for a woman who was mentioned on a Santos GoFundMe post. The person who answered said she was not that particular woman and had never met Santos, but since she had me, she wanted to note that she'd seen him on the media and he was "pretty outstanding." This was after Santos's lies had come out, but to her, he had stolen a spot from the rich and powerful people who are "supposed" to get these fancy positions. "It sucks that the elites are going after him, but it is what it is sometimes."

This woman, who had some time on her hands, explained that every politician steals taxpayers' dollars, and what's more, you can never trust what they say. She says she interned once for a Democrat in Congress who was against the war in Iraq, but voted to keep the troops in anyway, because the party told her to do it, and actually the order came from even higher than that. Higher than the president. The president is told what to do by a group of people who are really in charge, you know.

This is America, country of delusions. The establishment hasn't done itself any favors, to be sure, from Vietnam to the Iraq War to the financial crisis to accommodation of Trump. It's a little hard to take Mitt Romney too seriously about Santos not belonging when Mittens himself didn't mind sitting down to dinner with Trump, the chief not-belonger, when it seemed like such a dinner could get him secretary of state. But such ham-handedness doesn't fully explain the descent into mass lunacy flirted with by so many Americans, the ones who aren't exactly QAnon believers but still want you to do your research. In the run-up to 2020, it should be noted, Santos himself retweeted a QAnon slogan, telling me he didn't know what QAnon was. Yet it prompted me to talk to some other Long Islanders who rubbed up against that conspiracy in some form—like the East Meadow dad who thought the media got daily four a.m. emails with talking points for what to say. Or the Suffolk County man who believed that Jeffrey Epstein's driver also drove for Romney and used to pick up drugs and girls for Romney's son, Cole, and one time Cole "OD'd" one of the girls and dumped her body.

Romney does not have a son named Cole. The adjacent conspiracy that his number was found in Epstein's cell comes from a satirical website.

But facts are exhausting, hard-to-pin-down beasts.

Santos knew this, or he learned it. He once said on a podcast that his 2020 opponent, Tom Suozzi, did not "sling mud" at him.[7] The lesson for Santos was that here was just another field where lying worked fine. Just like customer service work at the Dish Network call center. Just like pet charities, and businesses that offered great financial opportunities. Here was just another place with weak penalties for faking.

So even after he'd been exposed, even after it all came out, he committed to the bit. He kept posting. Was it said of him in Washington circles that he was close to resigning, he was demoralized, he knew the jig was up? Did his body image issues still float to the surface, as when he brought up Ozempic again to an audience in the summer to cite the "92 pounds" he'd dropped?[8] So what? He kept going. So *Saturday Night Live* and Jimmy Fallon made fun of him with some impersonators, who donned his easy-to-recognize glasses, sweater, khakis, his cherry-red drag queen's dress: This was not a setback. This was the pinnacle of celebrity culture. "I have now been enshrined in late night TV history with all these impersonations, but they are all TERRIBLE so far," Santos posted. "These comedians need to step their game up." When the winner of season 3 of *RuPaul's Drag Race All*

*Stars* got in the mix on Twitter, saying the source material was "weak"—that was even better. Santos loved RuPaul, you could see it in his eyes the January day in Congress heading into an elevator when someone asked him if he'd watched and you know he did, the way he glowed. Now here was Santos joshing online with RuPaul's finest: "Clearly you know all about weak acting skills."

To be very honest, Santos was hardly the only one having fun with the whole George Santos situation. Everyone was. It's exhausting out there in the social media content mines of real life. We all need some enjoyment from time to time. This Santos thing was hilarious. A guy who made up literally everything—and he gets elected to *Congress*? Could he be—maybe—the GOATed con man? So flagrant that the scams breed admiration?

Hence the memes, the many memes, the one of him wearing a million WWII medals, the one photoshopping him into Yalta, or the Last Supper, or giving the "I Have a Dream" speech. The jokes about how we should really all leave him some space, his grandma died twice last week. The little scraps of script written for a modern *Seinfeld*:

KRAMER: I never said I was Jewish, Jerry.
JERRY: Then what did you say?!
KRAMER: I said I was Jew-ish *pop* they forgot the hyphen.
JERRY: They forgot the hyphen?!

It was a joke, but also this was his actual excuse when finally confronted with all his Jewish mishigas: he claimed he was simply being misunderstood and that he used to jokingly tell people he was "Jew-ish"—as in, kinda Jewish. How could this all not have gone viral? Santos was preparing the punch lines himself.

And what a punch line. A liar goes into politics, but no, *really* a liar. It was perfect. The story had something for everyone. You could know everything or nothing about local or national politics but still know, deeply know, George Santos. You could bash and sometimes even drift toward homophobia, let's be honest, playing on tropes of flamboyance and slipperiness and fashion choices, or you could just tune in for the headlines and enjoy the joke immediately. It could brighten anyone's day. There was the gentleman flight attendant on a recent trip back to New York, who delayed his drink service to hear a little more about the fabulist; the Brazilian woman outside a Queens church who said Santos the "deputada" made her very angry for what he represented, but she said this with a grin on her face. In the spring, I knocked on a door in Queens that once belonged to Santos's father and found not Gercino but an old Greek man who'd moved in afterward. Before I could leave, the Greek man had called over a couple of neighbors, so excited was he to know that they were all a little bit connected to this string of cons.

It is, after all, an addicting story. Everyone loves to be an amateur sleuth. I have been the recipient of more than one ophthalmological email from strangers suggesting I look into the issue of whether Santos's glasses are fake. I have been lectured by people, civilians, who think of themselves as Santos-ologists and could have honestly cowritten this book with me, so up on every twist of the saga were they.

There was a hint in all of this of . . . rooting for the man? Marveling? Shaking one's head with a smile, almost? Sure Santos was a liar and a thief, but you had to kind of hand it to him. You don't really have to hand it to, say, Hakeem Jeffries, or Mitt Romney. Those guys have their hands on everything already. They're all-stars, breathing out history. It's like handing it to the Yankees. As Jimmy Breslin once wrote, who does well enough to root for the Yankees, Laurance Rockefeller? Boring.

The Mets, Santos's Queens team, are "losers, just like nearly everybody else in life," Breslin claimed. That's where it's at. So they lose a lot? So they're messy? "Listen, mister. Think a little bit. When was the last time you won anything out of life?"[9] Watch the antihero and enjoy.

And Santos kept having fun, he really did. He had "brazened his way through the public shame of his own behavior," observed Shawn McCreesh in *New York* magazine, when he caught Santos at the Beach Cafe on East Seventieth Street in February. Friday night, the congressman's wrists full of Hermès and Cartier bling, all the right-wingers coming over for selfies.[10] He just kept posting. Like when he compared himself to Rosa Parks, that she didn't sit in the back of the bus and essentially hide, and so "neither am I gonna sit in the back."[11]

Or when he literally posted a video of himself with a Trump impersonator who said Santos was going to be his 2024 VP. "He's my favorite Brazilian Jew," the impersonator Trumps. And Santos laughs and laughs. He's in on the joke! Him sporting his soft blue sweater and blazer and khakis, practically a Halloween costume in waiting once he wore it all (plus backpack!) on his first days in the House. Iconic. Look how far he has come! "I'm not ruling it out!" he tweets, about the VP thing.

Did the fun and games coexist with all the trollish, right-wing stuff he was doing? Like the gun pin he took to wearing, the shouting about migrants and redirecting them "to 1 UN Plaza," the push to make the AR-15 the "National Gun of the United States"? Was it noteworthy to anyone that Santos with his shameless posting was both loosening the American grip on reality just a bit more and also paving new ground in American history—that not only could you have a figure with a longstanding cult following like Donald Trump be able to post through the bullshit, but now a random liar can keep lying and the gatekeepers can't even gatekeep him out? He'd won. He got seated. He served. This con artist—he was in Congress. If he could do it—there will be more.

But everyone was having fun. If you don't want to cry, you may as well laugh. Santos was part of the upper atmosphere now, mere months after being elected to Congress as one of 435. He was an answer on *Jeopardy!*, so Ken Jennings got to joke, "I don't get to say this very much, but George Santos is correct." He was a bobblehead. Then by March he was another version of the same bobblehead. He was on the tongues of both funnywoman Leslie Jones and Stephen A. Smith—ESPN's Stephen A. Smith. He was name-checked in a *New Yorker* story about animals. He was used as a fake blurb in theater advertisements on the subway. The New York subway, next to the Cop Shot posters and the iconic Dr. Zizmor. This kid of the Queens basement apartment. He won long before he was indicted.

———

*And sure, yes, the indictment* happened, in May 2023, the first round, out in Central Islip, the federal government, thirteen counts, could be twenty years, $500,000 bail. Waiting to get into the courtroom I found myself standing in front of Vish Burra, Santos's director of operations, who likes to piggyback his boss's attacks on Twitter. He has been busted for drugs and told a reporter he once built a drug dealing "empire";[12] he has also been a Steve Bannon staffer and tech helper for Rudy Giuliani with the whole Hunter Biden laptop situation.[13] In other words, he is a prince of gleefully posting through things. He was also wearing the kind of very loud royal blue suit and matching vest that you wear only if you're trying to draw attention. So I turned to him and introduced myself. He said, "C'mon man, I'm not gonna talk to you." This was followed by at least twenty minutes of talking, during which time he noted that his name comes from "king cobra," that he felt like he was in a snake pit (he was in a line of reporters), and did I know what king cobras eat? Other snakes, apparently.

He went on performing the Santos bravado. I complimented what appeared to be his breast pocket handkerchief and he showed how actually it was just the lining. This drew my attention to the pin on his chest, which from afar looked like the one worn by members of Congress, but actually it was for the US Space Force. I asked if he thought space had an ideology. He said certainly, and that the GOP was the party of space. He suggested that we'll run out of real estate down here on earth soon and there's only one place you can get more. I asked what're we talking here, the moon, Mars? He said, "Why limit ourselves?" The Democrats, he felt, were the party of babysitting, and that's what Joe Biden stood for too. People would wake up to this eventually, he warned. Around this point he asked if I wanted to touch the pin, which I did. It had an interesting texture. He then turned to a female reporter near me and said she could touch the pin too. "Oh, I know you wanted to touch it," he said, after she did. Some time later, he would post a range of sexually suggestive tweets in response to a different female reporter's own tweets from the courthouse.

Despite all the brave talk from Burra, Santos did look shaken a little when he walked into the courtroom to absorb his many charges. His hair looked combed. He wore his neat sweater-and-blazer outfit. He accepted the steadying hand of his lawyer, Joe Murray—a man who also knows all about posting through it, incidentally. This is a lawyer who appears to have been part of the January 6 crowd that surrounded the Capitol,[14] a lawyer and former cop who was arrested in 1993 for breaking another cop's jaw but, he has crowed, testified his way out of grand jury indictment; this is a lawyer who, in Santos's employ, would later argue on his client's behalf for bail terms to be modified to make it easier for Santos to shop and dine. But we digress. Santos's lawyer offered comfort as the accused walked through his "yes ma'ams" and "not guilty." The courtroom sketchers sketched.

The smell in the windowless courtroom, so full of press and prosecutors, was a moist human funk, and a good way to describe it was that it smelled how the inside of Rikers Island smells, a mix of proximity and water's-edge dampness. That was not what Santos wanted. That was the kind of place he'd avoided for so long. That was not the way he wanted to end his story. Indeed he wouldn't let it.

And the air was fresher outside, wasn't it? It revivified him. He recovered his brazenness outdoors. Suddenly the show became fun again, when he came outside the courthouse to address the cameras. My brother in Christ, he was wearing sunglasses. He was trim and his clothes fit well. He looked like a movie star. Someone had a LIES sign behind him, and he herded the reporters around to get a little space for himself, a good angle. Once again he was in control. "The reality is," he said with glee, "it's a witch hunt." It made no sense that he'd been indicted in so few months on the scene.

He ranted about Joe Biden, tossing off talking points about

"foreign destinations," bank account deposits. Where were the investigations into that? He preened and jousted, vowed to clear his name and said that he didn't know where the government was getting its information about his supposedly not-kosher application for COVID unemployment benefits. "I will present my facts," he promised. He was confident. It smelled like freedom. It smelled like party. Minute after minute, he kept talking. There is a pretty good rule that you don't say much after you've been indicted by the federal government. But this guy goes out and soliloquizes. The internet loved it. "Anna Delvey walked so he could STRUT," someone said.

Was he nervous? Had he been stressed? "I quite frankly don't believe I was stressed," he brags. "I was fine."

More than fine actually. Because nothing matters anymore. "The way I look at it," he said, "I'll be a chairman of a committee in a couple of years if you just look at the standards of Congress."

Santos's snake-eating staffer Burra stood protectively at his shoulder in aviators, like a bodyguard. It reminded me of something Burra had said just before we went into the room where Santos was charged. Burra avowed that he was paid to keep secrets, and I said, Until this is all over anyway. He said, We're not close to that. He seemed to mean not close to the end of George Santos's political career, and not close to the end of Santos's time as a free man, but perhaps he also meant this kind of insane patter, the swagger that passed for politics now. That was only getting started.

Santos had reclaimed his narrative. He loved the podium, seemed reluctant to leave it. He promised, leaning over the thicket of microphones, that this was not the end of his stories:

"This has been an experience, you know, for a book or something like that."

# Epilogue

One day in June 2023, I was driving up to Connecticut to speak to a woman who got conned by George Santos through one of his pet hustles. It was the usual story: she experienced his charming, ingratiating side, and then a cheeky attempt, and finally his bitter, curse-filled invective.

I was running barely on time to meet her and be granted access to her Facebook posts, but I had to stop quickly for gas around halfway there, near Stamford. While I pumped, a guy driving a gray SUV pulled up next to me.

"Brother," he said. "*Salam alaikum*, where you from?"

"Brooklyn," I said.

"Canada," he responded, smiling and gesturing collegially between us as if I'd said "Montreal." He then stuck his hand out of the car to shake mine, but I was too far away.

"What's up," I said.

Rather than respond, he pulled a thick NBA championship-style ring off his finger, gestured over and said I should have it.

By this time I know a scammy sale when I see one.

"I'm all good man, thanks," I said.

The man put the ring back on and then proffered a white box. "iPhone," he said.

"I'm good."

The man buzzed up his window and put the car into drive. As he pulled away I caught a glimpse of a woman and a small baby in the back seat. They were silent and stared forward. The license plate on the SUV was obscured.

This was one way Santos could have ended up, resorting more and more to the most desperate tricks to get money. Attempts with the lowest probability of success, selling CDs or Amway out of his trunk. Where the only thing going for the hustler is his relentless-ness, stamina, and lack of shame. Where there is no longer any thrill of the chase, only hunger. This could have been the end of Santos's story. But it wasn't.

———————

*In 2003, long before Santos* came on the scene, another Long Island Republican political contender had a story unearthed from his past, and it was pretty bad for his candidacy.

The story was that in 1987, the hopeful for Riverhead town supervisor had been charged with having sex with a fifteen-year-old boy. The candidate had taken an Alford plea—meaning he didn't admit or deny guilt, but took the punishment. The candidate re-peatedly said he did nothing wrong and that "one kid made a very ugly accusation many years ago." He didn't serve any jail time and went on to become a successful Suffolk County businessman. But this is not the kind of allegation you want to be defending during a campaign. The candidate had been pretty optimistic about winning—voters were angry about how things were going in the town, and as with Santos, an outsider wind was blowing. He performed surprisingly respectfully despite the past sex scandal, but ultimately he lost his primary.[1]

He then was forced to make a humiliating trip to the DMV, according to a Riverhead Democrat whose sister worked at that bureaucratic place of stifled dreams. The failed candidate had preemptively registered his car with the license plates "NXRHSUP."[2] Next Riverhead Supervisor. It wasn't to be. He traded them in.

This is another way Santos could have ended up, shamefacedly surrendering his dreams about fame and riches, escaping somewhere into hiding. Bowing his head in the face of scandal rather than, say, making fun of people on Twitter. Humility could have been the end of Santos's story. Obviously, it wasn't.

———

*The next chapters for Santos* were always heading in one direction. The federal government piled on even more charges in the fall of 2023, and a House Committee on Ethics report unveiled evidence of wildly unethical behavior such as using political money for purchases marked "Botox" and "Las Vegas." The investigators alleged that Santos also simply pocketed campaign money. Such revelations were just the tip of the iceberg, as readers of this book know, but they helped bring the drumbeat to a crescendo. That December, Santos was kicked out of Congress, becoming just the third member of the House to be expelled since the Civil War. But the final motions of his story very much remain to be written. He is already both more and less than the hustler on the turnpike, the politician laid low. His conduct, and that of his copycats, will be a signpost for the beleaguered democratic system he conned, a system whose fate is far more meaningful than one dissembling member of Congress.

Among the reasons that Santos eventually got caught in his wide range of lying was that the modern interconnected world brooks no secrets. Someone who knows something in Niterói doesn't have to wait for a reporter to travel to Niterói to reach millions. Politicians—people—have been lying and exaggerating forever. But the systems of revelation were not as strong. When Doris Kearns not-yet-Goodwin spent time with LBJ for her book *Lyndon Johnson and the American Dream*, it was already clear to the budding historian that Johnson's stories about, say, his ancestor's adventures at the Alamo were made up.[3] Years later, the dead president's lies were still being untangled by Robert Caro, who tried to check Johnson's stories with old associates of his and was told, "Well, that's not quite what happened."[4] Santos did not have the benefit of just a few professionals scrutinizing him. Everyone with internet access can dig into your background now. These days, it would have taken about twenty-five minutes from the time then-senator Joe Biden first removed attribution from a story about British politician Neil Kinnock's family to some bloke in Cardiff TikToking about it.

So we live in an unnerving world where everyone can have their turn in the panopticon, when the eyes of the world shift to them. But the same digital infrastructure makes it even easier for someone who is really committed to fabulism—someone who thinks about what they're doing and plots it all out—to fool people and fake everything.

An early taste of this can be seen in a very strange video posted to YouTube in 2020 that appears to be an acted-out press release for George Santos's elevation as "regional director for Harbor City Capital's New York City office." The video lays down a track of smooth techno music over images of Manhattan skyscrapers, along with photos of Santos and his boss at the fast-talking company. A quote attributed to Santos gets animated across the screen. The video has the high production value of a cable news segment or ad about a thriving business.[5] Yet Harbor City was far from a sure thing. Misleading pixelated creations like this will be even more convincing and easier to make with expanded digital and artificial intelligence tools. Such tools can be taken to the criminal extreme, even used by scammers to copy voices. Lina Khan, chair of the US Federal Trade Commission, warned earlier this year about AI abilities like this being able to "turbocharge" fraud and scams.[6] Santos got away with a bogus two-page résumé and GoFundMe posts featuring actual photos of another person's sick dog. How much easier a time would he have if he could fake a diploma or make some heart-wrenching pooch videos himself?

It's a losing game to predict future technology or AI's effects on society specifically—and there are some indications that AI software could help detect the kind of paperwork fraud that Santos was accused of committing. Detection tools could grow to match the scammers' toys. But such an arms race would mean plenty of chaos for regular people along the way. Nigerian-prince-style rip-offs are already blooming as more and more of our lives are interfaced with a screen. Imposter cons were the second-most-costly category reported in the United States in 2022, prompting $2.6 billion in reported losses.[7]

The road ahead also includes a lot more of the conspiracy

theories that Santos harnessed. Like lying, those fictions too have been around since the first bored rumormonger. But there's real money and platforms for mass delusions now, and Santos has shown how easily and unsubtly both can be courted. One of his earliest proposals in Congress was the MINAJ Act, which would prohibit the federal government from imposing mandates on relatively new vaccines, despite the significant benefits to American life wrought by the shots, plus the rigorous testing requirements already in place. The name was a jokey reference to the rapper Nicki Minaj, who became a hero to those who believe vaccine fables after she tweeted that a Trinidadian person she vaguely knew got the vaccine and his testicles swelled up. Santos is not alone among politicians in embracing conspiracy theories. His cosponsorless legislation was introduced two days before the presidential campaign launch of Robert F. Kennedy Jr., the antivax advocate, famous-family scion, and conspiracy fellow traveler who spent years elevating bogus theories before taking his pitch to America's highest stage in 2023. Kennedy has had plenty of monetary help to do so—including from a super PAC co-founded by John Gilmore, the Long Island antivax organizer who helped churn the red wave in suburban New York and spoke with Santos about their shared experience with autistic relatives.[8]

Gilmore's group took out full-page newspaper ads for Kennedy, but his cohort arguably reaches more people on social media, where fact-checking remains a joke and people can choose their own reality more easily than ever. On Facebook and Twitter and the rest, people do so. Cue misinformation about election fraud and George Soros and Jews and false-flag operations and more.

Conspiracies can be spread through a more polite, intellectual route, too. A common theme among the supporters who have rallied to Santos in the months since his exposure has been contrarianism: a feeling that, if all these officious liberals and moderates and even old-school Republicans hate him, then he's on the right track. This "but actually" impulse in American political life has been cresting since Trump's emergence. The former Birther-gate icon was of course a king of conspiracy theories but often cloaked them as just asking questions, from wind turbines to wiretaps. Then came the ultimate contrarianism of COVID, which Trump said could be treated with horse dewormer despite what the fussy experts claimed. It could be wacky, but he was a talented messenger, along with his Svengali right-wing aide Steve Bannon, Fox News personality Tucker Carlson, Sandy-Hook-wasn't-real showman Alex Jones, and Elon Musk, who bought Twitter basically to boost his philosophy of hot takes even more. The contrarians are big on Substack and are well funded thanks to the boom days of Silicon Valley, which built the fortunes of many libertarian "free thinkers" like Peter Thiel, whose intellectual journey away from liberal pieties is described pithily in Max Chafkin's biography, *The Contrarian*: "He'd chosen to reject those who'd rejected him."[9]

The political system itself has absorbed some changes thanks to Santos. His exposure led to a miniflurry of journalists guiltily going back to basics and digging up various lies and résumé embellishments of area politicians. Some were fun, like Tennessee representative Andy Ogles, who exaggerated about being an economist, and even a member of law enforcement who worked on human trafficking issues (he was actually, briefly, a reserve deputy with a sheriff's office and admitted to some condensing of his résumé on the campaign trail).[10] Santos's revelations have also prompted a little boom in the business of selling vulnerability reports, the kinds of deep dives that campaigns do on their own candidates to make sure they are aware of any skeletons in the closet.

This bubble of scrutiny is good, but history suggests it won't last forever. Watergate didn't scare off political trickery for too long. Soon, exaggerating politicians will go back to taking their chances, and juicy details will fall through the cracks as they always do—more so these days in a media ecosystem where 2,500 newspapers have closed in the United States since 2005, and more than one-fifth of Americans live in a place that is already or is at risk of becoming a news desert.[11]

One hopeful argument might be that Santos's saga would encourage political parties to screen their candidates more strictly and produce better elected officials. But that may turn out to be a naive wish. In parts of the country with weak party systems, where candidates buy a ticket to the annual Lincoln dinner and not much else, it's optimistic to believe that these creaky systems would do much if any work to weed out bad candidates and elevate good ones. Candidates who have money already—or who can raise it—to get their message up in un-fact-checked TV or digital ads will win. The other old-school vetting processes of the election cycle—the debates hosted by the Knights of Columbus, the screening questionnaires required by the Leagues of Women Voters, the endorsement interviews with newspaper editorial boards—draw fewer and fewer eyes. Santos skipped out on numerous engagements in his campaigns, or performed disastrously, and all that mattered was that people were pissed about alleged crime in New York City. All politics has become national, a truism that both boosted and then doomed Santos, when the whole political world focused on him, the liar of the moment, rather than their respective off-cycle village race. Even local contests and candidates are focused on the big hot-button issues. This is unfortunate, because those national issues are the hardest to solve, leading people to throw up their hands at all the paralysis.

Stronger political parties could certainly lay their fingers on the scale and give us, the voters, a better crop of candidates. In our two-party system, which gives a wild amount of power to what amounts to a pair of private clubs, don't we at least deserve a decent product? But the Santos situation shows the dangers of relying too much on parties. Republican organizations from national to local failed to expose him or push him aside in time. And they could have: enough of Santos's lies and shenanigans circulated among influential Republicans before his election that the massive pro-GOP Congressional Leadership Fund withheld support from Santos. Yet top Republicans did not come out against him and were happy to welcome him into the fold upon his win.

The party problem is broader than a little temporary cynicism to win a seat. The national GOP, at the time Santos intersected with it, found itself in the thrall of an established liar and institution-crasher. Aligning with Trump and the long tail of forces that created him, the party has given its imprimatur to wild claims and bizarre ideas that used to circulate on much lower platforms, if at all.

On the local level, county officials were quick to belatedly reassert their gatekeeper powers and turn against Santos. Indeed, some party regulars have whispered that Santos is exactly the kind of debacle that wouldn't have happened in the old days when the Nassau GOP was the strongest of machines. Used to be that politics was almost a family business, so that the young first-timer for town council had already been known to the bosses since he was twelve. His dad started on town council too before ascending to state senate. Two cousins work in the office. And by the way his name ends in a vowel. That kind of clannish system might mean a little more knowledge about candidates' backgrounds, but it is ripe for its own kind of abuses, and it certainly closes a door to outsiders who bring different experiences or ideologies to the body politic. If the ground-level operators of the party think the lesson from Santos is "clamp down more," does that lead to a better style of politics, or just an older one?

---

*So Santos has certainly disturbed* the complex world of American politics. His encounter with our funny little system of self-governance has also shaped him. After leaving a string of people behind him wrecked or squeezed for cash, he has been put through the wringer himself, opened up to the ridicule and abuse of the masses, and laid into the hands of federal law enforcement. He has been the victim of media pile-ons and given no benefits of the doubt. We are hard on our celebrities when they fall in this country, and our lawbreakers. Those who most fully enter the maw of the American media-entertainment or criminal justice systems tend to emerge similarly—broken.

In the year after his election, he lived a strange life. Once, in May 2023, late at night (maybe after a few drinks, it must be said), the formerly homeless veteran and dog lover Rich Osthoff decided to give Santos a call. He still had Santos's cell phone number, even years after the scam was pulled. It was basically a prank call, just for fun, but Santos picked up. "Who's this," Santos said. "I don't know who you are." Osthoff replied, "You sure do. We never met in person but . . ." They had a shared past, the ugly moment Santos had put him through, the navy man's beloved dog who died without the surgery that Santos promised. Santos had to listen to it. It was like the spirit from Christmas past calling Scrooge. Osthoff lit into his old nemesis, but it was not such a satisfying experience. Santos said eventually, "I'm going to end this conversation," and he hung up. He will always be dogged by those he screwed.

But he also helped write a new chapter in the book of American shamelessness, and even if he and his stories someday stop attracting attention, he will still have escaped anonymity for at least a moment, and he will still have captured something hilarious yet portentous about our politics. He has always seemed aware of this wild instant. Like at the 2023 Congressional Baseball Game for Charity, when he was mobbed in the stands by people who wanted to take selfies. And at that point, even after indictment, after exposure, he got to bask in a glow of celebrity and power thanks to nothing but lies. He gripped shoulders, he leaned in, he asked where ya from. When told "California" by someone, he said their state had terrible politics. He gave thumbs-ups and grinned professionally to the onlookers, but once, looking at the camera, his braggadocious mien dropped. His eyes widened in happy astonishment at the attention, that longed-for currency. "There's a line," he observed quietly about the people waiting to pose with him.

Some onlooker, maybe facetiously, maybe drunkenly, a little cleverly (but what is American politics but those anyway?) pointed back to the serial liar and scammer:

"He could literally win the presidential race, right now."

# A Note on Sources

*T*his book is based on conversations with more than one hundred people who knew or crossed paths with George Santos. Many spoke for hours on the record, while others spoke under the condition that their names not be used. As I've noted elsewhere, I interviewed Santos himself multiple times throughout his campaigns for office, but he did not participate in this book, refusing to speak or even agree to a standard fact-check procedure, which would have allowed me to incorporate his responses. Santos would not do this. Hence the lack of his affirmations or denials on the reporting here, though I have tried to include some of his public (and shifting) denials of previously reported allegations.

Even if he had submitted to an interview or to fact-checking, the process would have presented its own quandaries. Can we trust Santos's word alone without other forms of proof? That question hung over the entirety of my reporting. Further complicating the situation, many of Santos's associates, too, are slippery with the truth. To write this book, I therefore triangulated material and information received through many sources, including days of footage of Santos from his campaigns for office; hundreds of shared text messages; the copious imprints of Santos's life on apps, the internet, and social media; recordings that people made of him; and hundreds of pages of court filings and campaign finance records; as well as the many, many aforementioned and repeated interviews with people who knew him. Armed with all that, I tried as best I could to tell the true story of the habitual liar George Santos, but we will surely continue to learn more and more as Santos's time in the national spotlight stretches on. More lies will emerge; more truths will be revealed. And despite the fact that he refused many opportunities to help me get his facts straight, Santos will certainly look to belatedly highlight any detail he sees as unfair. Indeed, he promised me he would.

This book is based on my own reporting; when I rely on the reporting of others, or information beyond my own interviews and materials provided to me by sources, I note that in the endnotes. Direct quotes come from audio or text-based sources or the specific memory of someone present, unless otherwise noted.

I opted for purposes of clarity to call the gentleman from New York "Santos" in this book, with rare exceptions, such as if the person talking about him directly cites another variant of his full name.

# Acknowledgments

*I* am indebted, as are we all, to the crucial reporting of Grace Ashford, Michael Gold, Jacqueline Sweet, Marisa Kabas, Will Bredderman, Jake Offenhartz, Nicholas Fandos, Paul LaRocco, Scott Eidler, Andrew Silverstein, Andrew Kaczynski, Alex Calzareth, Lúcia Guimarães, and many more who have helped the public understand George Santos.

I am grateful to everyone who spoke to me as a source for this book, and also to the many people who aided this project in countless other, crucial ways.

That includes Caroline Curtin, a *Newsday* researcher whose diligence, curiosity, and interest in historical context has saved many, many reporters over the years. Her research help on this book was absolutely invaluable, which was no surprise to me since she has improved so many of my stories in the past, showing the importance of news libraries to reporters, editors, and readers.

Gustavo Werthein was my unparalleled Portuguese translator in and out of Brazil, and I would have been lost without him.

Thank you to my agent, Jackie Ko, who has been in my corner since the beginning, and I'm a lucky guy for that. Thanks to Julia Cheiffetz and Nick Ciani, Abby Mohr and Hannah Frankel and Joanna Pinsker and everyone at One Signal for shepherding this book and making it better by far. Nicholas Jahr was a swift and thorough fact-checker extraordinaire.

I first started reporting on George Santos while working for *Newsday*, where I was blessed with many great editors and colleagues, including Rita Ciolli, Eli Reyes, Michael Dobie, Randi Marshall, Lane Filler, Dan Janison, Amanda Fiscina, Larry Striegel, and Matt Chayes. Thank you to Lane and Randi too for reading chapter drafts.

Thank you to my incredible in-laws Emily Lazar—who is a true crime savant and knows just whom to call for any story—and Jonathan Alter, who read a draft of this entire book more quickly than should have been humanly possible and made it sharper and all-around better.

It is no political exaggeration to say that I have the best and most supportive family. My brother, Scott, has been an editor and literary partner since back when we were still pretty good at baseball. I would be nowhere without my parents, model educators and citizens who have been good sports about their two sons ending up in the strange world of journalism. My uncle Stephen heard a lot about this project before it was done, and I'm grateful for that.

I completed this book in a pediatric burn unit where my eighteen-month-old daughter, Rosie, was being treated. Thank you to all the nurses and doctors and hospital personnel who cared for her, for weeks. After spending these last months thinking about a dilettante trickster who never seemed satisfied with well-trodden career paths, it was comforting to be in the presence of so much graceful competence from people who have dedicated their lives to helping others.

The other person in that burn unit with me was my wife, Charlotte Alter, about whom full books should be written. She is the most loyal partner and tough-but-fairest editor; she has her finger on the pulse of American politics and culture and can both paint portraits like a professional and recite all the US presidents in order in under twenty seconds. She can entertain and take care of our daughter even while finding the weak point in one of my chapters (or writing her own). She took everything on and held up our family while I disappeared into Santos World. For the last decade-plus it has sometimes felt like we've been having one long, intense nonstop conversation about art, politics, family, and noncreamy pasta. Lucky me.

# Notes

## Introduction

1. Josh Kovensky and Hunter Walker, "Leaked Audio and Staff Dispute Show Chaos inside George Santos' Office," *TPM*, February 2, 2023, https://talkingpointsmemo.com/muckraker/leaked-audio-george-santos.

2. Kadia Goba, "For George Santos, Life in Congress becomes a Tread-mill," *Semafor,* January 6, 2023, https://www.semafor.com/newsletter/01/06/2023/semafor-principals-mccarthy-speaker-deal-jan-6.

3. Grace Ashford and Michael Gold, "Who Is Rep.-Elect George Santos? His Résumé May Be Largely Fiction," *New York Times*, December 19, 2022, https://www.nytimes.com/2022/12/19/nyregion/george-santos-ny-republicans.html.

4. Andrew Silverstein, "Congressman-Elect George Santos Lied about Grandparents Fleeing Anti-Jewish Persecution during WWII," *The Forward*, December 21, 2022, https://forward.com/news/529130/george-santos-jewish-lie-genealogy-records/.

5. Andrew Kaczynski and Em Stack, "More False Claims from George Santos about His Work, Education and Family History Emerge," CNN, December 29, 2022, https://edition.cnn.com/2022/12/28/politics/george-santos-false-claims-kfile/index.html.

6. Ashford and Gold, "Who Is Rep.-Elect George Santos?"

7. Laura Davison, "George Santos Produced Ill-Fated Spider-Man Musical. At Least, He Claims He Did," Bloomberg, February 3, 2023,

https://www.bloomberg.com/news/articles/2023-02-03/george-santos
-produced-broadway-s-spider-man-musical-at-least-he-claims-he-did.

8. "Police Off the Cuff After Hours #37 with Congressional Candidate George Santos," YouTube video, October 29, 2020, 1:06:17, https://www.youtube.com/watch?v=P2IF5bUsksQ.

9. Vanessa Friedman, "Clothes Make the Con Man," *New York Times*, January 17, 2023, https://www.nytimes.com/2023/01/17/style/george-santos-style.html.

10. George Santos for Congress NY-3, Facebook video, April 21, 2022, https://www.facebook.com/DevolderSantosforCongress/videos/713119466706883.

11. Robert Zimmerman, Financial Disclosure Report 10050208 (Washington, DC: Legislative Resource Center, 2022), https://disclosures-clerk.house.gov/public_disc/financial-pdfs/2022/10050208.pdf; Robert Zimmerman, Financial Disclosure Report 10044609 (Washington, DC: Legislative Resource Center, 2022), https://disclosures-clerk.house.gov/public_disc/financial-pdfs/2022/10044609.pdf.

12. "Rep. George Santos on GDNY: 'Most people lie on their resumes,'" YouTube video, 9:50, posted by Fox 5 New York, August 18, 2023, https://www.youtube.com/watch?v=duN_5PFeSRI.

13. Glen O. Gabbard, *The Psychology of the Sopranos* (New York: Basic Books, 2002), 40–41.

14. João Batista Jr., "An Avalanche of Fibs," *Revista Piauí* (Rio de Janeiro), January 19, 2023, https://piaui.folha.uol.com.br/an-avalanche-of-fibs/.

15. Snejana Farberov, "George Santos Claims He Survived 'Assassination Attempt,' Had Shoes Stolen off His Feet," *New York Post*, January 24, 2023, https://nypost.com/2023/01/24/george-santos-claims-he-survived-assassination-attempt/.

16. "Episode 276," *The Rory Sauter Show*, podcast, August 12, 2020, 2:22:00, https://www.blogtalkradio.com/therorysautershow/2020/08/12/the-rory-sauter-show--episode-276.

17. Andrew Silverstein, "George Santos' Latest Doozy: Records Show His Mom Wasn't in NYC on 9/11," *The Forward*, January 18, 2023, https://forward.com/news/532350/george-santos-congressman-lie-about-9-11-newly-released-documents/.

18. Grace Ashford, Miriam Jordan, and Michael Gold, "George Santos Mar-

ried a Brazilian Woman. House Is Asked to Find Out Why," *New York Times*, February 15, 2023, https://www.nytimes.com/2023/02/15/nyregion/george-santos-marriage-immigration.html.

19. "Episode 159," *Steak for Breakfast*, podcast, August 9, 2022, 3:07, https://podcasts.apple.com/us/podcast/episode-159/id1498791684?i=1000575587664.

20. Joshua Zitser, "George Santos Claimed to Be One of the First People in the US Diagnosed with COVID-19. That Looks to Be Bogus Too," Yahoo, January 11, 2023, https://news.yahoo.com/george-santos-claimed-one-first-121344222.html.

21. Jonathan O'Connell et al., "'I Felt Like We Were in *Goodfellas*'": How George Santos Wooed Investors for Alleged Ponzi Scheme," *Washington Post*, January 25, 2023, https://www.washingtonpost.com/investigations/2023/01/25/george-santos-ponzi-scheme-harbor-city/.

22. Decca Muldowney, "George Santos' Brain Tumor and COVID-19 Claims Questioned," *Daily Beast*, January 10, 2023, https://www.thedailybeast.com/george-santos-brain-tumor-and-covid-19-claims-questioned.

23. @RepSantosNY03, "Happy #OpeningDay," Twitter video, March 30, 2023, https://twitter.com/RepSantosNY03/status/1641550272085348354.

24. Jason Torchinsky, "New York Congressional Candidate Claims to Use an Absurd Amount of Gas," *Jalopnik*, December 13, 2021, https://jalopnik.com/new-york-congressional-candidate-claims-to-use-an-absur-1848207722.

25. "CPAC 2022: Interview with George Santos," *Loud Majority US*, podcast, n.d., 21:15, https://rumble.com/vwg4k9-cpac-2022-interview-with-george-santos.html.

26. Ashford and Gold, "Who Is Rep.-Elect George Santos?"

27. Marisa Kabas, "The Daily Santos: Vol. 7," *The Handbasket*, January 18, 2023, https://thehandbasket.substack.com/p/the-daily-santos-vol-7.

28. "Congressional Campaign Treasurer Pleads Guilty to Conspiring With a Congressional Candidate to Defraud," press release, US Attorney's Office, Eastern District of New York, Thursday October 5, 2023, https://www.justice.gov/usao-edny/pr/congressional-campaign-treasurer-pleads-guilty-conspiring-congressional-candidate

29. Harold I. Kaplan and Benjamin J. Sadock, *Kaplan & Sadock's Synopsis of Psychiatry* (Philadelphia: Lippincott Williams & Wilkins, 2003).

30. Michael Gold and Grace Ashford, "George Santos Admits to Lying about College and Work History," *New York Times*, December 26, 2022, https://www.nytimes.com/2022/12/26/nyregion/george-santos-interview.htm.

31. Jake Offenhartz, "Listen: George Santos Eviction Tapes Show Him Begging to Feed Pet Fish, Mulling Public Assistance," *Gothamist*, March 7, 2023, https://gothamist.com/news/listen-george-santos-eviction-tapes-show-him-begging-to-feed-pet-fish-mulling-public-assistance.

32. "Congressman George Santos Charged with Fraud," press release, US Attorney's Office.

## Chapter 1: Escape from the Tower of Babel

1. Michael Gold, Grace Ashford, and Ellen Yan, "George Santos's Early Life: Odd Jobs, Bad Debts, and Lawsuits," *New York Times*, December 23, 2022, https://www.nytimes.com/2022/12/23/nyregion/george-santos-republican-resume.html.

2. DISH Network Corporation, Form 10-K 20549 (Washington, DC: United States Securities and Exchange Commission, 2011), https://www.sec.gov/Archives/edgar/data/1001082/000110465912011853/a11-31127_110k.htm.

3. DISH Network Corporation, Form 10-K 20549.

4. Grace Ashford, Miriam Jordan, and Michael Gold, "George Santos Married a Brazilian Woman. House Is Asked to Find Out Why," *New York Times*, February 15, 2023, https://www.nytimes.com/2023/02/15/nyregion/george-santos-marriage-immigration.html.

5. Ashford, Jordan, and Gold.

6. "Episode 276," *The Rory Sauter Show*, podcast, August 12, 2020, 2:22:00, https://www.blogtalkradio.com/therorysautershow/2020/08/12/the-rory-sauter-show--episode-276.

## Chapter 2: Up from the Basement

1. "George Santos," *This Week's Long Island News*, WHPC, September 23, 2022, 28:41, https://www.spreaker.com/user/whpc/news-09-23-22.

2. Maureen Hack et al., "Very Low Birth Weight Outcomes of the National Institute of Child Health and Human Development Neonatal Net-

work," *Pediatrics* 87, no. 5 (May 1991): 587–97, https://publications
.aap.org/pediatrics/article-abstract/87/5/587/56988/Very-Low-Birth
-Weight-Outcomes-of-the-National.

3. National Center for Health Statistics, "Vital Statistics of the United
States, 1988" (1991), vol. II, mortality, part A, p. 496, https://www
.cdc.gov/nchs/data/vsus/mort88_2a.pdf.

4. "Police Off the Cuff After Hours #37 with Congressional Candidate
George Santos," *Police Off the Cuff After Hours*, podcast, October 29,
2020, 1:06:17, https://www.youtube.com/watch?v=P2IF5bUsksQ.

5. Juliette Fairley, "Man Charged in Race Attack," *Newsday*, June 24,
1988; Gale Scott, "Death Study Blasts 8 Hospitals: But Federal Statistics Challenged," *Newsday*, December 16, 1988.

6. George Santos, interview by Piers Morgan, *Piers Morgan Uncensored*,
TalkTV, February 20, 2023, https://www.youtube.com/watch?v=I7p
-6HHUgl4.

7. @MrSantosNY, "No need to . . . ," Twitter post, April 19, 2023,
https://twitter.com/Santos4Congress/status/1648875970927968256.
Isabela Dias, "Inside the Brazilian WhatsApp Group Exposing George
Santos," *Mother Jones*, January 26, 2023, https://www.motherjones
.com/politics/2023/01/george-santos-lies-have-short-legs-whatsapp
-group-brazil/.

8. Santos interview by Morgan.

9. "Live with Next Congressman of NY-03 . . . ," *Loud Majority US*,
podcast, July 22, 2022, 58:46, https://www.facebook.com/watch
/live/?ref=watch_permalink&v=463605262264959.

10. Selim Algar, "Queens Is Crowned Nation's Most Diverse Large County,"
*New York Post*, July 4, 2019, https://nypost.com/2019/07/04/queens
-is-crowned-nations-most-diverse-large-county/.

11. Clyde Haberman, "Life Lessons as Principal for a Day," *New York
Times*, May 8, 1998.

12. Marcia Kramer, "The Point: Rep. George Santos Wants to Use His
'Very Loud Voice' to Deliver Results for New York," CBS News, May
10, 2023, https://www.cbsnews.com/newyork/news/george-santos
-exclusive-interview-the-point-marcia-kramer/.

13. Santos interview by Morgan.

14. "George Santos: Reforming Education and the Coming Student Debt

Bubble Burst," *The Create Your Own Life Show*, podcast, May 17, 2022, 28:00, https://podcasts.apple.com/us/podcast/the-create-your -own-life-show/id1059619918?i=1000561772985.

15. Sherronna Bishop, "Immigrate to be Free," *America's Mom with Sherronna Bishop*, podcast, 26.53, https://frankspeech.com/video /immigrate-be-free.

16. Andrew Kaczynski and Em Stecl, "More False Claims from George Santos about His Work, Education and Family History Emerge," CNN, December 29, 2022, https://edition.cnn.com/2022/12/28/politics /george-santos-false-claims-kfile/index.html.

17. Jake Offenhartz, "Listen: George Santos Eviction Tapes Show Him Begging to Feed Pet Fish, Mulling Public Assistance," *Gothamist*, March 7, 2023, https://gothamist.com/news/listen-george-santos-eviction -tapes-show-him-begging-to-feed-pet-fish-mulling-public-assistance.

18. Michael Gold, "George Santos's Mother Was Not in New York on 9/11, Records Show," *New York Times*, January 18, 2023, https:// www.nytimes.com/2023/01/18/nyregion/george-santos-mother-911 .html.

19. "Constitutional Candidate Series [interview with Santos]," Facebook video, September 21, 2020, 38:33, https://fb.watch/mcYb-dRg8I/.

20. Kylie Blaine, "Immigration Records Contradict Santos' Claim His Mother Was at World Trade Center on 9/11," CNN, January 18, 2023, https://www.cnn.com/2023/01/18/politics/santos-mother-9-11-claim -immigration-records/index.html.

21. Fatima's immigration documents referenced here and elsewhere were received through a FOIL request by researcher Alex Calzareth.

22. "Charles Goodman, A Publisher, 55," *New York Times*, March 3, 1996, https://www.nytimes.com/1996/03/03/nyregion/charles-goodman-a -publisher-55.html.

23. Michael Schulman, "How the Marvel Cinematic Universe Swallowed Hollywood," *The New Yorker*, June 5, 2023, https://www.newyorker.com /magazine/2023/06/12/how-the-marvel-cinematic-universe-swallowed -hollywood.

24. Jacqueline Sweet, "Former Roommate 'Confident' George Santos' Mother Not in WTC on 9/11," *Port Washington, NY, Patch*, January 6, 2023, https://patch.com/new-york/portwashington/former-roommate -confident-george-santos-mother-not-wtc-9-11.

25. Sheena Samu, Pat Milton, and Erica Brown, "Priest Recalls George Santos' Financial Need—Saying Family Couldn't Afford Mother's Funeral," CBS News, December 24, 2022, https://www.cbsnews.com/news/george-santos-congress-mother-funeral/.

26. Santos interview by Morgan.

27. "Constitutional Candidate Series [interview with Santos]," 38:33.

28. Noah Lanard and David Corn, "George Santos Relative Says They Never Gave $5,800 Reported by the Campaign: 'I'm Dumbfounded,'" *Mother Jones*, February 1, 2023, https://www.motherjones.com/politics/2023/02/george-santos-campaign-funds-donors-scandal/.

## Chapter 3: Kitara at the Bingo Table

1. Ana Cristina Geyer de Moraes, "FALA, NITERÓI!," *O Globo*, June 26, 2005.

2. João Fragah, "George Santos em polêmica entrevista +1º Parada Gay de Niterói," YouTube video, May, 19, 2014, 6:05, https://www.youtube.com/watch?v=xUJuf4smRWk.

3. Marisa Kabas, "The Daily Santos: Vol. 7," *The Handbasket*, January 18, 2023, https://thehandbasket.substack.com/p/the-daily-santos-vol-7.

4. The article clipping itself is undated, but Rochard believes it was from 2007, which is backed up by other details from the page. Some outlets have dated the clipping to 2008.

5. Terrence McCoy and Marina Dias, "For George Santos, a Life in Brazil at Odds with His GOP Politics," *Washington Post,* August 31, 2023, https://www.washingtonpost.com/world/2023/08/31/george-santos-brazil/.

6. Stan Lehman, "A Look at Offensive Comments by Brazil Candidate Bolsonaro," Associated Press, September 29, 2018, https://apnews.com/general-news-1f9b79df9b1d4f14aeb1694f0dc13276.

7. Lehman.

8. Mike Gatehouse, "Ellen Page Confronts Jair Bolsonaro about Homophobia, in Rio de Janeiro," *Latin America Bureau*, March 6, 2019, https://lab.org.uk/ellen-page-confronts-jair-bolsonaro-about-homophobia-in-rio-de-janeiro/.

9. @MrSantosNY, "Really @newsmax…," Twitter post, July 15, 2021, https://twitter.com/Santos4Congress/status/1415680884775145481.

10. Santos4_congress, "USA & Brasil!!! Friends fighting…," Instagram

post, November 14, 2022, https://www.instagram.com/p/Ck91QlquMQr/?hl=e.

11. McCoy and Dias, "For George Santos, a Life in Brazil at Odds."

12. Matt Lavietes, Isabela Espadas Barros Leal, Kate Santaliz, and Olympia Sonnier, "Rep. George Santos Implies He Dressed in Drag but Denies Ever Being a 'Drag Queen,'" *NBC News*, January 19, 2023, https://www.nbcnews.com/nbc-out/out-politics-and-policy/rep-george-santos-denies-ever-drag-queen-rcna66414.

13. soniamaandrade, "Prefeitura de Niterói . . . Atenção! Parada Gay de Niterói!," YouTube video, August 28, 2007, 1:17, https://www.youtube.com/watch?v=ysmUy0Irt7Q; soniamaandrade, "Parada Gay de Niterói," August 28, 2007, YouTube video, 2:46, https://www.youtube.com/watch?v=xyn22Qp_ETE.

14. Jacqueline Sweet, "More George Santos Acquaintances Come Forward with Theft Allegations," *Port Washington, NY, Patch*, January 10, 2023, https://patch.com/new-york/portwashington/more-george-santos-acquaintances-come-forward-theft-allegations.

15. These and subsequent details about the check fraud case come from Santos's Brazilian court records: *Carlos Bruno de Castro Simoes vs. George Anthony Devolder Santos*, 0007984-78.2010.8.19.0002, Ministerio Publico do Estado do Rio de Janeiro, 2010.

16. Grace Ashford and Michael Gold, "Who Is Rep.-Elect George Santos? His Résumé May Be Largely Fiction," *New York Times*, December 19, 2022, https://www.nytimes.com/2022/12/19/nyregion/george-santos-ny-republicans.html.

17. "Explainer: Brazil's Clean Record Law," AS/COA, August 26, 2014, https://www.as-coa.org/articles/explainer-brazils-clean-record-law.

18. Sweet, "More George Santos Acquaintances Come Forward."

### Chapter 4: Grift City

1. Bill McIntyre and Jon Gallo, "Erase Racism NY and George Santos," *This Week's Long Island News*, podcast, 58:40, https://www.spreaker.com/user/whpc/news-06-03-22-final.

2. Bridget Read, "What George Santos Was Really Like as a Roommate," *Curbed*, January 25, 2023, https://www.curbed.com/2023/01/george-santos-roommate-nightmare.html.

3. Roger Sollenberger, "George Santos Planned 'Engagement Party'

with Man While Married to Woman," *Daily Beast*, January 20, 2023, https://www.thedailybeast.com/george-santos-planned-engagement -party-with-man-while-married-to-uadla-vieira-santos.

4. Offenhartz, "Listen: George Santos Eviction Tapes Show Him Begging to Feed Pet Fish, Mulling Public Assistance," *Gothamist*, March 7, 2023, https://gothamist.com/news/listen-george-santos-eviction-tapes-show -him-begging-to-feed-pet-fish-mulling-public-assistance.

5. Michael Gold and Grace Ashford, "George Santos Goes to Washington as His Life of Fantasy Comes into Focus," *New York Times*, January 1, 2023, https://www.nytimes.com/2023/01/01/nyregion /george-santos-congress-republican-new-york.html.

6. Will Steakin, "Promised Green Cards, Catfishing, Threats: How George Santos' Ex-Boyfriends Say They Were Left Feeling Trapped, Manipulated," ABC News, January 31, 2023, https://abcnews.go.com /US/promised-green-cards-catfishing-threats-santos-boyfriends-left /story?id=96797395.

## Chapter 5: And Then Came the Dogs

1. Jonathan O'Connell, Emma Brown, and Shayna Jacobs, "Amish Country Farmers Say George Santos Took Puppies, Left Bad Checks," *Washington Post*, February 10, 2023, https://www.washingtonpost .com/investigations/2023/02/10/george-santos-amish-puppies/; CNN, "Amish Dog Breeder Says George Santos Allegedly Stole Puppies," YouTube video, February 14, 2023, 3:37, https://www.youtube.com /watch?v=FE3hWw1xN5U.

2. Michael Gold and Grace Ashford, "About Those 2,500 Dogs That George Santos Claims He Saved," *New York Times*, February 6, 2023, https://www.nytimes.com/2023/02/06/nyregion/santos-pets-animal -charity.html.

3. Jacqueline Sweet, "Santos Was Charged with Theft in 2017 Case Tied to Amish Dog Breeders," *Politico*, February 9, 2023, https://www .politico.com/news/2023/02/09/santos-charged-theft-2017-dog -breeders-00082091.

4. Gold and Ashford, "About Those 2,500 Dogs."

5. João Batista Jr., "An Avalanche of Fibs," *Revista Piauí* (Rio de Janeiro), January 19, 2023, https://piaui.folha.uol.com.br/an-ava lanche-of-fibs/.

6. George Devolder, "Homemade Natural Dog Treats!," YouTube video, June 13, 2015, 4:52, https://www.youtube.com/watch?v=OkFiyyW FJMM.

## Chapter 6: Choosing Politics

1. "Résumé of George Santos," *New York Times*, January 11, 2023, https://www.nytimes.com/interactive/2023/01/11/us/resume-of -george-santos.html.

2. Jacqueline Sweet, "George Santos Masterminded 2017 ATM Fraud, Former Roommate Tells Feds," *Politico*, March 9, 2023, https://www .politico.com/news/2023/03/09/santos-masterminded-atm-fraud -feds-00086417.

3. *Retirement Benefits for Members of Congress,* Congressional Research Service, July 25, 2023, p. 2.

4. Randal C. Archibold, "Ex-Congressman Gets 8-Year Term in Brib-ery Case," *New York Times*, March 4, 2006, https://www.nytimes .com/2006/03/04/politics/excongressman-gets-8year-term-in-bribery -case.html.

5. "Veterans: The Hoax," *Time*, October 25, 1954, https://content.time .com/time/subscriber/article/0,33009,823567,00.html.

6. Lúcia Guimarães, "Homem que acusou George Santos está foragido sob acusação de torturar criança," *Folha De S.Paulo*, March 23, 2023, https://www1.folha.uol.com.br/mundo/2023/03/homem-que -acusou-george-santos-esta-foragido-sob-acusacao-de-torturar-crianca .shtml.

7. Dan Ladden-Hall, "George Santos' Brazil Lawyer Did Time for Gang Execution: Report," *Daily Beast*, February 2, 2023, https://www .thedailybeast.com/george-santos-brazil-lawyer-did-time-for-gang -execution-report.

8. "SEC Obtains Emergency Relief, Charges Florida Company and CEO with Misappropriating Investor Money and Operating a Ponzi Scheme," press release, US Securities and Exchange Com-mission, April 27, 2021, https://www.sec.gov/litigation/litreleases /lr-25082.

9. Michael Kaplan, Scott MacFarlane, and Graham Kates, "Newly Obtained George Santos 'Vulnerability Report' Spotted Red Flags

Long before Embattled Rep. Was Elected," CBS, September 6, 2023, https://www.cbsnews.com/news/george-santos-vulnerability-report-red-flags-long-before-embattled-rep-was-elected/.

10. Paul LaRocco and Scott Eidler, "George Santos May Have Inflated Role at Finance Company, Records Show," *Newsday*, January 19, 2023, https://www.newsday.com/long-island/politics/santos-linkbridge-lawsuit-hf4e6kjq.

11. *Securities and Exchange Commission v. Harbor City Capital Corp et al.*, Declaration of Steven Estle, 4-11 Exhibit 12 (2021).

12. "Congressman George Santos Charged with Fraud, Money Laundering, Theft of Public Funds, and False Statements," press release, US Attorney's Office, Eastern District of New York, May 10, 2023, https://www.justice.gov/usao-edny/pr/congressman-george-santos-charged-fraud-money-laundering-theft-public-funds-and-false.

13. Isaac Stanley-Becker, Jonathan O'Connell, and Emma Brown, "Harbor City Called George Santos a 'Perfect Fit.' The SEC Called the Company a Fraud," *Washington Post*, January 15, 2023, https://www.washingtonpost.com/investigations/2023/01/15/george-santos-harbor-city-capital/.

14. *Securities and Exchange Commission v. Harbor City Capital Corp et al.*, 6:21-cv-694-CEM-DCI (Orlando, FL, Court, 2021), https://www.sec.gov/litigation/complaints/2021/comp-pr2021-74.pdf.

15. Stanley-Becker, O'Connell, and Brown, "Harbor City Called George Santos a 'Perfect Fit.'"

16. J. P. Maroney, "How to Get MORE Done in LESS Time!," YouTube video, November 18, 2009, 3:26, https://www.youtube.com/watch?v=7IL48aezKro; J. P. Maroney, "Make BIG Money Attending Live Events," YouTube video, 17:01, https://www.youtube.com/watch?v=K1N29qE_oq4.

17. *Securities and Exchange Commission v. Harbor City Capital Corp et al.*, Declaration of James M. Halpin, 4-9 Exhibit 10 (2021), p. 36.

18. *Securities and Exchange Commission v. Harbor City Capital Corp et al.*, 6:21-cv-694-CEM-DCI.

19. Stanley-Becker, O'Connell, and Brown, "Harbor City Called George Santos a 'Perfect Fit.'"

20. @devolder, "I'm sorry I'm not...," Twitter post, June 28, 2020, https://web

.archive.org/web/20200628230552/https://twitter.com/Devolder
/status/1277376757230899201.

21. Jonathan O'Connell et al., "'I Felt like We Were in *Goodfellas*'":
How George Santos Wooed Investors for Alleged Ponzi Scheme,"
*Washington Post*, January 25, 2023, https://www.washingtonpost
.com/investigations/2023/01/25/george-santos-ponzi-scheme-harbor
-city/.

22. Stanley-Becker, O'Connell, and Brown, "Harbor City Called George
Santos a 'Perfect Fit.'"

23. "Our Supporters," USC Shoah Foundation, accessed August 4, 2023,
https://sfi.usc.edu/get-involved/our-supporters.

24. Grace Ashford, Alexandra Berzon, and Michael Gold, "How an Investor Lost $625,000 and His Faith in George Santos," *New York Times*,
January 19, 2023, https://www.nytimes.com/2023/01/19/nyregion
/george-santos-sec-intrater.html.

25. Isaac Stanley-Becker and Rosalind S. Helderman, "New Details Link
George Santos to Cousin of Sanctioned Russian Oligarch," *Washington Post*, January 16, 2023, https://www.washingtonpost.com
/politics/2023/01/16/george-santos-andrew-intrater-columbus-nova/.

26. Ashford, Berzon, and Gold, "How an Investor Lost $625,000."

27. Kadia Goba, "George Santos Tries to Explain His Wealth," *Semafor*,
December 28, 2022, https://www.semafor.com/article/12/28/2022
/george-santos-tries-to-explain-his-wealth.

28. Grace Ashford, "How George Santos Used Political Connections to
Fuel Get-Rich Schemes," *New York Times*, July 26, 2023, https://
www.nytimes.com/2023/07/26/nyregion/george-santos-money-donors
.html.

29. Rebecca Davis O'Brien and William K. Rashbaum, "George Santos's Role in Sale of $19 Million Yacht Attracts F.B.I. Interest," *New
York Times*, March 15, 2023, https://www.nytimes.com/2023/03/15
/nyregion/george-santos-yacht.html.

30. George Anthony Devolder-Santos, Financial Disclosure Report 10035761 (Washington, DC: Legislative Resource Center,
2020), https://disclosures-clerk.house.gov/public_disc/financial
-pdfs/2020/10035761.pdf; George Anthony Devolder-Santos, Financial Disclosure Report 10050385 (Washington, DC: Legislative

Resource Center, 2022), https://disclosures-clerk.house.gov/public
_disc/financial-pdfs/2022/10050385.pdf. "Congressional Campaign
Treasurer Pleads Guilty to Conspiring With a Congressional Candidate
to Defraud," press release, US Attorney's Office, Eastern District of
New York, Thursday October 5, 2023, https://www.justice.gov/usao
-edny/pr/congressional-campaign-treasurer-pleads-guilty-conspiring
-congressional-candidate.

31. Tori DeAngelis, "A New Kind of Delusion?," *Monitor on Psychology* 40, no. 6 (June 2009), https://www.apa.org/monitor/2009/06
/delusion.html.

32. Keith R. Billingsley and Clyde Tucker, "Generations, Status, and Party
Identification: A Theory of Operant Conditioning," *Political Behavior*
9, no. 4 (December 1987).

33. Andrew Kaczynski, "Inside George Santos' Transformation from
Anthony Devolder into a Political Figure," CNN, February 1, 2023,
https://edition.cnn.com/2023/02/01/politics/george-santos-anthony
-devolder-kfile/index.html.

34. Kaczynski.

### Chapter 7: The Excellent Messy Awesomeness of 2020
### Or, How Santos Got COVID and Learned to Stop the Steal

1. George Santos for Congress NY-3, "Very proud to join the movement!
#termlimits," Facebook video, November 11, 2019, https://www
.facebook.com/watch/?v=1919893338157546.

2. US Term Limits, "Devolder Santos NY Congressional District 3 Signs
Term Limits Pledge," YouTube video, October 18, 2019, 1:09, https://
www.youtube.com/watch?v=PGkHnZ5YYbw.

3. George Santos for Congress NY-3, "Corey Lewandowski Live at Queen
Village...," Facebook video, March 24, 2019, https://fb.watch/mc
-vcXxtMw/.

4. George Santos for Congress NY-3, "Trump Breakfast Fundraiser
Review!," Facebook video, September 26, 2019, https://fb.watch
/mc-xcrAHg4/.

5. "George Santos: A Corona Story," *Empire State Conservatives Podcast*,
March 29, 2020, https://podcasts.apple.com/us/podcast/empire-state
-conservatives-podcast/id1441178646?i=1000469913544.

6. Anna Merlan, "Everything I Learned Watching George Santos' Interminable Public Access Show," *Vice*, April 7, 2023, https://www.vice.com/en/article/z3mvd9/everything-i-learned-watching-george-santos-interminable-public-access-show.

7. "Special Episode: Evan Guests on Talking GOP w/ George Anthony Devolder Santos," *Empire State Conservatives Podcast*, January 29, 2020, 28:03, https://podcasts.apple.com/us/podcast/special-episode-evan-guests-on-talking-gop-w-george/id1441178646?i=1000464076314.

8. Andrew Silverstein, "Congressman-Elect George Santos Lied about Grandparents Fleeing Anti-Jewish Persecution during WWII," *The Forward*, December 21, 2022, https://forward.com/news/529130/george-santos-jewish-lie-genealogy-records/; Em Steck and Andrew Kaczynski, "Incoming Congressman's Claims His Grandparents Fled the Holocaust Contradicted by Genealogy Records," CNN, December 22, 2022, https://edition.cnn.com/2022/12/21/politics/george-santos-geneaology/index.html.

9. Matthew Kassel, "Brazilian Database Records, Historian Cast Doubt on Santos' Claims of Jewish Ancestry," *Jewish Insider,* December 21, 2022, https://jewishinsider.com/2022/12/george-santos-republican-congress-jewish-long-island-brazil-family/.

10. Errol A. Cockfield Jr., "Second-Generation Politics: After Watching His Father, Tom Suozzi Finds His Calling," *Newsday*, October 30, 2001.

11. Stephen Rodrick, "Tom Quixote," *New York*, April 11, 2019, https://nymag.com/news/politics/17665/.

12. "Problems at Northport VA," editorial, *Newsday*, September 1, 2016, https://www.newsday.com/opinion/editorials/problems-at-northport-va-b53203.

13. Paul LaRocco and David M. Schwartz, "The Grumman Plume: Decades of Deceit," *Newsday*, February 18, 2020, https://projects.newsday.com/long-island/plume-grumman-navy/.

14. "George Santos," *Sid & Friends in the Morning*, WABC, October 27, 2020, https://wabcradio.com/episode/george-santos-10-27-2020/.

15. "George Santos: A Corona Story," *Empire State Conservatives Podcast*.

16. Jesse O'Neill, "Did George Santos Lie about Being One of NY's First COVID Cases?," *New York Post*, January 11, 2023, https://nypost

.com/2023/01/11/how-lying-george-santos-changed-his-story-about-his-early-covid-19-case/.

17. Patrick Reilly, "George Santos Shares Photos to Back Up Sketchy Claims of Early COVID-19 Hospitalization: Report," *New York Post*, January 24, 2023, https://nypost.com/2023/01/24/george-santos-shares-photos-of-his-early-covid-19-hospitalization-to-back-up-sketchy-story-report/.

18. Kadia Goba, "George Santos Sent Us Some Photos of Him Sick with COVID," *Semafor*, January 24, 2023, https://www.semafor.com/article/01/23/2023/george-santos-sent-us-some-photos-of-him-sick-with-covid.

19. George Santos for Congress NY-3, "Hi everyone, in this video...," Facebook video, March 24, 2020, https://fb.watch/md1xgivdaE/.

20. "George Santos: A Corona Story," *Empire State Conservatives Podcast*.

21. Michael Ferrara, "Talking GOP Update," YouTube video, May 26, 2020, 4:13, https://www.youtube.com/watch?v=9uVEisI6b8M.

22. George Santos for Congress NY-3, "As a Covid19 survivor I understand," Facebook post, May 2, 2020.

23. Merlan, "Everything I Learned."

24. "George Santos," *Sid & Friends in the Morning*.

25. Myrto Pantazi, Mikhail Kissine, and Olivier Klein, "The Power of the Truth Bias: False Information Affects Memory and Judgment Even in the Absence of Distraction," *Social Cognition* 36, no. 2 (March 2018): 167–98, https://doi.org/10.1521/soco.2018.36.2.167.

26. Eugenio Garrido, Jaume Masip, and Carmen Herrero, "Police Officers' Credibility Judgments: Accuracy and Estimated Ability," *International Journal of Psychology* 39, no. 4 (August 2004): 254–75, https://doi.org/10.1080/00207590344000411.

27. Kyle Mattes, Valeriia Popova, and Jacqueline R. Evans, "Deception Detection in Politics: Can Voters Tell When Politicians Are Lying?," *Political Behavior* 45, no. 1 (March 2023): 395–418, https://doi.org/10.1007/s11109-021-09747-1.

28. Matthew Chayes, "Most Mayoral Candidates Back Rule Requiring New NYPD Cops to Live in NYC," *Newsday*, February 18, 2021, https://www.newsday.com/news/new-york/nypd-residency-requirement-nyc-mayoral-candidates-g83405.

29. Tom Brune, "George Santos Raised $265,000 for His Own 'Stop the Steal' Campaign," *Newsday*, March 11, 2023, https://www.newsday.com/long-island/politics/santos-trump-steal-congress-2020-suki5ik2.

30. Mark Chiusano, "Santos' 'Nice Check' for Capitol Rioters," *Newsday*, September 20, 2022, https://www.newsday.com/opinion/the-point/the-point-newsday-george-santos-lee-zeldin-raymond-j-dearie-capitol-rioters-o7kc32fw.

31. Brune, "George Santos Raised $265,000."

32. Jack Sirica, "Engel Has a Lesson in Ethics," *Newsday*, December 1, 1988.

33. George Santos for Congress NY-3, "Patriots the fight doesn't stop we must defend @KLoeffler seat!," Facebook video, November 21, 2020.

34. George Santos for Congress NY-3, "The highlight of my time in DC," Facebook video, Nov. 26, 2020.

35. Sherronna Bishop, "Immigrate to Be Free," *America's Mom with Sherronna Bishop*, podcast, 26.53, https://frankspeech.com/video/immigrate-be-free.

36. Petra Costa, director, *The Edge of Democracy*, Busca Vida Films, 2019, 2:01:00, https://www.imdb.com/title/tt6016744/.

## Chapter 8: The Coattail Candidate

1. George Santos for Congress NY-3, "Today I stood with parents wanting the ability…," Facebook post, January 31, 2022.

2. Mark Chiusano, "A Conversation with the First Vaccinated Nurse," *Newsday's Life Under Coronavirus*, podcast, December 2020, 10:25, https://open.spotify.com/episode/4EEGza86c9xbhwxO1mQ1WX?si=6if-DBiPS3GIC4a4sFjleg.

3. Ruy Castro, *Rio De Janeiro* (London: Bloomsbury, 2003), 178–79.

4. Denis Slattery, "New York Outlaws Religious Exemptions to Vaccination amid Epidemic National Measles Outbreak," *Daily News* (New York), June 13, 2019, https://www.nydailynews.com/news/politics/ny-vaccine-legislation-religious-exemptions-measles-outbreak-20190613-n7wudc2bcrdtbgdh624tabizzy-story.html.

5. Slattery.

6. Anya Kamenetz, "Want Your Kids to Opt Out of Standardized Tests?

The Constitution May Be with You," *Washington Post*, January 9, 2015, https://www.washingtonpost.com/opinions/want-your-kids-to-opt-out-of-standardized-tests-the-constitution-may-be-with-you/2015/01/09/bea151b4-973a-11e4-8005-1924ede3e54a_story.html.

7. Joie Tyrrell, "More than Half of Long Island's Students Opt Out of English Language Arts Testing," *Newsday*, May 10, 2021, https://www.newsday.com/long-island/education/op-out-exams-2021-english-ela-o93019.

8. George Anthony Devolder Santos, "Special Episode: Evan Guests on Talking GOP w/ George Anthony Devolder Santos," *Empire State Conservatives Podcast*, January 29, 2020, 28:03, https://podcasts.apple.com/us/podcast/special-episode-evan-guests-on-talking-gop-w-george/id1441178646?i=1000464076314.

9. Kate Anderson, "'It's Just Disgusting': Father of Antisemitic Attack Victim Rips Manhattan DA for Handling of Crime," *Daily Caller*, April 17, 2023, https://dailycaller.com/2023/04/17/disgusting-father-antisemitic-attack-victim-manhattan-da/.

10. James Barron, "Despite Fraud Conviction, Margiotta Remains a Political Power," *New York Times*, March 2, 1982, https://www.nytimes.com/1982/03/02/nyregion/despite-fraud-conviction-margiotta-remaims-a-political-power.html.

11. Marjorie Freeman Harrison, "Machine Politics Suburban Style: J. Russel Sprague and the Nassau County (N.Y.) Republican Party at Midcentury" (PhD diss., Columbia University, 2005), https://www.proquest.com/openview/27d49ec55404e0a9c3f5a22ea25d1dfc/1?pq-origsite=gscholar&cbl=18750&diss=y.

12. James Barron, "Despite Fraud Conviction, Margiotta Remains a Political Power."

13. John T. McQuiston, "Democrats Ask for Removal of G.O.P. Official," *New York Times*, May 2, 1995, https://www.nytimes.com/1995/05/02/nyregion/democrats-ask-for-removal-of-gop-official.html.

14. "George Santos," *Sid & Friends in the Morning*, 77 WABC, October 27, 2020, https://wabcradio.com/episode/george-santos-10-27-2020/.

15. Randi F. Marshall, "Santositis Hits Jericho School District Election," *Newsday*, May 16, 2023, https://www.newsday.com/opinion/the-point

/the-point-newsday-john-sarraf-jericho-school-board-george-santos
-todd-young-o7kc32fw.

16. George Santos for Congress NY-3, "We need help in #NewYork totalitarian....," Facebook video, December 12, 2020, https://fb.watch /md34G-kgEp/.

17. George Santos for Congress NY-3, "I feel like our entire country is stuck in a nightmare and can't wake up," Facebook post, February 21, 2022; George Santos for Congress NY-3, "Hochul in a mask alone in a cemetery," Facebook post, February 16, 2022.

18. "George Santos: A Corona Story," *Empire State Conservatives Podcast*, March 29, 2020, 1 hr., https://podcasts.apple.com/us/podcast/empire -state-conservatives-podcast/id1441178646?i=1000469913544.

19. George Santos for Congress NY-3, "I feel like our entire country is stuck in a nightmare and can't wake up."

20. George Santos for Congress NY-3, "'Don't say gay' is fiction!," Facebook post, April 16, 2022.

21. Half Hollow Hills Central School District, "Board of Education Meeting," Vimeo video, February 7, 2022, 1:25:25, https://livestream.com /accounts/8265235/events/10149571/videos/229194185.

22. George Santos for Congress NY-3, "Seen in Port Washington, NY today," Facebook post, February 9, 2022.

23. "Episode 286," *The Rory Sauter Show*, podcast, October 14, 2020, 2:30:22, https://radiopublic.com/the-rory-sauter-show-GAOKLn /s1!32b04.

24. George Santos for Congress NY-3, "Good morning to all except Kathy Hochul," Facebook post, January 26, 2022.

25. "Ep. 9/9/2020," *The Jiggy Jaguar Show*, podcast, August 31, 2020, 1:37:18, https://jiggyjaguar.com/ep-9-9-2020-the-jiggy-jaguar-show/.

26. "Episode 159," *Steak for Breakfast*, podcast, August 9, 2022, 3:07, https://podcasts.apple.com/us/podcast/episode-159 /id1498791684?i=1000575587664.

27. "Episode 276," *The Rory Sauter Show*, podcast, August 12, 2020, 2:22:00, https://www.blogtalkradio.com/therorysautershow/2020/08/12 /the-rory-sauter-show--episode-276.

28. Tom Brune, "George Santos Raised $265,000 for His Own 'Stop the Steal' Campaign," *Newsday*, March 11, 2023, https://www

.newsday.com/long-island/politics/santos-trump-steal-congress-
2020-suki5ik2.

29. Mark Chiusano, "Santos' 'Nice Check' for Capitol Rioters," *Newsday*,
September 20, 2022, https://www.newsday.com/opinion/the-point
/the-point-newsday-george-santos-lee-zeldin-raymond-j-dearie-capitol
-rioters-o7kc32fw.

30. Michael Kaplan, Scott MacFarlane, and Graham Kates, "Newly
obtained George Santos 'vulnerability report' spotted red flags long
before embattled Rep. was elected," CBS, September 6, 2023, https:
//www.cbsnews.com/news/george-santos-vulnerability-report-red
-flags-long-before-embattled-rep-was-elected/.

31. Nicholas Spangler, "Southern Poverty Law Center Lists 2 LI Groups
as Anti-Government," *Newsday*, May 2, 2022, https://www.newsday
.com/long-island/southern-poverty-law-center-report-ve8h0ryt.

32. "Capitol Under Siege," editorial, *Newsday,* January 6, 2021, https:
//www.newsday.com/opinion/newsday-opinion-the-point-newsletter
-w04758.

## Chapter 9: *The Producers*, Part 2

1. Scott Eidler and Anastasia Valeeva, "George Santos Far Outspent Other
Successful LI GOP Congressional Hopefuls for Food, Out-of-State
Travel," *Newsday*, December 30, 2022, https://www.newsday.com
/long-island/nassau/george-santos-campaign-spending-food-travel-steve
-israel-rick-lazio-anthony-desposito-nick-lalota-pete-king-vky1hoee.

2. "Episode 292," *The Rory Sauter Show*, podcast, December 23, 2020,
2:32:07, https://radiopublic.com/the-rory-sauter-show-GAOKLn
/s1!46ec4.

3. William Bredderman, "George Santos Took Donation from Migrant Smug-
gler Rocco Oppedisano," *Daily Beast*, January 11, 2023, https://www
.thedailybeast.com/george-santos-took-donation-from-migrant-smuggler
-rocco-oppedisano.

4. Alexander Sammon, "I Ate at the Italian Restaurant Where George
Santos Is Often, for Some Reason, Spending Exactly $199.99," *Slate*,
January 13, 2023, https://slate.com/news-and-politics/2023/01
/george-santos-il-bacco-campaign-spending-new-york.html.

5. Jonathan O'Connell, Isaac Stanley-Becker, Emma Brown, and Samuel

Oakford, "'I Felt Like We Were in *Goodfellas*'": How George Santos Wooed Investors for Alleged Ponzi Scheme," *Washington Post*, January 23, 2023, https://www.washingtonpost.com/investigations/2023/01/25/george-santos-ponzi-scheme-harbor-city/.

6. *Campaign Legal Center v. George Anthony Devolder-Santos*, Complaint Before the Federal Election Commission (2023), https://www.washingtonpost.com/documents/a523f2ca-d484-48d1-a0fc-79f0acd03fb8.pdf.

7. Jessica Piper, "The Improbability of George Santos' $199 Expenses," *Politico*, January 25, 2023, https://www.politico.com/news/2023/01/25/george-santos-199-expenses-00079334.

8. Eidler and Valeeva, "George Santos Far Outspent."

9. Grace Ashford and Dana Rubinstein, "How George Santos's Campaign Spent Its Funds: Rent, Flights and Hotels," *New York Times*, December 29, 2022, https://www.nytimes.com/2022/12/29/nyregion/george-santos-campaign-finance.html.

10. Scott Eidler, Paul LaRocco, and Candice Ferrette, "How George Santos Benefited from Sister's Rise NY PAC," *Newsday*, February 4, 2023, https://www.newsday.com/long-island/politics/rise-ny-pac-santos-rgmtkqvv.

11. Joseph Morton and Rebekah Alvey, "Van Duyne Says Santos-Related Cash Never Arrived," *Dallas Morning News*, April 17, 2023, https://www.dallasnews.com/news/politics/2023/04/17/van-duyne-camp-says-cash-from-joint-fundraising-committee-with-george-santos-never-arrived/.

12. Grace Ashford and Nicholas Fandos, "The Obscure GOP Bookkeeper at the Center of the George Santos Mess," *New York Times*, April 21, 2023, https://www.nytimes.com/2023/04/21/nyregion/nancy-marks-santos-treasurer.html.

13. Peter Marks, "Stand by Pete," GoFundMe page, August 3, 2018, https://www.gofundme.com/f/stand-by-pete.

14. Michael Gormley, "Santos Controversy: How Nancy Marks Became a Top GOP Campaign Adviser," *Newsday*, February 11, 2023, https://www.newsday.com/long-island/politics/nancy-marks-george-santos-republican-campaigns-fec-elections-treasurer-f0i1m1ra.

15. Robert E. Kessler, "Former Suffolk Legislator Fred Towle Jr. Sentenced to Supervised Release," *Newsday*, January 15, 2020, https://www.newsday.com/long-island/crime/fred-towle-corruption-prison-m05317.

16. Sandra Peddie, "Edward Walsh's Political Machine Influences Judge Picks," *Newsday*, March 12, 2016, https://www.newsday.com/long -island/politics/edward-walsh-s-political-machine-influences-judge -picks-c59874.

17. *Peter Zinno vs. Nancy Marks, Complaint of Peter Zinno*, 2014.

18. Ashford and Fandos, "The Obscure GOP Bookkeeper."

19. Isaac Stanley-Becker and Emma Brown, "George Santos Was Paid for Work at Company Accused of Ponzi Scheme Later than Previously Known," *Washington Post*, January 11, 2023, https://www.washington post.com/investigations/2023/01/11/george-santos-harbor-city -capital/.

20. William Bredderman, "George Santos Didn't Just Bilk Donors— GOPers Say He Conned Them Too," *Daily Beast*, May 18, 2023, https://www.thedailybeast.com/republicans-say-george-santos-lied -and-scammed-them-through-his-company-redstone-strategies.

21. Bredderman.

22. Kelli DeSantis, "Know Your Candidates: Jordan Hafizi, Volunteer, Writer, Running for Mid-Island City Council Seat," *SILive*, June 1, 2021, https://www.silive.com/politics/2021/05/know-your-candidates -jordan-hafizi-volunteer-writer-running-for-mid-island-city-council -seat.html.

23. Bredderman, "George Santos Didn't Just Bilk Donors—GOPers Say He Conned Them Too."

24. *United States of America v. George Anthony Devolder-Santos*, indict- ment, (2023); *Campaign Legal Center v. George Anthony Devolder- Santos*, Complaint Before the Federal Election Commission (2023), https://www.justice.gov/d9/2023-05/santos.indictment.pdf.

25. Rebecca Davis O'Brien and Michael Gold, "The George Santos In- dictment, Annotated," *New York Times*, May 10, 2023, https://www .nytimes.com/interactive/2023/05/10/nyregion/santos-indictment -annotated.html.

## Chapter 10: The Perfect-Storm Election

1. "George Santos: A Corona Story," *Empire State Conservatives Podcast*, March 29, 2020, 1 hr., https://podcasts.apple.com/us/podcast/empire -state-conservatives-podcast/id1441178646?i=1000469913544.

2. "Nassau County Police: Texts, Tweets Being Investigated in Nassau County Executive's Sexting Scandal," CBS News, February 14, 2016, https://www.cbsnews.com/newyork/news/nassau-county-sexting-scandal/.

3. Mark Harrington, "Karin Murphy Caro Files Federal Suit against Suffolk County, Spota," *Newsday*, January 5, 2017, https://www.newsday.com/long-island/suffolk/karin-murphy-caro-files-federal-suit-against-suffolk-county-spota-i33089.

4. Reuven Fenton and Bruce Golding, "My Wife Was Having an Affair—But Not with Nassau Exec," *New York Post*, February 15, 2016, https://nypost.com/2016/02/15/woman-accused-in-nassau-sext-scandal-divorcing-her-husband/.

5. Mark Chiusano, "Robert Mercer Is the Billionaire Next Door for Long Island Activists," *Newsday*, October 22, 2017, https://www.newsday.com/news/robert-mercer-is-the-billionaire-next-door-for-long-island-activists-x77102.

6. Nicholas Fandos, "Santos's Lies Were Known to Some Well-Connected Republicans," *New York Times*, January 13, 2023, https://www.nytimes.com/2023/01/13/nyregion/george-santos-republicans-lies.html.

7. Jacob Kornbluh, "Document Reveals Santos Boasted of Being 'Proud American Jew' during Campaign," *The Forward*, December 27, 2022, https://forward.com/fast-forward/529798/george-santos-jewish-american-republican-congress/.

8. Matthew Kassel, "Meet the Next Jewish Republican Congressman from Long Island," *Jewish Insider*, December 24, 2022, https://jewishinsider.com/2022/11/george-santos-long-island-queens-congress-midterms/.

9. Greg Owen, "Out Dem. Robert Zimmerman Wants to Be a Warrior for LGBTQ Rights in Congress," *LGBTQ Nation*, October 13, 2022, https://www.lgbtqnation.com/2022/10/dem-robert-zimmerman-wants-warrior-lgbtq-rights-congress/.

10. "George Santos (NY-03) Research Report," DCCC Research Department, July 2022, https://dccc.org/wp-content/uploads/2022/08/George-Santos-Research-Book.pdf.

11. Shira Toeplitz, "An Inside Look at the DCCC Research Department,"

*Roll Call*, April 20, 2012, https://rollcall.com/2012/04/20/an-inside-look-at-the-dccc-research-department/.

12. "The Case against George Santos," press release, Democratic Congressional Campaign Committee, August 24, 2022, https://dccc.org/the-case-against-george-santos/.

13. Frank Newport, "Abortion Moves Up on 'Most Important Problem' List," Gallup, August 1, 2022, https://news.gallup.com/poll/395408/abortion-moves-important-problem-list.aspx.

14. A brief sample of the pre-election Santos coverage: Maureen Daly, "Santos Filings Now Claim Net Worth of $11 Million," *North Shore Leader*, n.d., https://www.theleaderonline.com/single-post/santos-filings-now-claim-net-worth-of-11-million; William Bredderman, "George Devolder-Santos, MAGA House Candidate in New York, Haunted by Gig at Alleged Ponzi Scheme," *Daily Beast*, April 1, 2022, https://www.thedailybeast.com/george-devolder-santos-maga-house-candidate-in-new-york-haunted-by-gig-at-alleged-ponzi-scheme; Mark Chiusano, "For Santos, It's Not Over Yet," *Newsday*, December 11, 2020, https://www.newsday.com/opinion/newsday-opinion-the-point-newsletter-c36114; Chiusano, "Change of Address," *Newsday*, March 14, 2022, https://www.newsday.com/opinion/newsday-opinion-point-newsletter-w22146.

15. NSTV Long Island, "LOWV-US Congress 3 Debate—George A.D. Santos / Robert P. Zimmerman," YouTube video, October 21, 2022, 55:34, https://www.youtube.com/watch?v=dtXh1PI4UnQ&lc.

16. Marcia Kramer, "The Point: Democrat Robert Zimmerman, Republican George Santos Battle It Out to Replace Retiring Rep. Tom Suozzi," October 23, 2022, fifth video clip, 04:08, https://www.cbsnews.com/newyork/news/the-point-democrat-robert-zimmerman-republican-george-santos-battle-it-out-to-replace-retiring-rep-tom-suozzi/.

17. Matthew Kassel, "George Santos Claimed to Be 'Halachically Jewish' during Election Campaign," *Jewish Insider*, February 14, 2023, https://jewishinsider.com/2023/02/george-santos-jewish-election-campaign-israel-south-florida/.

## Chapter 11: Keep Posting

1. Grace Ashford and Michael Gold, "Who Is Rep.-Elect George Santos? His Résumé May Be Largely Fiction," *New York Times*, December

19, 2022, https://www.nytimes.com/2022/12/19/nyregion/george-santos-ny-republicans.html.

2. Grace Ashford and Michael Gold, "George Santos Admits to Lying About College and Work History," *New York Times*, December 26, 2022, https://www.nytimes.com/2022/12/26/nyregion/george-santos-interview.html.

3. Matt Young, "What Mitt Romney Really Said to George Santos at the SOTU," *Daily Beast*, February 7, 2023, https://www.thedailybeast.com/what-mitt-romney-really-said-to-george-santos-at-the-sotu.

4. Ellie Quinlan Houghtaling, "GOP Can't Decide on What to Do with Rep. George Santos' Tenure," *Daily Beast*, January 8, 2023, https://www.thedailybeast.com/gop-cant-decide-on-what-to-do-with-rep-george-santos-tenure.

5. Shayna Jacobs, "Aide for Rep. George Santos Accused of Defrauding Donors," *Washington Post*, August 16, 2023, https://www.washingtonpost.com/national-security/2023/08/16/santos-aide-miele-mccarthy-impersonate/.

6. Daniel Boguslaw, "One Night in Washington, D.C., with George Santos," *The Intercept*, April 27, 2023, https://theintercept.com/2023/04/27/george-santos-young-republicans/.

7. "Erase Racism NY and George Santos," *This Week's Long Island News*, podcast, June 4, 2022, 59:00, https://podcasts.apple.com/us/podcast/this-weeks-long-island-news/id1217015430?i=1000565205210.

8. Ian Mohr, "Rep. George Santos Touts Dramatic Ozempic Weight Loss at Bash, Source Says," *New York Post*, August 23, 2023, https://pagesix.com/2023/08/23/rep-george-santos-touts-dramatic-ozempic-weight-loss-at-bash-source-says/?utm_campaign=iphone_nyp&utm_source=com.facebook.Messenger.ShareExtension&fbclid=IwAR2ZNwzZeb0-rvTvy1qjXKZXwKscggUC0qcWQ5IAvIoePmjnwHW5MWSqu9s_aem_AWthnSqNpqFMsYjU9wrNohcJoFCnFciU3-3BDYY1wU1HUDWuwngF5RKScnvoxBfDxnQ.

9. Jimmy Breslin, *Can't Anybody Here Play This Game?* (New York: Viking, 1963).

10. Shawn McCreesh, "George Santos, MAGA 'It' Girl," *New York*, March 2, 2023, https://nymag.com/intelligencer/2023/03/the-plan-for-george-santos-magas-newest-it-girl.html.

11. Martin Pengelly, "Republican Fabulist George Santos Compares Himself to Rosa Parks," *The Guardian*, July 10, 2023, https://www.theguardian.com/us-news/2023/jul/10/republican-george-santos-rosa-parks.

12. Hunter Walker, "Meet the Man behind George Santos," *TPM*, January 31, 2023, https://talkingpointsmemo.com/news/vish-burra-george-santos.

13. McCreesh, "George Santos, MAGA 'It' Girl."

14. Jacqueline Sweet and David Corn, "George Santos' Lawyer Was Part of the January 6 Mob," *Mother Jones*, June 8, 2023, https://www.motherjones.com/politics/2023/06/george-santos-lawyer-joseph-murray-january-6-capitol-insurrection/.

## Epilogue

1. Gersh Kuntzman, "'88 Sex Offense Plagues L.I. Pol," *New York Post*, August 28, 2003, https://nypost.com/2003/08/28/88-sex-offense-plagues-l-i-pol/.

2. Lauren E. Hill, "Out from under the Rock: Riverhead Town Supervisor Candidate Confronts His Past," *Long Island Press*, https://web.archive.org/web/20040911153619/http://www.longislandpress.com/v01/i31030814/coverstory_02.asp.

3. Doris Kearns Goodwin, *Lyndon Johnson and the American Dream* (New York: St. Martin's Press, 1991).

4. Robert A. Caro, "The Secrets of Lyndon Johnson's Archives," *The New Yorker*, January 21, 2019, https://www.newyorker.com/magazine/2019/01/28/the-secrets-of-lyndon-johnsons-archives.

5. Global Research, "Harbor City Capital Corp. Announces Opening of New York City Office to be Fully Operational," YouTube video, June 1, 2020, 1:01, https://www.youtube.com/watch?v=4Dl_zr7xp1M.

6. Brian Fung, "FTC Chair Lina Khan Warns AI Could 'Turbocharge' Fraud and Scams," CNN, April 18, 2023, https://edition.cnn.com/2023/04/18/tech/lina-khan-ai-warning/index.html.

7. "New FTC Data Show Consumers Reported Losing Nearly $8.8 Billion to Scams in 2022," press release, Federal Trade Commission, February 23, 2023, https://www.ftc.gov/news-events/news/press-releases/2023/02/new-ftc-data-show-consumers-reported-losing-nearly-88-billion-scams-2022.

8. Brandy Zadrozny, "The Conspiracy Candidate: What RFK Jr.'s Anti-Vaccine Crusade Could Look Like in the White House," NBC News, June 19, 2023, https://www.nbcnews.com/politics/2024-election/rfk-jr-anti-vaccine-push-white-house-rcna89470.

9. Max Chafkin, *The Contrarian: Peter Thiel and Silicon Valley's Pursuit of Power* (New York: Penguin Press, 2021).

10. Phil Williams, "'My Body of Work Speaks for Itself,' Tennessee Andy Ogles Says in Response to Inflated Résumé Claims," News Channel 5 Nashville (WTVF), February 21, 2023, https://www.newschannel5.com/news/newschannel-5-investigates/my-body-of-work-speaks-for-itself-tennessee-andy-ogles-says-in-response-to-inflated-resume-claims.

11. Isabella Simonetti, "Over 360 Newspapers Have Closed since Just before the Start of the Pandemic," *New York Times*, June 29, 2022, https://www.nytimes.com/2022/06/29/business/media/local-newspapers-pandemic.html.

12. Kyle Mattes, Valeriia Popova, and Jacqueline R. Evans, "Deception Detection in Politics: Can Voters Tell When Politicians Are Lying?," *Political Behavior* 45, no. 1 (March 2023): 395–418. https://doi:10.1007/s11109-021-09747-1.

# Index

Abagnale, Frank, 107
abortion, 15, 199–200, 202–3, 206
Acevedo, Socrates, 73
Adams, Eric, 66
Alabama Securities Commission, 100
Almeida, Orlando, 38
Alvino, Tracey, 188, 189, 209
Amazon, 109
America First Warehouse, 162–63
*America's Mom* podcast, 136
Andrade, Mário de, 17
antivax movement, 144–46, 234
*Apprentice* (TV show), 108
Ariola, Joann, 122–23
Ashford, Grace, 213
ATM banking machine scam, 93
Autism Action Network, 145

"bail reform," 150–52, 157–60, 164
Bankman-Fried, Sam, 198
Bannon, Steve, 224, 235

Baruch College, 128, 155, 200, 215
Belfort, Jordan, 111
Benoit, Jayson, 183
Bernstein, Carl, 207
Bethpage Plume, 120
Biden, Hunter, 225
Biden, Joe
    Kinnock controversy and, 232
    State of the Union (2023),
        216–17
    2020 election of, 132
    2022 midterm elections and,
        197, 199, 203
bingo, 49–53
Black Lives Matter movement,
    109, 160–61
Blue Lives Matter movement,
    130–31
Boebert, Lauren, xxiii
Boehner, John, 217
Bogosian, Tiffany, 18–19, 31, 167
Boll, Mike, 85
Bolsonaro, Jair, 40, 43–44
Bond, Michelle, 163
brain cancer claim, 183

Bratton, Bill, 203
Brazil, lifestyle in. *see* Santos,
    George, Brazil lifestyle
Brennan, John, 163
Breslin, Jimmy, 223
Brooks, Mel, 132
Burra, Vish, 218, 224–25, 227
Bushnell, Candace, 195

Cairo, Joe, 92, 154, 155–57,
    214–15
campaign finance (Santos),
    165–85
  bookkeeping and, 133–34
  donations by Santos to other
    campaigns, 156, 170
  ECM Marketing/ECM
    Consulting and Marketing
    Inc., 178–79
  expenses incurred during 2022
    campaign, 165–70
  fundraising and Long Island
    political climate, 139–40
  fundraising consultants' pay,
    168
  Marks, campaign treasurer,
    business practices of, 170–75
  Marks-Santos dispute, 183–85
  Marks's lawsuits, 176–78
  Redstone Strategies LLC and,
    183–85
  Red Strategies USA and,
    180–83
  "$199.99 trick," 168
campaign issues (Santos)
  abortion, 15, 199–200, 202–3,
    206
  "bail reform," 150–52, 157–60,
    164
  climate change, 207–8

COVID, 124–26, 137, 141–47,
    159–61, 163, 233–34
Campaign Strategy & Consulting,
    187–91, 209–10
Campaigns Unlimited, 175
Carlson, Tucker, 235
*Carnivals, Rogues, and Heroes*
    (DaMatta), 48
Caro, Robert, 232
*Catch Me If You Can* (Abagnale),
    107
CBS2, 189, 208
Cervas, Jonathan, 193
Chafkin, Max, 235
Chiusano, Mark, xiv–xvi, 218
Choolfaian, Teodora, 139–42, 160
Cleaner 123, 169, 170
Clinton, Hillary, 196
Club 117 (Rio, Brazil), 46
Coacci, Thiago, 40, 41
Cohen, Michael, 101
Congress, US. *see also* 2020
    Congressional campaign;
    2022 Congressional campaign
Congressional Baseball Game
    for Charity (2023), 239
MINAJ Act proposed by Santos,
    233–34
new-member orientation,
    134–37
Problem Solvers Caucus,
    117–18, 122
Santos's swearing in by, 215
scammers in history of, 95
Conservative Party (New York),
    175
Conservative Political Action
    Conference (2020), 124
conspiracy theories, 218–20,
    233–35

# INDEX

*The Contrarian* (Chafkin), 235
Cornicelli, Robert, 182, 184
COVID
    antivax movement, 144–46,
        233–34
    Long Island political climate
        and response to, 141–47
    Santos's initial seriousness
        about, 124–26, 137
    Santos's reversed position on,
        159–61, 163
    Trump on, 126, 134
Crist, Charlie, 135
cryptocurrency trade, 163–64
Cunningham, Randy, 95
Cuomo, Andrew M., 143–44, 159,
    204
Cutrone, Jack, 189
Cyrus, Miley, 107

*Daily Beast* website, 166, 183, 205
D'Amato, Al, 154
DaMatta, Roberto, 48
De Blasio, Bill, 130
decision to enter politics (Santos)
    Devolder Organization and,
        102–5
    early interest in politics, 91–96,
        106–11
    Harbor City job and, 96–104,
        111
delusional behavior, politics and,
    106
Delvey, Anna, xxiii, 107, 227
Democratic Party. *see also* Suozzi,
        Tom; Zimmerman, Robert
    Democratic Congressional
        Campaign Committee, 123,
        148–50, 198–202
    opposition research, 198–203

DeSantis, Ron, 160
Deutermann, Jeanette, 147
Devolder, Anthony
        (George Santos), 20, 45
Devolder, Fatima
        (Santos's mother)
    bingo and gambling by, 49–53
    church of, 26–28
    death and funeral of, 27–28, 93
    financial support for family's
        lifestyle, Brazil, 47–55
    Queens lifestyle of, 59, 61, 63,
        65, 73
    son's childhood and, 16–17
    son's claim about 9/11/Wall
        Street career, 23–24, 69
    on son's lying, xviii, 69
    son's relationship with, 17,
        22–29
    work of, 16, 22, 25, 65–66,
        98
Devolder Organization, 102–5
Devolder Santos for Congress
        Recount committee, 133–37
Didion, Joan, 136
Dish Network, 1–13
dog hustles. *see* Friends of Pets
        United (FOPU)
Donnelly, Anne, 151
Dos Patins, Isabelita (drag queen),
    37–38, 40
Dowling, Michael, 143
drag performers, 37–38, 40,
    45–47

East Coast Marketing, 179
ECM Consulting and Marketing
        Inc., 179
ECM Marketing, 178
Elma (aunt), 17, 21–22, 30, 64

Elmhurst Hospital (Queens, New York), 16, 124
Engel, Eliot, 134
Epstein, Jeffrey, 161, 220
ESPN, 224

*The Fabulist* (Chiusano), xiv–xvi, 218
fact-checking, importance of, 236–37
Fallon, Jimmy, 220
Farley, Chele, 115
Federal Election Commission, 133
Federal Trade Commission, US, 233
Fitzgerald, F. Scott, xxiii
Florio, Mike, 127, 134–35
Floyd, George, 130, 151, 160
Flynn, Michael, 182, 184
Foley, Neil, 172
Forte, Stefano, 92, 183
Forte, Tina, 180
Four Seasons Total Landscaping (Philadelphia), 132
Fox Business, 124
Frankel, Bethenny, 107–8
Friends of Pets United (FOPU), 75–87
  dog breeding scams, 75–78
  lack of IRS documentation, 200
  vet bill scam, 78–87, 238–39
FTX, 163–64

Gabbard, Glen O., xxiii
Gavilla, Hector, xxvii–xxviii
Gillibrand, Kirsten, 115
Gilmore, John, 145–47, 234
Giuliani, Rudy, 23, 132, 225
Globo network, 17, 34, 60, 69
GoFundMe campaigns, 84, 86, 101, 173

Gold, Michael, 213
Goldberg, Isaac, 197
Goldman Sachs, 60, 92
Goldwater, Barry, xxv
Gomez, Selena, 107
Gonzales, Tony, 217
Goodman, Charles, 25
Goodwin, Doris Kearns, 232
Gosar, Paul, xxiii, 217
*Gothamist* website, 70
Greene, Marjorie Taylor, xxiii, 217, 218
Grumman, 120

Häagen-Dazs story, 208–9
Hafizi, Jordan, 180–82
Hall, KrisAnne, 149
Hampton, David, 107
Harbor City and Harbor City Capital, 96–104, 111, 180, 199, 233
Harris, Kamala, 159
Harrison, Marjorie Freeman, 153
Harvard, 61
Head of the Harbor, 190–91
Hilton, Paris, 107
Hochul, Kathy, 157, 159, 161, 203, 204, 206, 210
Holmes, Elizabeth, xxiii, 107
Holtz, Lou, 155
Hombres (New York City bar), 58
Horace Mann (NYC private school), 20–21
*The Hour of the Star* (Lispector), 36
Hurdas, Barbara, 2, 4, 10, 11

Il Bacco Ristorante, 166–68, 210–11
imposter cons, 233

Industry (New York City bar), 57

Intrater, Andrew, 101–2, 103, 185

iPad scheme, 70, 101

Isabelita dos Patins (drag queen), 37–38, 40

Israel, Steve, 123–24, 148–50, 207

Jacqueline (cousin), 72

Jeffries, Hakeem, 210, 222

Jennings, Ken, 224

*Jeopardy!* (TV show), 224

Jewish heritage claims, 11, 116, 193–94, 209, 221

*Jewish Insider* website, 193–94

Johnson, Lyndon B., 232

Jones, Alex, 235

Jones, David, 24

Jones, Leslie, 224

Jones, Steve, 24

Jordan (ex-boyfriend), 62

Kabas, Marisa, xxv, 36

Kaplan, Michael, 152

*Kaplan & Sadock's Synopsis of Psychiatry*, xxvi

Kappel, Brett, 167

Kearns, Doris, 232

Kennedy, Robert F., Jr., 234

Khan, Lina, 233

King, Pete, 197, 216

Kinnock, Neil, 232

Kinzinger, Adam, 215

Kitara Ravache (Santos's drag name), 38–39

Knights of Columbus, 236

Koifman, Fábio, 116

Kramer, Marcia, 208

Kumar, Ajit, 99

Lady Gaga, 107

Lafayette, Marquis de, 134

Lally, Grant, 117, 122–23, 125, 130

Lauder, Ron, 204

LaValle, John Jay, 171

LaValle, Kenneth, 171

Lazio, Rick, 168

League of Women Voters, 207, 236

Leandro (boyfriend), 71

legal cases against Santos
    check fraud case (Brazil), 53–55, 200
    federal indictment (May 2023), xxi, 185, 224–27

Lewandowski, Corey, 115

LGBT Network, 197

LGBTQ
    drag performers, 37–38, 40, 45–47
    gay pride parade in Niterói, Brazil, 33–39, 42, 45
    LGBTQ rights in Brazil, 40–43
    Santos and "Gays for Trump" sign, 108
    Zimmerman's candidacy and, 196–97

Liberty Education Forum, 169

Lincoln, Abraham, 208

Lincoln Dinner events, 115, 236

Lindsay, Sandra, 143

Ling, Daisy, 2

LinkBridge Investors, 97

Lino, Wellington, 59, 60, 70

Lipsky, Dave, 163

Lipsky, Gabrielle, 163

Lispector, Clarice, 36

Loeffler, Kelly, 135

Long Island Loud Majority, 163

*Long Island Patriots Radio*
(WRCN), 189
Long Island political climate,
139–64
"bail reform" and, 150–52,
157–60, 164
COVID backlash and, 141–47,
159–61, 163
fundraising and, 139–40, 156
Nassau County Republican
Party and, 152–58
New York gubernatorial race
(2022) and, 157–59, 161,
193
population profile and, 147–50
Santos's campaign rhetoric and,
139–40, 159–64
Lula (Luiz Inácio Lula da Silva),
41, 44, 136
lying
Congress scammers, historical
accounts, 95
conspiracy theories and, 218–
20, 233–35
delusional behavior and politics,
106
escalating problem of, 238–39
fact-checking for, 236–37
humility and, 230–31
imposter cons, 233
Internet and humility and,
230–31
*Kaplan & Sadock's Synopsis of
Psychiatry*, xxvi
political parties' responsibility
and, 237–38
pseudologia fantastica, xxvi
by Santos, overview, xvii–xxvii
Santos and, overview, xvii–xxvii
by small-time hustlers, 229–30

speed of uncovering lies via
Internet, 232
truth bias and, 128–29
*Lyndon Johnson and the
American Dream* (Kearns),
232

*Macunaíma* (Andrade), 17
Mangano, Ed, 189
Margiotta, Joseph, 152, 153
Marks, Nancy, 133
business practices of, 170–75
ECM Marketing/ECM
Consulting and Marketing
Inc., 178–79
lawsuits against, 176–78
Redstone Strategies LLC and,
183–85
Red Strategies USA and,
180–83
Santos in dispute with, 183–85
Marks, Peter, 173
Maroney, J. P., 96, 98–100
marriage
Santos on marriage ambition,
35
Santos's advice to friends about,
67–68
Santos's marriage to Uadla,
10–12, 68
Marvel Comics, 25
Mayorkas, Alejandro, 223
McCarthy, Kevin, 135, 217
McCreesh, Shawn, 223
McInerney, Jay, 195
McMahon, Linda, 155
Melville, Herman, xxiii
Mercer, Rebekah, 190–91
Mercer, Robert, 190
Minaj, Nicki, 234

MINAJ Act, 234
Mondello, Joe, 195
Monroe, Marilyn, 208
Morey-Parker, Greg, 57–63, 65, 68–69, 71–73, 94
Morgan, Piers, 20
Mo's Bagels & Deli, 209
MS-13, 149–50
Mueller, Robert S., III, 101
Murphy, Karin, 187–91, 209–10
Murray, Joe, 226
Musk, Elon, 218, 235

*Namaste* (yacht), 103–4
NASA, 120
Nassau County Republican Party, 92
Nassau GOP, 92, 152–58, 237
Nassau Off-Track Betting, 195
New Jersey Veterans Network, 85
*Newsday* (Long Island, New York), 118, 125, 168, 175, 205
news media
 fact-checking importance for, 236–37
 newspaper closings, since 2005, 236
 social media as news source, 164
New York, lifestyle in. *see* Queens, New York
*New Yorker* magazine, 224
*New York Post*, 189
New York (state). *see also* Hochul, Kathy
 "bail reform," 150–52, 157–60, 164
 Cuomo on COVID, 143–44, 159

gubernatorial race (2022), 157–59, 161
New York Third Congressional District. *see* Third Congressional District (New York)
*New York Times,* 102, 103–4, 172, 183, 213–15
9/11 terrorist attacks, 23–24, 148
Niterói, Brazil
 beauty pageant rumor, 37–38
 gay pride parade, 33–39, 42, 45
 government programs of, 48
 Santos's mother's address listed as, 24
 Santos's shopping in, 54
Nixon, Richard, 106, 218
Northport VA hospital, 120
*North Shore Leader* newspaper, 117, 130, 205
North Shore Towers, 119, 121–22, 127, 137
Northwell hospital network, 143
NYU, 60, 69, 92, 200

Obama, Barack, 106, 108, 119, 149
Ocasio-Cortez, Alexandria (AOC), 109, 130, 180, 188, 217
Occupy movement, 109
Ogles, Andy, 235
Oliveira, Pablo, 97
O'Nair, Deb, 79
Oppedisano, Joe, 166
Oppedisano, Rocco, 166
Oppedisano, Tina, 166
opposition research, 198–203
Osthoff, Rich, 78–87, 238–39

Page, Elliot, 43
Parizzi, Adriana, 28, 49–53, 55, 67–68, 71, 72
Parks, Rosa, 223
Pataki, George, 204
Pedro (boyfriend), 68, 71
Pelosi, Nancy, 206
pet hustles. *see* Friends of Pets United (FOPU)
Poitier, Sidney, 107
*Political Fictions* (Didion), 136
Ponzi scheme, SEC on Harbor City as, 98–100, 102
Posobiec, Jack, 218
post-election revelations (Santos), 213–27
  conspiracy theorists on, 218–20
  federal indictment (May 2023) of Santos, 224–27
  negative publicity and Santos's response, 213–15, 220–21
  *New York Times* article on, 213
  public fascination with, 222–24
  Republican Party's reaction to, 215–18
Prince (friend), 58
Problem Solvers Caucus, 117–18, 122
*Producers* (Brooks), 132
Proud Boys, 110
pseudologia fantastica, xxvi
*The Psychology of the Sopranos* (Gabbard), xxiii
public opinion. *see* post-election revelations (Santos)
Putin, Vladimir, 139

QAnon, 219
Queens, New York, 57–73
  Amazon HQ project, 109

Republican Party of, 110, 156
Santos's apartment evictions, 70–72
Santos's childhood and early life in, 16–20, 22–31
Santos's evictions, 61, 70, 192, 200
Santos's home address, 2020 campaign, 127
Santos's lifestyle in, 57–59, 66–69
Santos's roommate churn, 59–60, 64
Santos's roommates, stealing from, 62–63, 69–73

Rabello, Yasser, 59–60, 63–65, 68–69, 71
Ravache, Kitara (Santos's drag name), 38–39
Ravitch, Richard, 207
Reagan, Ronald, 106, 153
Redstone Strategies LLC, 183–85
Red Strategies USA, 180–82, 183
Republican Party. *see also* Long Island political climate; Santos, George, political career; Trump, Donald
  on COVID, 126
  Lincoln Dinner events, 115, 236
  Nassau County, 92
  on post-election revelations about Santos, 215–18
  Queens Village Republican Club, 110
  Whitestone Republican Club, 146, 166
Rijo, John, 2–3, 12
Rise NY, 169

Ritchie, Marcia, 3–4, 6–7, 13
Rochard, Eula, 35–43, 45–47, 51
Rockefeller, Nelson, 204
*Roll Call* publication, 201
Romney, Mitt, 78, 216, 219, 220, 222
Ronald Reagan Republican Club, xix–xx, xxvii–xxviii
Roosevelt, Eleanor, 208
RuPaul, 220–21
Russia-Ukraine war, 139, 161

Saint Rita's (Queens, New York), 26–28, 44
Salabert, Duda, 40
Salame, Ryan, 163–64
Santos, Gabriela, 20
Santos, George. *see also* Santos, George, early life; Santos, George, names of; Santos, George, political career
  ambition of, xix
  anger and threats by, 19, 23, 72
  check fraud case (Brazil), 53–55, 200
  cosmetic procedures/weight loss of, xvii–xviii, 188, 220
  on *The Fabulist* (Chiusano), xiv–xvi
  federal indictment of, xxi, 185, 224–27
  lying by, xvii–xxviii
  marriage of, 10–12, 68
  rise of, xxii–xxiii
  sexual orientation of, 10–11, 18–19
Santos, George, Brazil lifestyle, 33–55
  Bolsonaro's rise and, 43–45

  Brazil birthplace claim, 11
  drag performers and, 37–38, 40, 45–47
  financial support for family's lifestyle, 47–55
  gay pride parade in Niterói, Brazil, 33–39, 42, 45
  lawyer to Santos, 96
  LGBTQ rights in Brazil, 40–43
  Parizzi and Devolder Santos family, 49–53, 55
  *transformistas,* 40
Santos, George, childhood and family, 15–31. *see also* Devolder, Fatima
  birthplace, Queens, 16
  father's relationship with, 28–31
  mother's relationship with, 17, 22–25
  Queens upbringing of, 16–20, 22–31
  stealing allegations, 21–22, 25, 27–28, 31
Santos, George, early life, 1–87. *see also* Friends of Pets United (FOPU); Queens, New York; Santos, George, Brazil lifestyle; Santos, George, childhood and family; Santos, George, heritage and background claims
  Brazil lifestyle of, 33–55
  childhood and family, 15–31
  Dish Network job, 1–13
  Friends of Pets United (FOPU), 75–87
  Queens, New York lifestyle of, 57–87

Santos, George, heritage and
  background claims
Black father, 115
Brazil as birthplace, 11
education, 20–21, 60, 61, 69,
  92, 128–29, 200, 215
Häagen-Dazs story and,
  208–9
on his premature birth, 15
Jewish heritage claims during,
  11, 116, 193–94, 209, 221
trust fund and inheritance, 2,
  10–11, 65, 194
Ukraine roots, 116, 129, 161
Santos, George, names of
Anthony Devolder, 20
birth name, 29
Kitara Ravache, 38–39 (see also
  Santos, George,
  Brazil lifestyle)
Santos as political choice, xxviii,
  156
Zabrovsky, 20
Santos, George, political career,
  89–227
anti-abortion stance of, 15
campaign finance of, 165–85
decision to enter politics,
  91–111
Long Island political climate
  and, 139–64
MINAJ Act proposed by,
  234
2020 Congressional campaign,
  113–37
2022 Congressional campaign,
  187–212
2023 revelations about, 213–27
  (see also post-election
  revelations (Santos))

Santos, Gercino (father), 16–17,
  21, 24, 28–31, 40, 49, 64
Santos, Tiffany (sister), 22, 23,
  30, 59, 73, 169
Sapphire (dog), 78–87
Saturday Night Live (TV show),
  220
Schumer, Chuck, 206
Schwartz, Bernard, 206–7
Schwarzman, Stephen, xxiv
Securities and Exchange
  Commission (SEC), 98–100,
  102
Shoah Foundation, 101
Small Businesses for Santos
  Coalition, 166
Smith, Stephen A., 224
social media
  beauty pageant video and, 45
  Devolder name used for, 45
  Facebook, 22–23
  negative publicity and Santos's
    response, 213–15, 220–21
  as news source, 164
  Orkut, 44
  Santos as "anti-AOC reply guy,"
    109
  Santos's blocking of reporters
    on, xiii, 218
  Santos's celebrity mentions on,
    107–8
  speed of uncovering lies,
    232
  2020 Congressional campaign
    and, 113–14, 125–26,
    135–37
Southern Poverty Law Center,
  163
South Shore Press (Long Island),
  175

Spitzer, Eliot, 118
Sprague, J. Russell, 153
Springsteen, Bruce, 82
State of the Union (2023), 216–17
Stone, Roger, 218
#StopTheSteal, 131–32
Stringfellow, Doug, 95
Suozzi, Tom
  gubernatorial bid of, 193
  2020 election of, 117–19,
    121–22, 127, 129, 131, 133,
    137, 220
Sweet, Jacqueline, 49

Taglienti, Tom, 19
*Talking GOP* (TV show), 115
Tea Party movement, 148, 149,
  203
Therapy (New York City bar),
  57–58
Thiago (shoe gift recipient), 54
Thiel, Peter, 235
Third Congressional District
    (New York). *see also*
    Long Island political
    climate; Suozzi, Tom; 2020
    Congressional campaign;
    2022 Congressional campaign
  redistricting of, 193, 194,
    197
  territory/constituents of,
    119–24, 127, 130, 137
Towle, Fred, 174–75, 179
Trainor, Meghan, 61
*transformistas,* 40
Trelha, Gustavo, 92–93, 96
Trump, Donald
  on COVID, 126, 234–35
  Long Island political climate
    and, 149, 161–63

  psychological makeup,
    speculation about, xxv
  as role model to Santos, xxiii,
    84–85, 101, 108–11, 214, 224
  Romney and, 219
  Stone and, 218
  2016 media coverage of, 205
  2020 election and, 127,
    131–32, 135
  2022 midterm elections and,
    190, 191, 197, 202, 204
Trump, Melania, 169
2020 Congressional campaign
    (Santos), 113–37. *see also*
    decision to enter politics
    (Santos)
  announcement about running,
    113–15
  Baruch College claims during,
    128–29
  Blue Lives Matter movement
    and, 130–31
  bookkeeping for, 133–34
  campaign overview, xi–xii, 94
  COVID bout during, 124–26,
    137
  election results, 131–32, 137,
    162
  Jewish heritage claims during,
    116
  lack of knowledge about
    territory/constituents,
    119–24, 127, 130, 137
  new-member orientation
    attendance, 134–37
  recount, 132–37
  social media use during,
    113–14, 125–26, 135–37
  Suozzi as incumbent in, 117–19
    (*see also* Suozzi, Tom)

2022 Congressional campaign (Santos). *see also* campaign finance; post-election revelations (Santos)
   campaign overview, xiii–xiv
   campaign rhetoric of, 139–40, 159–64, 193–94, 203–4, 207–9
   Democratic Party opposition research, 198–203
   election results in other campaigns, 205–7
   Jewish heritage claims during, 193–94, 209, 221
   media coverage of, 204–5
   results of, 210–12
   Santos supported by Nassau County Republican Party, 155–58
   Zimmerman's candidacy and, 194–98

Uadla (ex-wife), 10–12, 68
unmask movement, 141–47
US Space Force, 225

Van Duyne, Beth, 170
Vekselberg, Viktor, 101
Victoria (aunt), 26
"vulnerability study," 192

Warwick, Dionne, 40
*Washington Post,* 100, 167
Weingarten, Randi, 210
Whitestone Republican Club, 146, 166
WRCN radio, 189

Zabrovsky (George Santos), 20
Zambelli, Carla, 44
Zeldin, Lee, 133, 157, 176, 203–4, 205
Zimmerman, Robert
   campaign media coverage, 204–5
   candidacy of, 194–98
   Democratic Party opposition research, 198–203
   loss of, 210–12
   Santos's campaign rhetoric and, 193–94, 207–9
Zinno, Peter, 176–77

# About the Author

MARK CHIUSANO started covering George Santos in 2019 as a columnist and editorial writer at *Newsday*. His story collection *Marine Park* received a PEN/Hemingway Award honorable mention in 2015. His writing has appeared in places like *The Atlantic, Time, The Paris Review, McSweeney's, The Drift,* and *Guernica,* and he teaches at CUNY City Tech. He lives in his native Brooklyn with his wife and two daughters.